THE LONG YEAR
A.D. 69

WELLESLEY, Kenneth. The long year, A.D. 69. Westview, 1977 (c1976). 234p ill map index 76-5390. 16.50 ISBN 0-89158-609-1. C.I.P.

CHOICE JULY/AUG.'77
History. Geography &
Travel
Ancient (Incl.
Archaeology)

The year when four emperors vied for the Roman throne has attracted considerable attention recently. One full-length book has already appeared in English, P.A.L. Greenhalgh's *The year of the four emperors* (1975), others in other languages, and more are promised. But Wellesley is particularly suited to write about that year; he has authored numerous learned articles, translated Tacitus's *Histories* (our main source) for Penguin Classics, and produced an annotated edition of *The histories, book III* (CHOICE, Jan. 1973). His book is a sober, scholarly, and readable account, but there is no bibliography (Wellesley refers the reader to his translation) and only five pages of notes. Stronger than Greenhalgh on the military aspects of the situation (Wellesley has visited the sites), the book also reassesses the four emperors politically, often less convincingly than Tacitus, and it may stick a little too closely to A.D. 69 to be entirely comprehensible to beginners. The numerous plates are unhelpful, and there is a dearth of maps (not even one of Rome itself). Worth consulting by specialists and definitely a good buy for undergraduate libraries even if they have already invested in Greenhalgh.

Galba (top), Vitellius (bottom left) and
Vespasian (bottom right)

THE LONG YEAR
A.D. 69

Statue . . . illum Galbae et Othonis et Vitellii
longum et unum annum.
TACITUS, *Dialogus de Oratoribus*

KENNETH WELLESLEY

WESTVIEW PRESS · BOULDER · COLORADO

Copyright © Kenneth Wellesley 1975

Published in 1975 in London, England by Paul Elek Ltd.

*Published 1976 in the United States of America by
    Westview Press, Inc.
 1898 Flatiron Court
 Boulder, Colorado 80301
 Frederick A. Praeger, Publisher and Editorial Director*

Printed and bound in Great Britain

Library of Congress Cataloging in Publication Data
Wellesley, Kenneth.
    The long year, A.D. 69.

    Includes bibliographical references and index.
    1. Rome—History—Civil War, 68–69.   2. Galba,
Servius Sulpicius, Emperor of Rome, d. 69.   3. Otho,
Marcus Salvius, Emperor of Rome, 32–69.
4. Vitellius, Aulus, Emperor of Rome, 15–69.
5. Vespasianus, Emperor of Rome, 9–79.   I. Title.
DG286.W44   1976   937'.07   76–5390
ISBN 0–89158–609–1

Contents

Figures

Plates

Galba, Vitellius, Vespasian   *frontispiece*
(a) Onyx head of Galba, 21 × 25 mm, British Museum. cf. H. B.
Walters, *Engraved Gems and Cameos, Greek, Etruscan and Roman, in the
British Museum*, no. 3606, pl. xlii. By courtesy of the Trustees. (b)
Silver denarius of Vitellius once in the Herzogliches Münzkabinett,
Gotha. Legend: A(ulus) VITELLIVS IMP(erator). After L. M.
Lanckoronski, *Das römische Bildnis*, 1944, pl. xiv. (c) Red jasper
laureate head of Vespasian, 14 × 12 mm, British Museum. cf. H. B.
Walters, op. cit., no. 1989. By courtesy of the Trustees.

1. Coins of Galba and Otho   *facing page* 48
(a) Billon tetradrachm of Alexandria, year 1 of Galba (July–August 68),
Fitzwilliam Museum, Cambridge. Obverse: ΛΟΥ ΛΙΒ ΣΟΥΛΠ
ΓΑΛΒΑ ΚΑΙΣ Lᴬ Head of Galba; reverse: ΚΡΑΤΗΣΙΕ Kratesis.
cf. J. G. Milne, *Catalogue of Alexandrian Coins in the Ashmolean Museum*,
1933, no. 314. By courtesy of the Fitzwilliam Museum. (b) Aes
dupondius of Rome, Fitzwilliam Museum. Obverse: IMP SERV
GALBA AVG TR P Head of Galba; reverse: LIBERTAS PVBLICA
S. C. Libertas draped, carrying pileus and sceptre. cf. H. Mattingly,
Coins of the Roman Empire in the British Museum I, 329, no. 121. By
courtesy of the Fitzwilliam Museum. (c) Aureus of Rome, Hunter
Coin Cabinet, Glasgow. Obverse: IMP M OTHO CAESAR AVG
TR P Head of Otho; reverse: SECVRITAS P R Security, draped,
holding wreath and sceptre. cf. A. Robertson, *Roman Imperial Coins in
the Hunter Coin Cabinet* I, 172, no. 3. By courtesy of the Court of the
University of Glasgow.

2. Coins of Vitellius and Vespasian   49
(a) 'Military Class' silver denarius of Lyon (?), Fitzwilliam Museum.
Obverse: FIDES EXERCITVVM Clasped hands; reverse: FIDES
PRAETOR(IANORVM). cf. H. Mattingly, op. cit. I, 306, no. 65;
C. Kraay, 'Revolt and Subversion', *Numismatic Chronicle*, 1952, 78ff.
By courtesy of the Fitzwilliam Museum. (b) Silver denarius of Lyon (?).
Obverse: A. VITELLIVS IMP GERMAN Head of Vitellius;
reverse: FIDES EXERCITVVM Clasped hands. cf. H. Mattingly,
op. cit. I, 391, no. 114. By courtesy of the Fitzwilliam Museum.

(c) Silver denarius of Rome, Hunter Coin Cabinet, Glasgow. Obverse: A VITELLIVS GERM IMP AVG TR P Head of Vitellius; reverse: L VITELLIVS COS III CENSOR Head of Lucius Vitellius, the emperor's father, with eagle-tipped sceptre, alluding to the combined censorship (as colleague of Claudius) and third consulate of A.D. 47. cf. A. Robertson, op. cit. I, 177, no. 14. By courtesy of the Court of the University of Glasgow. (d) Aureus of Rome, 69/70, Hunter Coin Cabinet, Glasgow. Obverse: IMP CAESAR VESPASIANVS AVG Head of Vespasian, laureate; reverse: CAESAR AVG F COS CAESAR AVG F PR Bare heads of Titus (on left) and Domitian (on right). cf. A. Robertson, op. cit. I, 186, no. 2. By courtesy of the Court of the University of Glasgow.

3. An inscription commemorating Piso and his widow Verania   80
Squeeze of grave-altar inscription commemorating Lucius Cal-purnius Piso Frugi Licinianus (ll. 1–4, soon after 15 January 69) and his wife Verania (ll. 5–8, about 96–100: cf. Pliny, *Ep.* ii, 20, 1–6), 77 × 83 cm, Museo Nazionale Romano ('Terme'), Rome. The photograph is reproduced by courtesy of A. E. and J. S. Gordon from their *Album of Dated Latin Inscriptions*, 1958, I, pl. 53c (no. 126).

4. The text of a decree by Lucius Helvius Agrippa, Governor of Sardinia   80
CIL x, 7852 = *ILS* 5947 = MW 455 = Smallwood 392. Drawing made by the author from a photograph, kindly supplied by Dr David Ridgway, of a bronze tablet now in the museum at Sassari. It was discovered in 1866 near the village of Esterzili in south-east central Sardinia and is a locally made copy of an entry in the official register of the governor of the province. Another copy would have been sent to Rome and inscribed on a bronze tablet there. cf. T. Mommsen, *Gesammelte Schriften* v, 325–51, F. F. Abbott and A. C. Johnson, *Municipal Administration in the Roman Empire*, no. 58, and A. C. Johnson, P. R. Coleman-Norton and F. C. Bourne, *Ancient Roman Statutes*, no. 181.

5. Otho as Pharaoh of Egypt   81
Sunk relief (Lepsius, *Denkmäler* IV, 81a) on the south side of the propylon, outer face, of the Temple of Isis at Deir esh-Shelweit, Western Thebes. Otho, named in the cartouches as 'Mrqs Autuns Kysrs Autukrtr' according to his Greek title, stands on the left facing right, and offers two pots of milk to two of the temple gods, Horus-Prē' and Horus-Shu, to be understood as standing side by side. The former replies, 'I cause thy popularity to be great among everyone, that thou mayest rejoice in repeated years', the latter, 'I have placed love of thee among the people, that thou mayest be elevated through thy strength.' (This note is based on a full description and translation kindly supplied by Mr Cyril Aldred and Mr Vivian Davies.)

6. **Papyrus Fouad 8**   81
Fragment of papyrus, end of first century A.D., 215 × 75 mm, Cairo
Museum. It appears to record an announcement by Tiberius Julius
Alexander to the people of Alexandria. cf. p. 122 and V. A. Tcheri-
kover and A. Fuks, *Corpus Papyrorum Judaicarum*, no. 418a, L. Koenen,
Gnomon 40 (1968), 256, and R. Coles, A. Giessen and L. Koenen,
Zeitschrift für Papyrologie und Epigrafik 11 (1973), 235. Photograph
supplied by courtesy of Dr Coles and the Palaeographic Commission
of the Association International de Papyrologues, and reproduced by
kind permission of the Director of the Cairo Museum.

7. **A Roman secondary road in the Vosges**   144
Section of the 'Chemin d'Allemagne' recently cleared in the wooded
hills near the Donon north of Raon-les-Leau (French 1:25,000 staff
map 'Cirey-sur-Vezouze 3–4', ref. 3592 5378). The road leads from
the south-east towards Tarquimpol (?Decempagi), where it once met
the Reims–Strasbourg high road. Photograph supplied by courtesy of
Monsieur G. Viard of Saint-Dié.

8. **The Postumian Way in northern Italy**   144
The photograph was taken by the author in the month of April and
looks eastwards at a point 10 miles east of Cremona. On the left the
canalized Delmona follows the ditch on the north side of the road;
that on the south is a slight depression or virtually non-existent.

9. **Auxiliary infantrymen in conversation**   145
A scene (cxi, Cichorius) from the spiral of reliefs adorning Trajan's
Column, Rome. Photographed by the author from the cast of the
Column by courtesy of the Victoria and Albert Museum, London.

10. **Part of the bronze facing of a military chest belonging to a
unit of the Fourth (Macedonian) Legion, lost at Cremona on
25 October 69**   145
This fragment, 31 × 22 cm, was found with others near the Porta
Venezia on the north-east edge of Cremona (cf. Fig. 3). The inscription reads: LEG(io) IIII MAC(edonica)/M(arco) VINICIO II/
TAVRO STAT(ili)O CORVINO (co[n])S(ulibus)/C(aio) VIBIO
RUF/INO LEG(ato)/C(aio) HORATIO (. . .)O PRINC(ipe)
P(riore?). The chest was thus made between January and April 45,
and the lower gap, which obliterates the inscription, was cut later
when the lock was changed. The emblems (bull and goat) on the
standards may identify the company and cohort to which the chest
belonged. cf. F. Barnabei in *Notizie degli Scavi*, 1887, 209–21 with
Tavola iv, here reproduced. The fragment is now in the museum at
Cremona.

Detail (top right corner) of pen-and-ink drawing, 27·7 × 40 cm, by
Leonardo da Vinci, Royal Library, Windsor (no. 12684). cf. A. E.
Popham, *The Drawings of Leonardo da Vinci*, 1946, pl. 287, and K.
Clark, *The Drawings of Leonardo da Vinci in the Collection of Her Majesty
the Queen at Windsor Castle* I, 170f., with plate in II. Rather less than a
quarter of the drawing is shown here. The route taken by the
Vitellian attackers (cf. pp. 163 ff.) is visible. The drawing is reproduced
by gracious permission of Her Majesty the Queen.

CIL vi, 930 = *ILS* 244 = MW 1; cf. A. E. Gordon in *Greece and
Rome* 20 (1951), 80–2 with pl. cvi. The bronze tablet, 163 × 115 cm,
in the Capitoline Museum, Rome, contains part of the text of a law
reproducing the wording of the antecedent decree of the Senate
passed in the last days of December 69. Photograph by courtesy of
the German Archaeological Institute, Rome.

Preface

The present work seeks to provide a plain narrative of the events of one crowded year. Interwoven by cause and effect, framed in time and space, they embraced the whole Mediterranean world and created the second dynasty of imperial Rome. The web is intricate and colourful. That an attempt to retell the story nineteen hundred years later is possible at all is largely due to the chance survival of the early books of Tacitus' *Histories*, supported by other information in as generous (or as meagre) a bulk as the historian of ancient Rome can now hope to enjoy. But the Long Year provides us with a thousand problems—dark corners into which only a dim light penetrates from feeble candles, and which we think we can explore by inference, conjecture and imagination. We dispose of no exhaustive official records or revealing memoirs. All the literary sources are liable to be rhetorical, partisan, moralizing or trivial. From the rest industry and scholarship can glean a few straws in a field whose once abundant harvest has irrevocably vanished.

It might seem an enterprise of folly and conceit to tread in the footsteps of Tacitus, whose narrative of this time often withstands the sharpest criticism. But his readers are not senators of Rome living forty years after the Long Year. Expansion or contraction is called for. Yet I have not scrupled on occasion to echo his words and emulate, if with a difference, the way in which he cunningly arranges his material. Unlike some of his successors, he is invariably an elegant writer, easier to parody than imitate. But in him drama and emotion, the sly thrust, the style that dominates the matter, above all the *studium* and *livor* from which he imagined himself to be free—these are too overpowering for modern taste. Such elements, therefore, I have reduced, assuming that Roman politicians and leaders were no less open to cool reason than we, no less guided in their day-to-day decisions by careful calculation based on available knowledge and resources. This assumption, which is merely an act of faith, seems not infrequently to suggest verdicts and solutions rather different from those of Tacitus, and, when supported by evidence he did not use, helps to fill some of his silences.

I should like to express my very sincere thanks to all who have so readily offered their assistance, especially in the matter of illustrative material, and in particular to Dr Cyril Aldred; Dr R. A. Coles; Mr Vivian Davies; Dr Karin Einaudi; Professor A. E. Gordon and Mrs Gordon; the late Dr Ernest Nash; Dr David Ridgway; Dr Anne S. Robertson; Dr E. Savova; Dr Beatrice Schneider; Dr E. Mary Smallwood; Professor Eric Turner; Monsieur G. Viard; Dr T. R. Volk; and Professor Alan Watson. To this list must be added those whom I have repeatedly plagued with sudden demands always generously met: my immediate colleagues in the University of Edinburgh, and the members of my family. Nor must I forget the University itself, which in years gone by has assisted me to travel in Tacitean territories, and more recently in respect of typing facilities. It is unnecessary to state that all errors and shortcomings in this book are due to myself alone.

If it were fashionable to observe the formality of a dedication, mine would be twofold: first, to the *manes* of Cornelius Tacitus, Roman consul, orator and historian; secondly, to the memory of a later historian of Rome, whose brilliance was equalled only by his courtesy and who many years ago suggested that this book should be written: Jérôme Carcopino.

Edinburgh
December 1974   *Kenneth Wellesley*

Sources

The principal ancient literary sources for A.D. 69 are the excerpts of Cassius Dio, Books lxiii–lxv (most conveniently in the Loeb edition, with translation by H. B. Foster and E. Cary); Plutarch, *Lives of Galba and Otho*, edited in 1890 by E. G. Hardy; Suetonius, *Galba, Otho, Vitellius* and *Vespasian*; and Tacitus, *The Histories*. In the 1972 and 1975 re-issues of the Penguin Classics translation of the last-named will be found a fairly complete bibliography of modern studies of the period and the topics involved.

The contribution made by epigraphy and specialist studies of all kinds to our understanding of the year is sufficiently obvious. But a special mention must be made of the enormous utility of McCrum and Woodhead's *Select Documents of the Principates of the Flavian Emperors, Including the Year of Revolution: A.D. 68–96* (Cambridge, 1961) which expertly conveys the resources of many large and inaccessible *corpora* to the non-expert. But it possesses no index and provides (of set purpose) the barest minimum of comment.

PLACE-NAME EQUIVALENTS IN LATIN AND THE VERNACULAR LANGUAGES

Achaia	Greece	Fanum Fortunae	Fano
Adua, fl.	Adda, R.	Ferentium	Ferentino
Aenus, fl.	Inn, R.	Forum Julii	Fréjus
Albingaunum	Albenga	Forum Alieni	? Legnago
Altinum	Altino	Gallia Belgica	Belgian Gaul
Anagnia	Anagni	— Lugdunensis	Central Gaul
Antipolis	Antibes	— Narbonensis	Southern Gaul
Aquinum	Aquino	Gelduba	Gellep
Aquitania	Gaul, South-	Hadria	Adriatic Sea
	western	Haemus, Mons	Balkan Range
Arar fl.	Saône, R.	Herculis Monoeci	
Aricia	Ariccia	Portus	Monaco
Ariminum	Rimini	Hierosolyma	Jerusalem
Ateste	Este	Hispalis	Seville
Atria	Adria	Hispania Citerior	Spain, Nearer
Aventicum	Avenches	— Baetica	Spain, Southern
Augusta		Hostilia	Ostiglia
Taurinorum	Turin	Interamna	Terni
Baetica	Spain, Southern	Leucorum civitas	Toul
Berytus	Beirut	Lingonum civitas	Langres
Bonna	Bonn	Lucania	Lucania and
Bononia	Bologna		S. Campania
Brixellum	Brescello	Luceria	Lucera
Brundisium	Brindisi	Lucus	Luc-en-Diois
Byzantium	Istanbul	Lugdunum	Lyon
Calabria	Province of	Lupia fl.	Lippe, R.
	Lecce	Lusitania	Portugal and
Campania	Lazio and		Western Spain
	Campania	Massilia	Marseille
Chobus fl.	Khobi, R.	Mauretania	Morocco
Colonia		Mediolanum	Milan
Agrippinensis	Cologne	Mediomatrici	Metz
Cythnus	Kythnos	Mevania	Bevagna
Divodurum	Metz	Misenum	Miseno
Dyrrachium	Durrës	Mogontiacum	Mainz
Emerita	Merida	Mosa fl.	Meuse (Maas),
Eporedia	Ivrea		R.

Mutina	Modena	Tarentum	Taranto
Narnia	Narni	Tarracina	Terracina
Novaesium	Neuss	Tartarus fl.	Tartaro, R.
Novaria	Novara	Ticinum	Pavia
Ocriculum	Otricoli	Tingitana	Morocco near
Opitergium	Oderzo		Tangier
Padus fl.	Po, R.	Tolbiacum	Zülpich
Paeligni	Abruzzi	Trapezus	Trabzon
Patavium	Padova (Padua)	Treviri	Trier
Perusia	Perugia	Urvinum Hortense	Collemancio
Picenum	Marche &	Vascones	Basques
	Abruzzi	Vercellae	Vercelli
Placentia	Piacenza	Vicetia	Vicenza
Poetovio	Ptuj	Vienna	Vienne
Saxa Rubra	? Grottarossa	Vindonissa	Windisch
Stoechades Insulae	Iles d'Hyères	Vocetius, Mons	? Bözberg

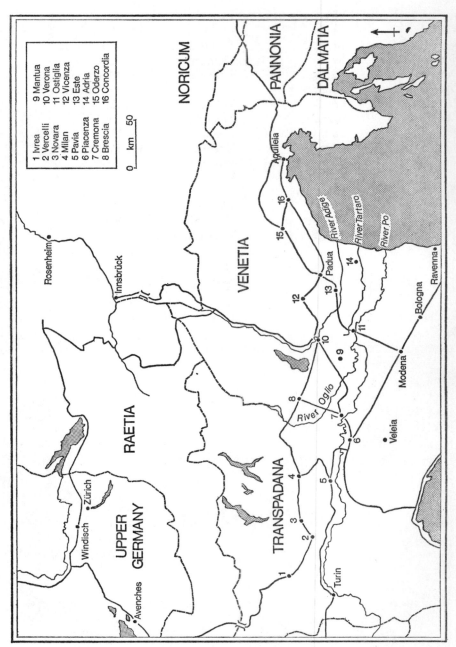

Fig. 1 Northern Italy

1 Ivrea
2 Vercelli
3 Novara
4 Milan
5 Pavia
6 Piacenza
7 Cremona
8 Brescia
9 Mantua
10 Verona
11 Ostiglia
12 Vicenza
13 Este
14 Adria
15 Oderzo
16 Concordia

0 km 50

I

Prospect and Retrospect

On 1 January A.D. 69, in the eight-hundred-and-twenty-first year of the City, the emperor Servius Sulpicius Galba Caesar Augustus and Titus Vinius Rufinus entered office as consuls, the former for the second time.

At the start of the year a careful ritual was observed to ensure success in public and private affairs. The first words you spoke on rising in the morning, the first actions performed within the house must be happy and uncomplaining. Laurel and saffron, around the door or burning on the little household altar, would bring luck. Outside in the city, the temples, normally kept shut, were open to worship, and fire burned on the altars that stood before them. But this was no holiday. As the year started, so would it continue. One must be up and doing. By all means visit and receive your friends; exchange good wishes and little gifts of dates, figs and honey to sweeten the coming year; but then off to work. Wherever Roman citizens lived throughout the circle of the lands, everything done and said would—or might—set the pattern for the year: above all at Rome itself, head and mistress of a civilized and peaceful world. In the capital city the solemn and annual procession of Roman notables was once more to make its way up to the Temple of Jupiter Best and Greatest to seek a blessing on the community.

No rational observer could possibly have suspected the anger of the gods. No one could have supposed that the great triple shrine on the hill towards which the company moved would in this year sink into ashes and rubble, a symbol no longer of Rome's eternity but of its seemingly imminent extinction. That Italy should be twice invaded by Roman armies, that its cities and capital should be taken by storm, that three successive emperors should die by assassination, suicide or lynching, and that the whole empire, from Wales to Assouan and from the Caucasus to Morocco, should be convulsed and disarrayed, were matters beyond imagination or surmise. More than a century, after all, had passed since the bad old days of the republic. Yet the long and single year now beginning would provide a spectacle of calamity, endurance and survival without parallel, so far, in Rome's history.

Within the structure of the Roman principate instituted by Augustus the ghost of the republic lived on in formalities. Annual magistrates, or magistrates in relays within the year, were still elected by, and accountable to, the whole citizen body. Occasionally, to honour his fellow-senators or a particular friend, the emperor himself, as now in 69, assumed the consulship. So early in the day the crowds had gathered in the Forum Romanum near the palace, the senator wearing his heavy, newly-fulled and pure-white woollen toga over the broad-stripe of his tunic, the patrician shod with scarlet shoes, cross-gartered. Of the total of 500 or so senators perhaps 300 were present on such a special occasion—all those not hindered by illness or absent on the public service in or outside Italy. Then there were representatives of the middle class of 'knights': men rich enough in simpler days to afford the expense of mounted service in the army, now merchants, bankers and contractors, men of solid financial status, second estate in a community where rank and privilege were not imagined to be incompatible with the liberty of the individual. These men you could distinguish by the narrow purple stripe beneath the toga. Next, the *populus Romanus* at large: artisans, shopkeepers, labourers, servants, farm folk in for the day from the nearby country; and almost as numerous and not outwardly distinguishable, the freedmen and the unfree, immigrants or indigenous, climbing to citizenship. The ceremony was rather a special one: Nero's successor, old Servius Galba, had only two months before come with Vinius from Tarragona in Spain, and the public was still curious about the newcomer.

The emperor had blue eyes, a hooked nose and a square jaw; he had lost most of his hair. Of medium height and stocky build, he walked with a limp, victim of arthritis in foot and hand, so that he found it difficult to unroll or even hold a book. After Nero, who had died at the age of thirty, an emperor in his seventies must have seemed strange. Yet, as Romans had already discovered, Galba was no weakling in character. His was the green and vigorous old age of a man who had never lived a soft life. His manner suggested the habit of authority and a capacity to rule. He was no stranger to greatness.[1]

The palace he had known from childhood, changed though it now was by the building activities of Gaius and Nero. As he emerged from it, descended the steps, and walked down the ramp leading to the Forum, he must surely have thought back over the years to the first day of his first consulship, when by favour of the dowager-empress Livia, Augustus' widow, he had been allowed, though not really a member of the imperial family, to show himself to Rome from the palace on his way to the Capitol. Now, thirty-six years later, he did so in his own right. The prophecy of Livia's son, the second emperor Tiberius, had been strangely fulfilled: he had once called the young Galba to him, asked him a number of questions and finally produced as horoscope a short sentence in

Greek: 'One day, my boy, you too shall have a brief taste of power.' This was the kind of prediction that one believed after the event; but the event, incredibly, had happened.

The procession formed up as Galba and Vinius, dressed in the purple and embroidered togas of consuls, appeared in public. At the front moved the senators and knights; then, immediately preceding the consular pair, their lictors, each with the traditional bundle of rods strapped round an axe and supported in left hand and on left shoulder. Behind Galba and Vinius were carried the ceremonial Etruscan folding stools of metal inlaid with carved ivory, the simple thrones of Roman magistrates. The apparatus of the age-old sacrifice was there: priests, herald, flute player, *victimarius*, assistant and young boy (both his parents of course must be alive), together with the victims: white oxen from the Faliscan heights or the watery plain of Clitumno, their horns gilded. At the foot of the slope the company turned to the left, away from Nero's columns and the 120-foot statue of the vanished megalomaniac which stood before the Golden House, and moved north-westwards towards the Capitol, past Julius' basilica and the high podium of the Temple of Saturn, and up the steep slope of the paved, slightly curving way that led along the south face of the Capitoline Hill. Once through the gate and into the sacred area, they squeezed into position among the columns fronting the Temple of Jupiter, Juno and Minerva. Within the doorway of the central shrine, that of Jupiter, Galba and Vinius took their places for the first time upon their *sellae curules*, facing outwards to the altar, the assembly and the roofs of Rome.[2]

It was necessary to take the auspices and make sure, as far as possible, that heaven would accept the coming sacrifice. The cage containing the sacred chickens, kept conveniently hungry, was superintended by a special official, the *pullarius*. Gossip afterwards alleged that the birds scuttled away instead of greedily pecking at the cakes of pulse thrown to them. If true, this was a bad sign—and during the actual sacrifice Galba's laurel garland slipped from his head. But no doubt the *pullarius* was equal to the emergency. He reported in due course that the birds had fed. The altar fire crackled with saffron, casting a slight glow on the gilded coffers of the shaded pronaos. In the presence of the toga'd consuls, and of the Senate and People of Rome, keeping holy silence, the purple-veiled priest offered prayers for the state, formulae carefully repeated from a written exemplar and checked for correctness by a listener appointed for the purpose. Any slip of the tongue, any stumble or mispronunciation vitiated the proceedings; to drown unlucky noises a piper played. Then the head of the ox was sprinkled with meal by the priest, and turned sideways; the animal was felled or its throat was slit; the victim was disembowelled and the entrails laid upon the altar. Only if the ritual repeated undeviatingly that of past years could another year of success be expected to take its place in the long tale. Afterwards came a second offering, this time made by the twelve Brethren of the Fields, an ancient and exclusive body, of which the emperor was president, and whose members constituted a kind of order of chivalry. Its origin lay in the remote and unknown past, when Rome or some other Italian community was a little town dependent on the yield of a little land—a yield that might be guaranteed by piety or magic. Now a few nobles carried on the fossilized rituals, celebrating clubbable occasions with a certain pageantry at Magliana down the Tiber or at Rome itself.[3]

The ceremony concluded, the procession re-formed and descended the slope it had climbed. The consuls, magistrates and senators made their way to the Senate House in the north-east corner of the Forum for the first meeting of the year. Here the magistrates, and then each senator in turn, swore an oath to observe the ordinances of the sacred Augustus and his successors, and to be faithful and true to Servius Galba, Emperor, Caesar, Augustus, Pontifex Maximus, Holder of the Tribunician Power, Father of His Country.

As Galba gazed around at the great assembly gathered to pay homage, the thought of the events of the past nine months gave him satisfaction: a sense of gratitude that, late though it was, he had been chosen to end a long political decline. He had not fallen a victim to the dagger of Nero's assassin after all, and the prophecy of greatness had not been in vain. Almost overnight, a hundred-year-old dynasty had vanished, its place taken by himself: old, childless, a widower, a blunt soldier, he had yet become, while governor of Nearer Spain, the choice of the troops, the Senate and, by tacit consent, the world. There would be renewal and reform.

Certainly Rome could not have endured Nero much longer; his death, self-inflicted in unbalanced and perhaps premature despair, signified the end of the Julio-Claudians, for he had no son. The last ten years had seen a series of disasters and disgraces: the murders of Agrippina and Octavia, the fire of Rome, the conspiracy of Piso with the enforced deaths of Seneca and Lucan, the virtual execution of Corbulo, Nero's tour of Greece as charioteer and poet, and finally the revolt of Vindex and of Galba himself. By 68 no prominent Roman could be sure that he would not be the next to be struck by the bolt of an insane Jupiter: service and obedience like Corbulo's were themselves fatal. Galba, too, had believed that his life was in danger, and had connived at the treasonable plans of Julius Vindex, governor of Central Gaul, who had written to him for his support. Instead of transmitting the correspondence to Rome as strict duty required, he had maintained it. In March, Vindex rose; and early in April, Galba's troops at Cartagena, clearly with his permission, had saluted their commander not as

'Caesar's Legate' but as 'Caesar'. Galba preferred for the moment to regard himself as an officer of the Senate and People of Rome, a comparatively prudent form of protest against Neronian autocracy. Perhaps, even now, some semblance of the old liberty would be restored.

In Spain Galba was liked and respected for his strict but just rule. In eight years the people had grown attached to the old noble who stood no nonsense and believed in principles of honesty, duty and discipline. They welcomed his proclamation, which was supported by Titus Vinius Rufinus, latterly an upright governor of Southern Gaul, by Caecina Alienus, financial secretary in Southern Spain, and by the neighbouring province of Lusitania. Its governor, Marcus Salvius Otho, had been husband or lover of Poppaea before she became empress, and he had his own compelling reasons for disliking Nero, who had sentenced him to a ten-year stretch of virtual exile in this remote Atlantic province. Thus Otho, once the friend and associate of Nero, was one of the first provincial governors to go over to Galba, and, as he did so, the thought of succeeding the old man at no very distant date cannot have been absent from his calculations. He was still only thirty-seven, still remembered in Roman society. He could consider his future prospects good. But all these hopes of Galba, Otho and Vinius received a rude shock at the end of May. The governor of Central Gaul was dead, his rebellion crushed.

When Vindex rose against Nero in March, he had no legions at his disposal. He had gathered together some kind of militia force from the Gallic tribes, and finding his capital of Lyon too firmly attached to Nero and the Rhineland legions, many of whose veterans had taken up residence in the city they knew so well, had set up his headquarters at Vienne, eighteen miles downstream. From here he conducted an unsuccessful siege of Lyon. In May, hearing that Verginius Rufus, commander of the legions of Upper Germany, had assembled a force in Mainz from all the Rhine legions and auxiliaries to deal with him, Vindex went to meet him when he besieged Besançon, the capital of the Sequani, a vital stronghold in a tight loop of the Doubs. By a misunderstanding, it seems, a conference between the two governors, Vindex the enemy of Nero and Verginius the ambiguous constitutionalist, had become a confrontation between their two armies. There was a fight outside Besançon which ended in a débâcle for Vindex, who committed suicide. But in this confused situation, Verginius himself was repeatedly offered the principate by his troops, and had repeatedly —but with varying degrees of decisiveness—rejected it.

For Galba the situation was now obscure and alarming. He had only one legion, the Sixth. However, he put a bold face on the matter, appointed a young and vigorous officer, Quintus Pomponius Rufus, later consul and provincial governor, to patrol the coast of Nearer

Spain and Southern Gaul against a possible naval attack by Nero, and recruited infantry and cavalry among the sturdiest inhabitants of his province, notably the Basques and the mountaineers of north-west Spain. On 10 June at Clunia, near Coruña del Conde, in Old Castile north of the Upper Duero and not far from a site famous in Roman history—Numantia—he presented its eagle to a new legion, the Seventh (Galbian). The ceremony would have been a happier one if Galba had known that on the previous day the Senate in Rome had already recognized him as emperor. Within a week he heard the news from his confidential servant Icelus, who travelled fast. The whole of Rome had put on the cap of liberty, like slaves manumitted in Feronia's temple.[4]

Quite apart from his following in the west, Galba must have seemed to the Senate in June 68 an unobjectionable, indeed highly desirable, candidate for the principate. He came of a rich and noble family, had a career of public service behind him and was believed to possess old-fashioned virtues, still, for instance, summoning his servants twice each day to exchange morning and evening greetings individually. Despite his years he was full of vigour. In the nature of things, however, he could scarcely be expected to live long: and this too was a commendation. Galba would certainly serve as a stop-gap, and his remoteness from Rome would give the Senate time to think and debate, time perhaps to wipe off scores long chalked up. A greater contrast between the late emperor and the present one could scarcely be imagined. After his first consulship under Tiberius at the age of thirty-six, he had been governor of South-West Gaul, general officer commanding the military district of Upper Germany, victor over the Chatti in 41, participant in the invasion of Britain in 43, proconsul of Africa (roughly modern Tunisia), and for the last eight years governor of Nearer Spain. Galba's memories reached back to the divine Augustus himself, who had pinched his childish cheek in playfulness. Livia Augusta and Tiberius, as we have seen, had been his friends. Neither Rome nor the rest of the empire had any hesitation in accepting the new Augustus, however novel his rise to power. So, like the creator of the principate, he could claim that though nominated by the army he had been accepted by the Senate and People, that he was a democratic emperor.

By late summer, having dealt summarily with a few obdurates, notably the governor of Africa, Clodius Macer, who had thought to dislodge Nero by cutting off the corn supply upon which the capital was heavily dependent, the new emperor was ready to leave Tarragona for Rome. A route march would toughen up his troops, and have the advantage of showing the flag in southern Gaul and northern Italy. Only the new legion, VII Galbiana, accompanied him; but as was fitting, a sovereign's escort of the Praetorian Guards had been sent out from Rome by sea. Dislodged from comfortable ceremonial duties in the capital or the seaside resorts around the Bay of Naples, these fine warriors now found themselves toiling up the slopes of the Pyrenees and the Alps in the company of raw Spanish legionaries and a lame emperor riding in a carriage often shared by Otho. Marcus Fabius Quintilianus, a bright young rhetorician who, after study in Rome, had recently returned to his home at Calahorra, travelled with the column: Galba himself was a man of few words, and it would be useful to have a speech-writer on hand. At Narbonne, at the beginning of August, Galba had been met, very properly, by an honorific deputation of senators. He entertained them at an official banquet, and the guests were surprised, and perhaps pleased, to note that no use was made of the splendid plate despatched from Rome: they were to dine off the more modest equip-ment of a serving officer's canteen. The march was orderly and unevent-ful. Wherever he appeared, Galba received a cordial welcome from the populace, who now, after many years, saw in their midst an emperor who corresponded with their ideal. This esteem for Galba was indeed to survive him and become a political force used by others. In late September or early October—no precise dating is possible—came the entry into Rome. It was slightly marred by a fracas caused by some Neronian recruits for whom Galba said he had no employment.[5]

The Senate had given him a good reception. It was true, of course, that the exuberance marking the first few months of senatorial liberty of speech had now to be decently muted in the presence of the new master. A determined and bigoted republican, Helvidius Priscus, had already commenced a vendetta against those involved guiltily, as he thought, in the trial and condemnation two years before of his father-in-law, the respected Thrasea Paetus Even good emperors, however, welcomed a certain moderation in public expressions of opinion, and it is certain that the orators of the immediate post-Neronian days had not minced their words. Neronian exiles had returned clamouring for justice and retribution. More than once it was necessary for a Roman emperor to deprecate recrimination of this sort. Inevitably such squabbles were unwelcome to the man who in the last resort, bore the responsibility of running the world, and had despite past associations to employ such talent as was available. The constitution of the Roman state entrusted large and imprecise authority to its emperor, shared with Senate and People. Towards the end of the year 68, it seemed that power was once more being concentrated in the hands of the emperor, or rather, as some critics believed, of a small coterie of privy councillors and civil servants, accountable only, if at all, to the emperor. Behind a republican façade, which seemed to proclaim that power was delegated by the Roman people, the operation of the imperial prerogative demon-strated that it was in fact delegated by the Augustus.

As for the Roman mob, for them there would be fewer cakes and less ale. The days of lavish largesse and spectacle were past. More intelligent or better informed observers must have realized that the state treasury was empty, and that, Galba or no Galba, there would have to be economies. Nero had squandered enormous sums on acting, architecture and athletics. Galba ordered the recipients of the imperial bounty to be sent demands for repayment of 90 per cent of what they had received. But they had barely 10 per cent left, for they had spent other people's money as freely as their own, and no longer disposed of any real estate or capital investments: only the minor trappings of dissipation remained. The collection of the money was to be supervised by an equestrian committee of thirty, but their functions were without precedent and rendered onerous by the ramifications of the business and the number of individuals to be dealt with. The auctioneer and the dealer were everywhere, and Rome was distracted by lawsuits. Yet there was also intense satisfaction at the thought that the recipients of Nero's generosity would in future be as poor as those he had robbed.[6]

The financial stringency had other and more dangerous consequences. The Praetorian Guards, twelve cohorts of infantry and cavalry, each 500 men strong and largely concentrated on the north-east outskirts of Rome in a huge fortified barracks area, were—or considered themselves to be—a corps d'élite. Certainly they were paid at a rate disgracefully higher than that of the ordinary serving soldier in the legion, who faced monotony and danger on the frontiers; and they had by now grown used to being offered a handsome gratuity by each new ruler on his accession. Such a donative had been promised in Galba's name, but without his authority, before October. It had not been paid, and Galba had now decided that it never would be: 'I levy my troops,' he said; 'I don't buy them.' His own conception of discipline, the prejudices of a legionary commander who had served for years far from Rome, and the undeniable destitution of the state treasury combined to render this decision both rational and final. Officialdom temporized. It began to dawn upon the Praetorians that they had been the losers by the change of régime. Mutterings were heard, and disregarded.

Apart from the Praetorians and the other paramilitary forces of the Rome garrison, the city was crowded to an unusual extent by drafts from the northern legions, summoned by Nero in the last months of his reign for the projected Caucasus expedition, and then on Vindex' revolt halted in Italy or returned to it. These men had sworn allegiance to Nero and the house of the Caesars. They could hardly be expected to be enthusiastically devoted to an ex-governor of Spain whom they had never seen and whose German command had been held before they entered the army. But they were not actively disloyal.

There was thus an undertow of discontent whose pull it was hard to estimate. Among the disgruntled, the names most often mentioned with

envy and hostility were those of Titus Vinius, now—despite his good
record in Gaul and Spain—denounced as corrupt; Cornelius Laco,
Galba's choice for the invidious post of Praetorian prefect, but felt by
his subordinates to be arrogant and deaf to advice; and Galba's
freedman Icelus, as a civil servant more powerful than many senators
and detested accordingly. With what justice abuse of power may be
attributed to them we cannot say, since we have only the voice of
hostile propaganda on the matter. If faults existed, it seems clear that
Galba was ignorant of them, for his own standard of honesty was high;
they were certainly much exaggerated by interested parties, though it
would be ingenuous to deny that some adherents of the emperor may
have decided to make hay while the sun briefly shone. On the whole,
and rightly, Galba believed himself and his régime to be acceptable to
the Senate and People of Rome and Italy, and this belief is not proved
to have been ill-founded by any of the events that followed.

Nor, as Galba looked at the provinces, could any serious threat to
his position be descried. Military intervention, to be successful, could
only come from governors of provinces possessing legionary garrisons.
In the Lower Rhine military district, four legions, two at Vetera near
Xanten, one at Neuss and one at Bonn, were controlled by a lethargic
but noble nonentity, Aulus Vitellius. He had only recently assumed
command, appointed by Galba to fill the sudden vacancy as a safe
and amiable person of distinguished ancestry though the two men were
not personally known to each other. The army of Upper Germany,
two legions at Mainz and one at Windisch, had presented more of a
problem. In June, fresh from the victory or massacre at Besançon,
preferring as emperor their own commander to the ally of Vindex,
they had been slow to acknowledge Galba. It was difficult to read the
mind of Verginius Rufus, whose pious professions of fidelity to the
decisions of the Senate rang hollow, and were scarcely believed by his
own troops. Of a stature suited to empire, he had refused offers which,
while Nero still lived, were treasonable, and immediately thereafter
premature. But whether these offers were welcome or unwelcome nobody
but Verginius knew. For the rest of a long life he dined out on the glory
acquired by doing nothing and calling it patriotism; and it is difficult
to feel much sympathy for a man who composed for himself a boastful
epitaph:

> Here Rufus lies, once Vindex' conqueror: he
> Claimed empire not for self, but Italy.

So ambiguous a figure, commanding spirited legions so near to Italy,
must be removed. As the emperor passed through Gaul, Verginius
received a flattering invitation: he was to join Galba as a member of

his privy council. His place was taken by a safer man, Hordeonius Flaccus, who suffered badly from gout and tended to issue his daily orders from a sickbed; but his deficiencies would perhaps be supplied by the lively Caecina, who was put in command of IV Macedonica, one of the two formations at Mainz. Thus, despite its seven legions, Germany could hardly represent a threat.

Beyond the Channel, the barbarians of Wales and Yorkshire were restive enough, on the edge of Roman-held territory, to preoccupy the governor of Britain, Trebellius Maximus, and his three legions at Gloucester, Wroxeter and Lincoln. As for the long Danube frontiers of Pannonia and Moesia, six legions guarding 900 miles of river were shared between two senior officers, Lucius Tampius Flavianus and Marcus Aponius Saturninus. They had honourable careers behind— and to some extent before—them, but no political ambitions. Syria was governed by a more interesting and perhaps more dangerous man, Gaius Licinius Mucianus, commander of three legions and with personal gifts of diplomacy, oratory and literary competence. Luckily, he was too intelligent to act rashly, and as it happened, hardly on speaking terms with his neighbour in Judaea, Titus Flavius Vespasianus, a rough diamond but a good and cautious soldier, who after two campaigns had now largely broken the back of the Jewish revolt. But Jerusalem and some few fortresses still held out, and Vespasian had too much upon his shoulders to nourish delusions of grandeur. As for Egypt, it had for some years possessed a competent prefect in Tiberius Julius Alexander, an Egyptian Jew, who could have no imperial or political aspirations. Despite its two legions and its efficient governor, the country remained a pawn, however valuable, over which the emperor reigned as Pharaoh by the will of heaven. Africa, after its unfortunate experience with L. Clodius Macer, was content even with such an uninteresting governor as Gaius Vipstanus Apronianus. Finally, in Spain, which retained the Sixth Legion, Galba left behind a cultured but unmilitary character, Cluvius Rufus. His ambition was modest: he hoped to be an historian.

Granted this satisfactory picture, it remained true that the succession question would have to be settled before long. Galba had no living son, or son-in-law, who could be publicly presented as the next presumptive ruler, as Augustus had presented Tiberius after years of partnership. Galba would make a virtue of necessity. You did not have to be a student of politics or competent in law—though our man was both— to know that what providence has taken away adoption could supply. Why should Rome not have a ruler chosen not by birth or by the hazard of revolt or by any manipulation of the long-discredited mechanisms of the republican oligarchy, but by the considered judgment of a predecessor? Selecting the best candidate in an unrestricted field might reasonably be expected to succeed where so many other methods had demonstrably failed.

The qualities ideally required of a Roman emperor could be developed in a mind receptive of instruction and in a character capable of firm action; but they were undeniably considerable. Immense areas were controlled by too simple mechanisms: and the burden of responsibility resting upon the individual governor, and *a fortiori* upon the emperor, was heavy. A small army and a rudimentary civil service discharged functions now requiring many times more men and the refinements of an industrial and technological revolution which still lay in the remote future. It was long since Rome had ceased to be a city-state. The extension of control from Lazio to Italy and from Italy to the Mediterranean basin had destroyed the old republic. If one left out of account the ramshackle empire of the Parthians and the remote and mysterious people from whom came silk, the Roman state was now almost coextensive with the civilized world. Multilingual, it acknowledged two common tongues as supreme: Latin, the language of the law, the government and the western literates; Greek, the lingua franca of the eastern half. But the peoples of this motley empire presented every variety of culture and local government, of indocility or tractability, of poverty or wealth, of colour, creed and education. In the absence of firm statistical records, its population has been estimated at little more than 50 million. Vastly smaller than today's figures, it yet included a greater density—as is obvious to any traveller—in North Africa and in Anatolia. Italy may have possessed 7–10 million inhabitants. We are on slightly firmer ground (though only slightly) in thinking that the capital, the circuit of whose walls measured more than thirteen miles, contained perhaps a million souls. After Rome, whose size was quite exceptional, the most considerable cities were Lyon in the west, Alexandria and Antioch in the east; outside a few great centres, we must think in general of a peasant economy serving to support small market towns whose inhabitants could often be counted in four figures. Agriculture, trade, transport, personal services, and—to a very much lesser extent—small-scale manufacturing engaged the toilers and tillers, and provided a relatively handsome return for a restricted class of landowners, businessmen, financiers and officials. Extremes of wealth and poverty were to some extent offset by a tradition of state, municipal and private benevolence encouraged by enlightened law, by a community sense, by the teachings of philosophy or merely by the prospect of those ultimate rewards for good works: fame, a statue and the immortality of the written record in book or inscription. While not deficient in inventive capacity or the incentives of greed and patronage, the Mediterranean world was spared the fatal juxtaposition of coal and iron, and its profounder speculations were directed to rhetoric, law,

literature, history, philosophy and religion. It was also free from nation-
alism and the colour-bar, though rich in superstition, quackery and
magic.[7]

The obligations of the ruler of such an empire were massive and
multifarious. Chief among them was the defence of the long frontiers
against the enemy without (mercifully primitive as he still was) and
the maintenance of internal peace assailed or assailable by rivals,
revolutionaries or mere brigands and pirates. Tradition, prudence and
convenience compelled him to work in harness with a Senate now
composed less and less of the great families of the republic and more
and more of men advanced by his predecessors and himself according
to the rough justice of apparent acceptability or real performance.
The Senate was divided not on political issues (except in so far as a
republican opposition group can be held to exist) but by personal
rivalries and jealousies, thanks to which antagonism towards the
princeps could be denounced as treason and approval of him vilified, at
any rate after his death, as flattery. It was a body about which it is
impossible to feel much enthusiasm, though all the talents of the empire
should have been assembled in it. Senators were uncertain about the
degree of subservience and liberty appropriate towards an emperor
upon whose favour their own careers depended. They often lacked a
strong sense of what the realities of the political situation demanded or
permitted. Hence a real partnership between emperor and Senate
resting upon mutual liking and trust was only rarely achieved. Nor
could the Senate claim to be in any way representative of the scattered
citizen and non-citizen populace; and at any one time many of its
leading members would be absent from Rome and from its deliberations
in the capacity of provincial governors, military commanders, financial
secretaries, members of missions and so forth. Long-term policy and
day-to-day administration alike were believed, and inevitably believed,
to be influenced by the imperial civil service of knights, freedmen and
slaves: a state, some thought bitterly, within a state, certainly a phenomenon unknown to the republic. Prosecutions arising from the mis-
conduct of provincial officials might be dealt with by the Senate or
the emperor or the two in concert. The objects upon which money was
principally spent were the armed forces, the *annona* or subsidized food
supply of the capital, public works throughout the empire and sub-
ventions to disaster areas: and all these lay almost entirely within the
emperor's competence. More and more the Senate tended to become
an assembly of imperial officials rather than a mouthpiece of public
opinion, a prophet of woe or a voice inviting change and reform. Having
lost the dominant position it had often enjoyed and abused under the
republic, it was slow to accept the no less challenging role of mentor
to a virtually all-powerful emperor. Upon the latter rested a personal

responsibility which it is not surprising many failed adequately to sustain. But that a practical common sense and a technique of ruling, only dimly perceived by us beneath the froth of events, guided the operations of the world-wide empire, is obvious from the continued life and health of that empire as a whole, and from its very survival in A.D. 69.

For the understanding of the history of the Long Year—indeed often for its recovery from a defective record—it is important to remember the limitations and opportunities presented, despite generally peaceful conditions and the excellence of the Roman road system, by the slowness of travel in a large area enjoying, or at least demanding, coordination and cohesion. Official newsbearers, if granted diplomas signed by the emperor or by one of his governors (which guaranteed the bearers the services of the public posting system), could find relays of horses waiting for them at the *mansiones* on their route, and might thus achieve a maximum of 100 Roman miles a day, though 50 would be nearer the average if no urgency existed. The hobnailed boots of the long-enduring legionary could carry him along main roads only some 15–18 miles daily, though higher speeds (up to 35) might be briefly achieved in a crisis. By sea the speed of travel was equally slow and equally variable. It depended upon the type of craft, the season of the year and the direction of travel. We have seen that Icelus got to Clunia in seven days (but it was summer); contrariwise a heavy merchantman sailing from Alexandria to Rome could take as long as two months. In winter you enjoyed, like St Paul, a fair chance of shipwreck and the virtual certainty of unpredictable delays, like those of Fielding on his last journey to Lisbon. An average speed under sail might vary between 1 and 4 knots, with a maximum approaching 6 in the most favourable conditions. It was, for instance, at this leisurely average speed that news proceeded up the Nile from Alexandria, and there is plenty of evidence that for information to reach Thebes from the coast a month was necessary. This slowness of communications, intolerable to us, had an important consequence in the relative weakness of the central authority and the relative independence of the provincial governor, despite his accountability to the emperor and Senate and the by no means unreal risk of impeachment by injured provincials. Nor did the annual tenure of the home magistracy apply in the majority of the provincial posts, and governors might be left, like Otho and Galba, for several years in the same command. An ordinary degree of common sense and fair dealing could win a man considerable *gratia*; but his absence was remembered and unpopularity recorded.[8]

So Galba's survey of his world left him reasonably content. The first day of January seemed to promise the chance of a new and better era. On the second, no business could be transacted, for the day was unlucky.

On the third the Senate met again, beginning its business with yet another traditional act of homage: this time the offering of prayers on behalf of the reigning monarch and the eternity of Rome. And the minutes of the noble Brethren of the Fields contain an entry under this day:

On the third day of January, in the presidency of Servius Galba, Emperor Caesar Augustus, and the vice-presidency of Lucius Salvius Otho Titianus, in the name of the College of the Brethren of the Fields, members offered vows for the well-being of Servius Galba, Emperor Caesar Augustus Pontifex Maximus Holder of the Tribunician Power. By the immolation of victims upon the Capitol the College paid what the president of the previous year had vowed and it formulated new vows for the coming year according to the form of words dictated by the vice-president L. Salvius Otho Titianus, as follows: 'To Jupiter a bull, to Juno a cow, to Minerva a cow, to the Goddess of Survival a cow; in the new temple, to the sacred Augustus a bull, to the sacred Augusta a cow, to the sacred Claudius a bull.' Members present: L. Salvius Otho Titianus, M. Raecius Taurus, L. Maecius Postumus.

Would deities so lavishly bribed carry out their part of the bargain? It was hard to be certain when you reflected that last year's vows, now so meticulously fulfilled, had been offered for the well-being of Nero.

2

The Five Days' Caesar

On 9 January a fast messenger arrived at the palace in Rome from Pompeius Propinquus, financial secretary of the province of Belgian Gaul, whose headquarters were at Trier on the Mosel. He brought with him grave news. On the morning of 1 January, at the military parade at which—at Mainz as at every other military station throughout the empire—the soldiers' annual oath of loyalty was to be renewed, the Fourth and Twenty-Second Legions, who were encamped together, had refused to swear allegiance to Galba. There had recently been mutterings against him. If one Spanish legion could make an emperor, why could not seven German ones? It was intolerable that Galba had punished the Gallic tribes who had opposed the rebel Vindex and shown favour to the supporters of the man whom they themselves had defeated and crushed at Besançon. Nor, by all accounts, did the new emperor promise to be an easy chief. He belonged to the old school. He was a martinet and a stickler for the regulations. What was more, he had probably engineered in the autumn the death of the popular and easy-going governor of Lower Germany, Fonteius Capito. To crown all, their own candidate for the empire, Verginius Rufus, had had to give way, as general officer commanding the Upper Rhine, to the gouty and feeble Hordeonius Flaccus.[9]

On this occasion the general and his legionary commanders had taken up their position as usual on a raised tribunal, surrounded by the eagles and standards before which—and before the emperor's statue— the oath was to be administered. Flaccus had had to look on helplessly as a party of activists from the Fourth Legion rushed the platform. Four centurions of the Twenty-Second Legion, whose loyalty was at first less undermined, tried to protect it, but were overwhelmed in the stampede and hustled off to confinement. The statue was overturned, the portrait medallions torn from the standards, and a chaos ensued in which some of the officers joined. Eventually the troops did take the oath, not to Galba, but to the Senate and People of Rome—a convenient political slogan already employed by Vindex, Verginius Rufus and Galba himself. It perhaps meant little, and certainly invited the nomination of a candidate to be retrospectively accepted by the authorities in

Rome. At this stage no name had emerged, and no one attempted to harangue the troops.

Later that day the officers of the two legions had held a secret emergency meeting. It seemed necessary to take urgent steps to prevent a complete breakdown of discipline and the risk of civil war. It was clear that the upper army would have none of Galba. Hordeonius Flaccus was out of the question. The obvious remaining candidate was the officer governing Lower Germany, Aulus Vitellius. But there were differences of opinion on this, too. Vitellius was scarcely known, and though he seemed to have made a favourable impression on his own men in the short month since taking up his command, it was impossible to judge his qualifications for empire. But the commander of the Fourth, Caecina Alienus, who had his own reasons for disliking Galba, came out strongly in favour of an approach to Vitellius, and though the meeting had come to no clear decision, he had secretly sent off the standard-bearer of his legion to carry the news of the revolt against Galba to Vitellius at Cologne.

Of Aulus Caecina Alienus we know little beyond what the history of the Long Year tells us. He belonged, like the commander at Bonn, Fabius Valens, to a type of army officer afflicted by political or rather personal ambitions not easily satisfied by the slow advancement of a regular army career. He was born at Vicenza in northern Italy, and in April 68, as we have seen, was financial secretary of the province of Southern Spain and as such had quickly rallied to Galba. In the summer or autumn he was rewarded with the command of the Fourth (Mace-donian) Legion. But almost immediately his past caught up with him. Galba, it seemed, had given orders, not yet executed, for his prosecution on the charge of having misappropriated public funds, a weakness not to the liking of the new emperor. The alleged offence had presumably been committed in Spain, and was perhaps revealed when his books were examined by his successor there; but whatever the details, Caecina had a strong motive for swapping allegiance at speed.

His *aquilifer* covered the 120 miles rapidly and entered Cologne after dusk on the same day at an hour when Vitellius was entertaining a large and distinguished company to a New Year dinner. The governor had to come to an immediate decision on a situation for which he was not perhaps entirely unprepared. It is hard to resist the suspicion that he had already been tentatively sounded by the two men who were to figure so prominently in his future reign, Caecina Alienus and Fabius Valens. But now the fateful decision was his. He must either countenance, or else crush, a scandalous breach of loyalty to the reigning emperor. The oath of allegiance to the Senate and People was a transparent fiction. The safest thing, he considered, would be to report the events in a neutral tone to his legionary commanders in Lower

Germany and await their reaction. He could then declare himself one way or the other. Power and privilege had some attractions for the impoverished Vitellius; but they were not overwhelming.

But of these calculations Pompeius Propinquus' messenger could know nothing. All he could report to Rome was that the legions of Upper Germany had broken their oath of loyalty, inviting thereby a change of emperor. Pompeius had acted immediately on hearing the news. His messenger was instructed to use the utmost speed in this calamitous situation. In eight days he covered 1,000 miles, posting along the main roads that connected Trier, Besançon, the Great St Bernard, Milan and Rome.

Galba's reaction was equally prompt. He was anxious, if not unduly alarmed, about the recalcitrance of the two legions, and could know nothing of the length to which the Rhineland plots had gone. He was in no position to repel an invasion of Italy. His troops in the capital were a mixed bunch of drafts of varying quality, and he had already sent off the formation in which he could have fully trusted, VII Galbiana, dispatched under its enterprising commander Antonius Primus to Petronell on the Danube to take the place of the Tenth, transferred to Spain. It was clearly high time to put into operation a move which he had been contemplating in recent weeks: the public adoption of an heir, a co-Caesar, selected and trained to take over power whenever the moment came. This was how Augustus had proclaimed Tiberius his heir and presumptive successor ten years before his own death, and in A.D. 14 power had passed smoothly to the new emperor. For Galba the choice was not difficult. Gossips believed that Otho was the obvious candidate, and Otho shared their view. He was backed by the emperor's consular colleague, Titus Vinius, who may have hoped to marry off his daughter to Otho. But Galba, though grateful for the support of the governor of Lusitania in the early days, could see flaws of character: the man was designing, selfish, a spendthrift, a popularity-hunter. He wore a wig, and on the march to Rome it was suspected that he studied his appearance in a mirror, like an actor in his dressing-room. No, it was little use having inherited power from Nero if this were to pass to Otho. The name of another possible candidate had been canvassed: Cornelius Dolabella came of a famous line and was closely connected with Galba. But the emperor thought little of Dolabella's prudence, though the latter's status was high enough to earn him exile at the hands of Otho and death at the bidding of Vitellius.

The tenth day of January was an unpleasantly stormy day, pronounced of ill omen by those who were wise after the event: there was thunder, and lightning filled a sullen sky. But idle superstition meant nothing to Galba. He summoned a privy council consisting of Vinius, Laco, Ducenius Geminus, prefect of the city and *ex-officio* commander of the

B

Urban Cohorts, and finally of one of the consuls designate, the excellent and loyal Marius Celsus who managed to serve—and survive—a succession of emperors. After a few remarks on his advancing years and childlessness, and the need for a young heir, Galba summoned his choice. The great secret was revealed. A thirty-year-old man was presented: Lucius Calpurnius Piso Licinianus, the next emperor, it seemed, of the Romans.

He came of an unlucky line. He was the fourth son of Marcus Licinius Crassus Frugi, consul in 27 under Tiberius and crony of Claudius, who honoured him with triumphal ornaments and the pontificate, and then executed him together with one of his sons. Another brother had died a year or so before 69 as victim of Nero. A third survived Nero and the Long Year to share the family fate a little later, probably in 70 and at the command of Mucianus. His sister was married to the Piso who was governor of Africa in 69/70 and who despite his extreme caution was to be assassinated by a military colleague anxious to curry favour with the new régime. Piso himself, Galba's choice, had been exiled by Nero. Such a grim record of persecution and extermination argues family pretentions and prominence dangerous under suspicious rulers; names too famous—and descent on the maternal side from the great Pompey, on the paternal from the great Crassus—proved a damnable inheritance under Julians and Flavians alike.

The young man's appearance was presentable, even handsome; his demeanour was modest; and nothing was known against his character. In January 69 he enjoyed the considerable advantage of having been one of Nero's victims, not, like Otho, one of his favourites, for that emperor had had him denounced by the notorious informer, Regulus, no doubt in connection with the witch-hunt that followed the conspiracy of 65. On coming to power, Galba had brought him back to Rome from exile and as supreme pontiff had given him what often accompanied office, and now served as a substitute for it, a priesthood. It was not generally known that Piso was already named in Galba's will as his private heir. The emperor now took the young man by the hand in token of intent to give him public and political adoption, offering some sensible advice on the tasks that lay ahead. 'You are called,' he said, 'to be the leader of a people that can tolerate neither total servitude nor total liberty.' Tiberius, in Galba's youth, had said the same thing more brutally: being emperor was like holding a wolf by the ears. The advice given, the privy council offered their congratulations, taking the consent of Senate and People for granted. Piso, it was noted with approval, betrayed no indications of elation now or afterwards. He addressed his adoptive father and sovereign in respectful language, and gave the impression of being competent, rather than eager, to be emperor. Piso was clearly a man after Galba's own heart,

possessing old-fashioned virtues which Rome had not seen in its rulers
for many a day. Even now we cannot deny that, if fortune had allowed
him survival, he might have gone down in history as one of the 'good
emperors'. His lack of political experience, inevitable in a young man
and an exile, would have been rectified by office and time.

The selection of Piso as heir and presumptive emperor was then
announced in the Praetorian barracks, earlier than in the Senate. This
attempt to placate the restless Guard was not entirely unsuccessful.
Beneath a leaden sky, Galba delivered a prepared speech of military
brevity, saying that in adopting a successor outside his own family and
the circle of his military men, he was following, indeed improving upon,
the example set by Augustus in his choice of Tiberius. To stop exaggerated rumours, he openly admitted that the Mainz legions had failed
to swear fealty, but added that this was merely a matter of words: they
would soon return to duty. Unfortunately, there was still no mention
of a donative. Despite this curt and unaccommodating announcement,
the officers and front ranks cheered. Those who did not needed only a
token inducement to join in. No such inducement was offered.

Piso was then presented to the Senate in an equally brief ceremony,
and received a warm welcome, much of it genuine, some of it perfunctory. He was now officially Servius Sulpicius Galba Caesar, son of
Augustus, and in honour of his adoption under this name (which,
however, owing to the briefness of his reign appears in no other extant
source), the minute book of the dutiful Brethren of the Fields notes the
inevitable sacrifice upon the Capitol to Jupiter, Minerva and the
well-being of Rome. The oxen were slaughtered to no purpose. Piso's
reign was to last just five days. His record is brief—and good.

These events were a severe shock to Otho. As one of the first provincial governors to support Galba in the spring of 68, as one familiar—
though at the distance of ten years' exile in Lusitania—with Roman
society, a member of a family distinguished for public service (his
father had been greatly honoured by Claudius), with a good record as
a provincial governor and of an easy and affable manner, he had believed
it inevitable that he would be chosen to succeed on the death of the
elderly stop-gap. Looking ahead, Otho had already ingratiated himself
with Galba's Praetorians, both on the march to Rome and now in the
capital, as men recollected afterwards. He had secured the friendship
of Plotius Firmus, commander of the Watch, and his methods of corruption were enterprising. For instance, a member of the emperor's
bodyguard, Cocceius Proculus, happened to be in dispute with a
neighbour over part of the latter's land: Otho bought up the whole of
the neighbour's farm and presented it to Proculus as a gift.

Until 10 January he seems to have had no inkling of the great
disappointment to come. Yet without realizing it, he had by now ceased

to belong to the inner circle of Galba's advisers. His reaction to the choice of Piso makes this conclusion inevitable. Otho's repugnance for civil war, revealed in the coming months, makes it likely that he would never have sought the principate if Galba had revealed to him the increasingly serious news from Germany. Otho was not the man to advance knowingly into a head-on confrontation with the most powerful and coherent army group in the Roman empire. In ignorance of the danger from outside Italy, he had eyes only for the preservation of his career in the capital. He was thirty-six years old, the new Caesar thirty. This similarity in age, no less than their difference in character, was such as to render an eventual succession in the last degree improbable, even if Otho could wait so long. For their own reasons his followers played upon his mortification, and even persuaded him that his life might be in danger. With these alarmist suggestions Otho half agreed: they salved his conscience. In a fit of pique and desperation, he decided upon a gambler's throw—all or nothing. Galba was old, Piso as yet untried and unknown. He, Otho, would strike hard and strike at once. If the treason succeeded, he would be emperor. If not, there was always a quick way out.

Otho put his confidential freedman Onomastus in charge of the plot, and the latter produced two non-commissioned officers of the imperial bodyguard, whom by careful sounding Otho found to be both competent and unscrupulous. They were handsomely bribed, and given money for bribing others. The men, Veturius and Proculus (their names survive, carefully consigned to eternal infamy), played upon the anger and anxiety of those of the Praetorians who were disgruntled at Galba's tightening of discipline, greedy for the donative or fearful of being under a cloud as supporters of the unsuccessful putsch of Nymphidius Sabinus in 68. A few were let into the inner counsels of the plot. Some attempt was also made to seduce all the scattered legionary detachments and auxiliary regiments. Early in January, for reasons that cannot be unconnected with his suspicion of Otho, Galba had cashiered two tribunes of the Praetorian Guard, and a tribune each of the paramilitary Urban Cohorts and Watch, respectively Aemilius Pacensis and Julius Fronto. One of the cashiered Praetorian tribunes, Lucius Antonius Naso, must certainly have stood well in Otho's esteem. An inscription found at Baalbek tells us that he had already had an honourable and lengthy military career. Decorated by Nero as a company commander in two legions, he had been senior company commander of a third, staff officer of a fourth, and had then been given a cohort of the Watch and in succession two Urban Cohorts. Now, by January 69, he was in command of the Ninth Praetorian Cohort. As a reward for his support of Otho he was destined to be advanced to the command of a good fighting formation, the Fourteenth Legion. Whatever the part played by Naso in the complicated activities of this legion in our year, he continued his career unimpeded by the changes of emperor. Still to come were the posts of tribune of the First Cohort of Praetorians and an imperial secretaryship in the Anatolian province of Pontus and Bithynia. As late as 77 or 78, another stone (from Bursa in that province) records his road-building activities in the neighbourhood. That Galba had thought it necessary to discharge a man of this calibre shows that Otho could rely on some solid support among the Praetorians. The sequel, indeed, was to prove it. As Plutarch remarks (and perhaps read in his Roman source), 'a loyal army could not have been corrupted in four days, which was the extent of the interval between the adoption and the assassination'. Less certain is the suspicion that Titus Vinius was implicated. Though a friend of Otho, he had received the signal honour of sharing the consulship with the emperor, and he had little to gain by treachery that loyalty had not already secured him. He opposed advice that proved fatal to Galba on 15 January, and his own death (given high priority in the instructions to the assassins) might seem to attest his innocence. But Vinius gets hostile treatment in our sources. He was perhaps selected by the Othonian pamphleteers for the role of Galba's evil genius, a propaganda stroke by which they hoped to excuse the Othonian treason and account for Vinius' perhaps unintended death.[10]

But the numbers involved in the conspiracy were not great, and Tacitus may be forgiven his sally: 'Two ordinary soldiers took it upon themselves to award the Roman Empire to a usurper: and they succeeded.' A wild idea to carry Otho off from a banquet on 11 January in order to be declared emperor in the barracks was rightly scotched by Onomastus. He proved to be a good organizer. On 15 January Otho was to stay by the emperor's side until the very last minute, find a pretext for leaving him when all was ready, move to the Praetorian barracks and make a bid for the support of the guards as a whole. If this succeeded, it would be easy to surround the palace, and, to make assurance doubly sure, key accomplices had been found in the very cohort that would be on duty there at the time. No speedy or effective intervention was likely from the legionaries and auxiliaries scattered through Rome in temporary quarters; in any case they hardly rivalled the Praetorian Guard in strength or prestige. And seizing the barracks had an additional and vital advantage. Arms were not normally worn by troops within the city; their issue in an emergency would take time, and indeed the principal armoury of Rome lay precisely within the area of the Praetorian barracks. If Otho dominated these, he dominated Rome, and Galba —at any rate temporarily—would be helpless.

At dawn on 15 January a ceremony took place at the altar before the Temple of Apollo on the Palatine, most commonly, but not beyond dispute, identified with a shrine on the south-west flank of the hill overlooking the Circus Maximus. Servius Sulpicius Galba, Emperor Caesar Augustus Pontifex Maximus, was performing his morning sacrifice. He was no doubt attended by his suite, and certainly by Otho himself. When the court diviner Gaius Umbricius Melior examined the lobes and markings of the liver of the victim, he prophesied doom: a plot was imminent, the traitor was within the gates. Otho, standing immediately behind Galba, overheard the prophecy, and was as much delighted by a prediction that seemed to promise success to himself as others were alarmed by the menace to their emperor. A few minutes later, Onomastus appeared and whispered to Otho: 'The architect and contractors are waiting for you at home.' This was the prearranged code message indicating that the moment had come, and that a party of troops was waiting to take Otho from the north-west end of the Forum Romanum, where their presence would evoke no comment, to the Praetorian barracks. As Otho made to move away, someone said, 'Why are you going?' Otho had his reply ready: he was proposing to buy some decayed property, which had to be surveyed before the deal was complete. Then without impediment he slipped to the rear of the temple, hurried along beside the Palace of Tiberius by the 150-foot gallery where Nero's stucco putti looked down upon him, descended to the rear of the Basilica Julia and from there passed in a moment to the Golden Milestone near the Temple of Saturn. From this cylinder of marble faced with gilded bronze, centre of the civilized world, departed all the great roads of an empire studded with its humbler and more functional brethren. For Otho, too, this was a beginning. He must follow his road to a new and unknown destination.[11]

But on reaching the Miliarum Aureum he was appalled by the fewness of the troops awaiting him. They were twenty-three *speculatores*, members of the imperial bodyguard. Still, they saluted him briskly as Imperator, quickly placed him in a closed chair, drew their swords and carried him away. Otho himself was on tenterhooks with anxiety, repeatedly urging on the bearers: unless they hurried, all would be lost. A somewhat greater number joined in with the party while it was in the Forum or else further on the way—some in the know, many bewildered, a few shouting and flourishing their swords, others in silence, prudently. The officer on duty at the barracks was the tribune Julius Martialis. Whether he lost his nerve when confronted with an inconceivable coup, or whether he was an accomplice of the mutineers, no one was ever able to discover. What is certain is that he—and the other officers present—offered no resistance. Nobody knew for certain the extent and ramifications of the movement, and there was no individual who had the resolution to challenge the determined little band of plotters. Gradually, at first in ones and twos, compelled by the rebels that surrounded them, then contagiously in a growing stream, sheeplike, afraid to be left behind, the other ranks joined the men gathered round Otho. The pretender greeted each newcomer with a handshake. When general support seemed assured, he climbed on to a platform, from which the ceremonial golden statue of Galba had been hastily removed, and against a background of massed flags and standards acknowledged the plaudits of his men, less like an emperor than a popular entertainer. He raised his hands in acknowledgement of the applause of the audience, bowed to the mob, and even threw kisses to them, aping the servant in order to become the master. His inflammatory speech dwelt heavily upon Galba's failure to pay the promised bounty, his severity and the undue influence of his inner clique of advisers. It was plausibly argued, well delivered and received with acclaim. The armoury was then opened at Otho's order and weapons hastily distributed. Preparations were made to occupy key points in the city.

Meanwhile, at the altar of Apollo, Galba continued to pray to the gods of an empire no longer his. Suddenly news came that a senator of unknown identity was being conducted by an armed retinue to the Praetorian barracks. After a while the man was identified as Otho. So this was a coup d'état. Galba consulted his immediate entourage. It seemed advisable that Piso should explore the loyalty of the Praetorian cohort on duty at the palace. He addressed a parade in sensible language, stressing the unsuitability of Otho as an emperor and the Praetorian tradition of loyalty to the sovereign and concluding with an undertaking that the long-delayed donative would now be paid. The speech was well enough received, and preparations were made for the emergency, though precisely what action to take was less obvious, and the élite of the cohort, the *speculatores*, had slipped away, evidently to join Otho or carry out some traitorous task assigned to them. A second step was to probe the attitude of the motley collection of troops scattered in the city. The faithful Marius Celsus, who had commanded a legion years before, was sent off to the drafts called up by Nero from the Danube armies and brought back by him to Rome at the time of the Vindex crisis in March 68. They were bivouacked among the cloistered laurels of the Portico of Agrippa, a mile to the north, on the east side of Broad Street beyond the aqueduct. But here Onomastus and his officers had done their work well. The men had hoped to serve Nero in the East. They declared for Nero's one-time friend, and drove Celsus away at the point of the *pilum*. Three Praetorian cohort commanders— one at least, Subrius Dexter, survived the year and turns up as governor of Sardinia in 74—had a more difficult task. They were dispatched upon the desperate, and, as it proved, hopeless, errand of seeing if the situation in the barracks could be retrieved. Subrius and one other were greeted with threats, and the third, a known friend of Galba, roughly handled and put under close arrest. Nearer at hand, Liberty Hall behind the Senate House served as quarters for the contingents from the armies of Germany. Two centurions sent to approach them found these forces less hostile, for Galba had given them considerate treatment as a recompense for enduring the agonies of boredom and seasickness entailed by the useless winter voyage to and from Egypt. But even these troops were divided in their sympathies. After all, they came from formations in an area which seemed to be supporting neither Galba nor Otho, but Vitellius, and owing to their proximity to the palace, some individuals among them had been given special instructions by Onomastus. As for the naval legion, quartered we know not where—perhaps by the lake in the grounds of Nero's abandoned Golden House—Galba's rough treatment of it on his arrival in Rome had successfully killed its loyalty. To this formation no approach was made. It was a pity that the Seventh had been sent off. As it was, Galba seemed to have only a handful of men upon whom he could call.[12]

It was some little time before the forlorn envoys returned to announce failure. They were surprised to find a mood of jubilation in and around the palace. In the interval a mob, alerted by the strange passage of Otho to the barracks, had gathered in the Forum and even within the palace grounds on the hill, vociferous, buoyant and surprisingly pro-Galban. They clamoured for Otho's head. Within the palace itself, the emperor was still closeted with Piso, Vinius, Laco and Icelus, debating his course of action. The council of war was split. Vinius held that the Palatine Hill should be defended until the mutineers had had time—and such things had happened more than once before—to come to their senses and return to duty. It would still be possible to venture out if the situation improved, but a premature exit might jeopardize everything irremediably. Critics of Galba's reign later alleged that Vinius was implicated in the plot. We have seen that this is improbable. His advice now was good, though he can hardly have known how good. Even with some inkling of the activities of Otho and Onomastus, he could not have foreseen the crucial synchronisms. But the pompous Laco, with Icelus' support, pooh-poohed the danger and asserted that honour and fortitude demanded a bold front and a confident appearance in public. In this they had a telling argument. Galba valued duty more highly than life, and a long career might well have taught him that courage in a crisis was the policy of success. With a friendly public around him and protected by a cohort believed to be loyal, Galba could surely risk encountering a few mutineers. Whatever else he was or was not, Galba was not a coward, and it seems that Piso agreed with his adoptive father. Now, after his apparent success with the Palatine cohort, the young Caesar was given the chance of trying his persuasive powers and the prestige of his rank upon the main body of

the Praetorians in their barracks. Galba had sent his officers in vain.
He was now sending his son. In the last resort he would face the men
himself.

Soon after Piso left the palace, Othonian agents planted in the Forum
spread the bogus report that the pretender had been killed. Then certain individuals claimed to have witnessed his death. At this point, it
seems, some senators and knights burst open the palace gates and poured
on Galba a torrent of congratulation. The multitude everywhere
lapped up the pleasant news. Finally one of the imperial bodyguard,
Julius Atticus, obviously acting a part, came in to the now crowded
palace and called out to Galba that he had done the deed himself,
flourishing a blood-stained sword as if that were proof. He did not
know his Galba. The emperor's retort was immediate and incisive:
'And who gave you the order, my man?' The remark was relished by
the retailers of anecdotes. But Galba, however anxious to preserve
military discipline, had not bothered, or was not able, to interrogate
the braggart more closely, nor had he reckoned with Onomastus'
cunning. It seemed that Otho was dead and that Piso's mission had
been unnecessary. Galba put on a light protective garment and had
himself carried in the imperial litter through the clapping and jubilant
throng on his way, not now to face the mutineers in the barracks, but
to express thanks for deliverance to the god who punishes traitors and
guarantees the life of Rome.

The emperor had not reached the Forum when Piso met him with
bad news. Celsus too returned with information of his failure. As hope
faded and Otho's control of the barracks was confirmed, chaos set in
among Galba's followers. Laco and many of the loud-mouthed champions quietly melted away. But for Galba himself there was no going
back now. The euphoria of the mob or its uncertainty, flowing this
way and that, swept the litter and its occupant irresistibly forward
into the scuffling press of bodies in the piazza. The guards appeared
to be useless. Galba was carried this way and that, the helpless victim
of adulation and treachery. Yet the mob was strangely quiet. Their
faces bore a look of vague bewilderment, their ears were strained to
catch the latest rumour. There was no shouting, only an indistinct
murmurous rumour of expectation, neither fearful nor angry. Those
who looked on from the podia of the temples seemed to be spectators at
a show that was about to begin, as if the Forum were a circus or a
theatre.

Galba had made his slow progress past the little round Temple of
Vesta, moving to the north-west end of the square whence the road
led up to the Capitol. By the seventh arch of the Basilica Julia he was
close to the Basin of Curtius, that spot of many legends almost in the
middle of the Forum, where, by a monumental well-head, a fig tree,

an olive and a vine provided loungers in the piazza with welcome shade. A body of cavalry appeared to the right, in the opening of the Argiletum alongside the Senate House. They were Praetorians, but Galba noticed that they were improperly dressed. Then through the columns of the Basilica Aemilia there emerged infantry. These must have been men of the drafts from Germany, quartered just behind. They had clearly been waiting their moment. The cavalry, Praetorian or auxiliary, charged across the Forum, driving their way through high and low, making a desolation. The crowd scattered before them towards the balcony of the Basilica Julia, or the steps of the Temples of Castor, Saturn, Julius Caesar and Concord, deities now condemned to contemplate impassively an unarmed old man, a consul, a pontifex maximus, an emperor, murdered without warning or mercy by his own guards. The litter stood isolated. The cavalry paused. Then Atilius Vergilio (so most authorities say), an ensign of the cohort which should have protected Galba, ripped the medallion carrying the emperor's effigy from the pole of his standard and dashed it to the ground. This was the prearranged gesture to which Otho, in his speech at the barracks, had made reference in the words, 'When the cohort on the Palatine catches sight of you, when it receives my signal, you will know that all the troops are with you. The only struggle that awaits you is a competition to see who can earn my deepest gratitude.'[13]

The nature of this competition was now revealed: it was to select the speediest assassins. First some *pila* were hurled by the infantry at the litter, but they missed it. Then the men drew their swords, obeying the familiar drill of battle. But this time there was no danger. One soldier alone on Galba's side did his duty—Sempronius Densus, a Praetorian centurion who accompanied the little group as Piso's personal bodyguard. He stood in front of Galba's litter and raising his centurion's vine rod shouted to the advancing infantry to spare their emperor. They tried to push past him. He then drew his sword and entirely unaided engaged Galba's assailants for some time until he was brought to the ground by a knee-blow and killed.

During the scuffle the bearers had set down their burden in a panic, and had fled. The chair was overturned in the confusion, and Galba was thrown to the ground, sprawling. He offered his throat to the assassins, telling them to get the business over quickly: 'Strike—if this is what is best for Rome.' A soldier of the Fifteenth Legion from Vetera (if the usual version is right) thrust his sword deep into Galba's throat. Others hacked at the unprotected arms and legs in a frenzy. Vinius quickly suffered a similar fate. In front of the Temple of Julius Caesar, he was struck by a blow on the back of the knee and transfixed from side to side by a legionary. As for Piso, the heroic resistance of Sempronius Densus had given him time to cover the 100 yards to the Temple

of Vesta, where he hoped to find sanctuary. But the goddess of the
eternal fire, whose life typified Rome's own life, no more protected him
than she had the Pontifex Maximus, Quintus Mucius Scaevola, 150
years before. The temple officer, a state slave, took pity on Piso and
concealed him in a tiny room, perhaps the *penus* in which the sacred
Palladium was kept. But two of Otho's men had been detailed to
dispatch his hated rival. One was Sulpicius Florus, member of an
auxiliary cohort serving in Britain who had just been given Roman
citizenship by Galba. The other was the imperial bodyguard, Statius
Murcus. Even assassins have their scruples. They dragged Piso out and
murdered him at the door of the temple. So perished violently Servius
Sulpicius Galba, sixth emperor of Rome, his heir Piso and his fellow-
consul Vinius.[14]

The bodies of Galba, Piso and Vinius were decapitated, and the heads
carried to the barracks to be displayed to Otho. They were then impaled
and paraded round the square in a grisly procession backed by the
cohort standards of the Praetorians and the legionary eagle of the
marine legion. A number of men claimed without justification the merit
of participating in the slaughter, and demanded a prize for an infamy
they had not achieved. Indeed, it is said that more than 120 petitions
demanding a reward for some 'service' on 15 January later fell into
the hands of Vitellius.

The mob and some magistrates now hastily made their way to the
barracks, where Otho awaited the issue of the day, and lavished on the
new master the compliments with which, a few hours before, they had
been so free towards the old. Among those who presented themselves
the most considerable was Marius Celsus, a loyal supporter of Galba
to the last and consul designate for July and August according to that
emperor's dispositions. The troops, or some of them, were aware of his
appeal to the Danubian contingents to defend Galba, and demanded
his execution, a request which Otho properly and successfully resisted
by alleging that Celsus must first be interrogated. He thus managed to
save, and soon publicly honoured, a man of character and integrity,
qualities of which the new régime stood sorely in need. Fresh Praetorian
prefects, Plotius Firmus and Licinius Proculus, were chosen by the
troops themselves, and Flavius Sabinus, the elder brother of Vespasian,
was given the prefecture of the city, a position which he had already
held for many years under Nero. This appointment was judicious: it
seems to have been designed to win the support of Vespasian and yet
maintain a link with Nero. Demands for reforms in the military regulations were voiced, and in due course amendments were made, and
indeed retained as beneficial by later emperors. The ex-prefect Laco,
who had made himself scarce during the confusion in the Forum, was
given the impression that he would be exiled, but Otho arranged for

him to be put to death. Icelus the freedman was publicly executed on the spot.

Then the Senate met at the summons of the city praetor, both consuls being dead. Otho made a speech in the chamber seeking to exculpate himself by claiming that he had been made emperor willy-nilly by the troops; and a subservient Senate—what else could it do?—hastened to award him the imperial titles of Imperator Caesar Augustus. Motions were passed recommending him for the consulship, the enjoyment of tribunician power, and the post of Pontifex Maximus. These three still lay theoretically in the gift of the Roman people, and formal elections were necessary. They are alluded to in the minutes of the Brethren of the Fields under the respective dates 26 January, 28 February and 9 March. It will be observed that Otho was apparently in no mood to hurry on the formalities. The reasons for this caution may become apparent as our narrative proceeds.

From the Senate House Otho passed across the Forum to the Capitol, presumably for the mockery of invoking Jupiter's blessing upon the day's work, and thence along the Basilica Julia and Nero's Colonnade to the Clivus Palatinus that gave access to the palace. The headless bodies of Piso, Vinius and Galba still lay where they had fallen. The new emperor gave permission for the relatives of the former two to bury their dead. Titus Vinius' body was carried away by his daughter Crispina, whose name had once been linked by gossips with Otho's. Piso was laid to rest by his widow Verania Gemina, daughter of the distinguished soldier Quintus Veranius, who had been governor of Britain from 57 and had died there the following year. Visitors to the Terme Museum in Rome may read the simple and dignified inscription, handsomely lettered, of a grave altar erected by her in quieter times and completed at her own death thirty years later:

TO THE DIVINE SPIRIT

OF L. CALPURNIUS PISO

FRUGI LICINIANUS

MEMBER OF THE COMMITTEE OF 15 IN CHARGE OF SACRIFICES

AND OF VERANIA

DAUGHTER OF Q. VERANIUS CONSUL AND AUGUR

GEMINA

WIFE OF PISO FRUGI

There is no mention here of 'Caesar', of old unhappy things of long ago; but the brief description of Piso as member of a sacred college recalled the whole grim story to the observer. The stone, with two others relating to the Crassus family, was found in 1884 in a sepulchral chamber on the Via Salaria between the Colline and Salarian Gates, in the grounds of the former Villa Bonaparte. Both Crispina and Verania had been compelled to search for the heads and pay a ransom for them.

As for Galba, he had no wife or family to care for his remains. The truncated body lay disregarded for many hours, and in the darkness ghoulish marauders offered it further outrage. Finally, by means not entirely clear, it was buried in a humble grave in the grounds of Galba's villa on the Via Aurelia, on the western outskirts of Rome. The head had been impaled like the others, and was found next day in front of the tomb of a creature of Nero's sentenced by Galba. It was then laid to rest with the ashes of the body which had already been cremated.

Grisly as these details are for modern readers, they were even more shocking to the ancient observer. Dignity in death and burial was if anything more important than decorum in life and action. The events of 15 January provided, and provide, a painful example of the ease with which an inhuman barbarity could without warning shatter the fragile façade of order, loyalty and decency which Rome claimed as her peculiar qualities.

The judgment of historians upon Galba has been too often determined by the brilliant but superficial obituary notice—a concatenation of artful antitheses—which in Tacitus immediately follows the account of the emperor's cremation and burial. It concludes with a forced and famous epigram: 'So long as he was a subject, he seemed too great a man to be one, and by common consent possessed the makings of a ruler—had he never ruled': *omnium consensu capax imperii, nisi imperasset.* The Roman historian has the weakness that he is not only seduced by epigram but given to *post eventum* condemnation. It is assuredly a fault to allow oneself to be assassinated in a palace conspiracy: it shows ignorance and recklessness. But the lapse tells us little about the victim's qualities as man and emperor. Our questions relate to the life, not the death, of Galba.[15]

Of his qualifications for the principate there could be no doubt. He had known, and had been on friendly terms with, all the Julio-Claudian emperors, except—latterly—Nero. He enjoyed distinguished ancestry and a very considerable inherited fortune which he husbanded almost as carefully as, at the end of his life, he controlled the finances of the state. He owned the country house at Fondi where he was born, and a suburban villa. These imply capital invested in landed property, and the family possessed the immense and immensely profitable granaries at Rome known as the Horrea Sulpicia. Physically he was as hard as nails. During his German command, he impressed Gaius during a visit of inspection in 39 by doubling for twenty miles behind the emperor's chariot while directing a route-march with shield signals. He had been awarded the triumphal ornaments and three priesthoods — the highest military honours and orders of chivalry of ancient Rome. By 68 his career had been, as we have seen, long and distinguished. His strictness, regretfully criticized by Tacitus as unsuited to the degenerate modern age, was the subject of many anecdotes no doubt embroidered in the telling. He is said by Suetonius to have sentenced a money-changer of questionable honesty to have both hands cut off and nailed to the counter. He crucified, it seems, a man who had poisoned his ward to inherit the property. When the murderer protested that he was a Roman citizen and therefore could appeal to Caesar, Galba ironically remarked, 'Let the Roman hang higher than the rest, and have his cross whitewashed.'[16]

The success of Otho's plot, carefully planned though it was, was due in large part to a very practical weakness in Galba's position as emperor. To the Senate and People he was as acceptable as an old man of strict principle can be; but he lacked something which on any reasonable expectation he should never have needed in the city of Rome—a body of troops personally devoted to him. The situation on 15 January might have been very different if the legion he had recruited in Spain and brought with him to Rome, VII Galbiana, had still been there. A force of this kind competently handled could have defended the palace area and swung the undecided garrison solidly behind it and against the plotter; and Otho's task of persuading the Praetorians that they had everything to gain by treason would have been immeasurably harder. It may legitimately be claimed, therefore, that Galba was ill-served and over-confident. But if he is to be condemned as a failure, the charge must be a weightier one than this, and Otho's resentment, the motive force of revolt, arose from decisions of Galba's which can easily be defended.

His traducers and, we may assume, Otho in his speeches of self-justification echoed by Othonian scribblers, pointed to brutality, meanness and senility. The last charge may be dismissed out of hand. Galba had a mind of his own and did not shrink from unpopular decisions. The amount and speed of the business transacted in his short reign is impressive. Equally inapposite is the accusation of brutality. The rebel Clodius Macer—other names are cited, less known to us, and in circumstances more mysterious—could hardly complain if the extreme penalty was exacted. Many crocodile tears were shed by the Othonians for the naval petitioners scattered at the gates of Rome by Galba's cavalry; but the casualties were grossly exaggerated by propagandists and their citation comes particularly badly from traitors prepared to practise butchery in the Forum. Galba might be strict: he was not vindictive. Julius Civilis, the Batavian noble sent to Nero for judgment on suspicion of rebellion, was set free. In an effort to curb corruption and to limit its consequences, the emperor fixed a two-year limit on provincial appointments. Galba also deprecated the prolonged witch-hunt begun immediately after Nero's death by those senators who had wrongs to avenge upon the Neronian prosecutor Eprius Marcellus, and in this attitude of realism, as in other respects, he resembles Mucianus and Vespasian.

The charge of meanness is even more senseless. After the extravagances of Nero's latter years, symbolized by the blatant ostentation of the Golden House and the Colossus, retrenchment was inevitable and inevitably unpopular. At the best of times the financial resources of the empire were hardly adequate to meet the immense charges upon it. This is the fundamental reason—apart from questions of military discipline—for Galba's reluctance to grant a donative to the Praetorians, who had done less than nothing to deserve it, or to encourage the prolongation of an evil into the future. For Galba himself the results of this inflexible insistence upon correct behaviour were fatal. Contemporary historians believed that if he could have brought himself to sacrifice principle to expediency even to the extent of a small token gift to the Praetorians and legionaries, he might never have lost his life. So evenly balanced, it was thought, were the scales of fortune; and Otho's own diffidence, if such was rightly attributed to him, seems to bear out the view of the critics.

The emperor's attempt to recover some of Nero's 'benefaction' from his cronies was perhaps expedient, and some people were gratified by the spectacle of retribution; but not much of substance was achieved. Another similarly laudable attempt at reform was the appointment of a reliable soldier, Gnaeus Julius Agricola, the future father-in-law of Tacitus, to make an inventory of the gifts deposited in the temples of Rome—a hint that the administration of a valuable patrimony had become lax. Measures of this sort clearly did little to enhance Galba's reputation except in the eyes of that tiny minority which had some concern for the public good; and they provided opponents with a useful propaganda weapon. Much was made of Galba's *avaritia*: 'covetousness' in one sense, 'economy' in another.

However, in one respect Galba was generous, perhaps ill-advisedly. A toll of 2·5 per cent was exacted on goods passing through the numerous customs posts lying on main roads in an extensive area of the west comprising modern Belgium, France, portions of Germany, Switzerland and northern Italy at such points as Lyon, Langres, Grenoble, Geneva, St Maurice-en-Valais, and Zürich. Galba's Gallic and Spanish coinage proclaimed its abolition. The measure was no doubt designed as some sort of compensation for the rough treatment handed out by the Rhine armies to Galba's ally Vindex, though the concession must have affected a much vaster public, traders and consumers, for instance, in Britain and central Italy. This was a blunt, indiscriminate and costly concession. There is no doubt that it was scrapped by Vespasian. A similar move to reward old allies imposed fiscal punishments on Lyon, which had remained pertinaciously loyal to Nero in the spring of 68, and granted fiscal concessions to Vindex' supporters—Vienne, the Aedui and the Sequani (whose capital Besançon had been the scene of Vindex' defeat and death). These breaches of Galba's own principles did nothing but harm, for they encouraged jealousies between the Gallic communities, always spiteful towards their immediate neighbours, prolonged old resentments and directly stimulated the movement which is dignified by the title of the Batavian War. Less undesirable was the grant of Latin rights (giving Roman citizenship to magistrates) made to Digne, for this method, whereby the peregrine was gradually admitted to the full privileges of *civitas*, was one traditionally practised by Rome to her own and the recipient's benefit.[17]

An essential qualification in a leader is the ability to choose good lieutenants. One gains the impression that Galba had few reserves to draw on in this respect. Eight years in the comparative remoteness of Spain had to a certain extent isolated him, and of set purpose he had avoided, during the bad and later years of Nero, contact with his equals. Nor was his judgment as prescient as the armchair historian requires. Sometimes he chose well: we have observed the preferment of Antonius Primus and Julius Agricola. Nor was much harm done by placing a pliable and mild-mannered Valerius Marinus upon the list of future consuls. But Laco and Vinius, whatever the truth behind the violent attacks upon them, gave Galba little help in his hour of need; and his two chief appointments in Germany were disastrous. That they had serious consequences, not for Galba but for Rome, was due to the presence among their subordinates of ambitious and designing legionary commanders.

For Galba himself the momentous choice was that of a successor. He could not expect a long reign, and he had no intention of allowing Rome to fall into the hands of Otho, assiduous as the latter had been in his support. When Tacitus places in Galba's mouth a long and eloquent speech on imperial adoption, he is clearly thinking of a contemporary event, the choice of Trajan by Nerva. By selecting a young man of promise from outside his own family, Galba introduced a method of appointment which marked a new step in constitutional development. The first Caesar, Julius, had chosen his grand-nephew Octavian. Augustus (Octavian) had selected a succession of heirs, all related to him by blood or marriage. Galba himself had been appointed by the acclaim of the troops, and the subsequent consent of the Senate and People. In now recommending his previously adopted private heir as his political successor, Galba might claim that he had solved the problem of reconciling irreconcilables—freedom and the principate. The mere fact that emperors were no longer born, but elected, and that their initial selection proceeded from the free choice of the reigning monarch among the best available talent irrespective of birth, approved by Senate and People, seemed a solution well suited to the empire, nor was Rome destined to find an answer that was better. There was general agreement before, during and after his reign that Galba was worthy and competent to be emperor; and the successful conspiracy of a disappointed courtier backed by a handful of desperadoes gives the historian no right to question the correctness of this judgment.

The fifteenth day of January in the year in which Servius Sulpicius Galba held the consulship for the second time with Titus Vinius as his colleague drew to its end. No one then living had experienced a day like it, and what the future held no one could guess. The ancestral curse, the inheritance of Romulus and Remus, was not yet exorcized.

3

Caecina and Valens

Early on 2 January Vitellius sent messengers from his headquarters at Cologne to the four legionary commanders of Lower Germany at Bonn, Neuss and Vetera, reporting the mutinous attitude of the Fourth and Twenty-Second Legions at Mainz communicated to him late on the previous evening. He put it to his lieutenants that they must either fight the rebels and remain faithful to their oath of loyalty to Galba, or, if the unity of the forces in Germany was thought worth preservation, nominate their own emperor. Prompt choice of a ruler, he added, would be safer than a prolonged search for one.

This well-weighed and diplomatically-phrased dispatch earned an immediate and enthusiastic response. At midday the commander of the First Legion, stationed at Bonn only twenty miles away, entered the walled city of Cologne at the head of his legionary and auxiliary cavalry, made his way to the governor's palace on the bank of the Rhine, and hailed Aulus Vitellius as Imperator. Vitellius accepted the acclamation and was carried in procession through the busiest streets of the city, holding a drawn sword, allegedly that of Julius Caesar, which someone had taken from the Temple of Mars and thrust into his hand.

In offering Vitellius the purple, the hard-headed and unscrupulous Fabius Valens must have known that his action would not be unwelcome. This in turn implies prior discussions between Vitellius and the two officers who were to be his marshals, Caecina and Valens, and the speed with which the movements gathered way points in the same direction. The lead offered was eagerly followed by Fabius Fabullus and Munius Lupercus, commanding respectively the Fifth and Fifteenth Legions stationed at Vetera, and by Numisius Rufus of the Sixteenth at Neuss. On the third day of January the Mainz garrison dropped its protestation of loyalty to the Senate and People of Rome and recognized Vitellius as emperor; and in due course the adherence of the outlying Twenty-First at Windisch was confirmed.

It is not difficult to reconstruct the considerations that induced Vitellius to accept this dangerous eminence. Some rational and not entirely selfish calculations may be attributed to him. If Galba on the strength of the acclamations of a single legion believed—and rightly believed—that he had a duty and a capacity to replace Nero, might not similar confidence and a similar duty be felt by the chosen candidate of seven legions? Legionaries were after all Roman citizens, spokesmen of the community at least as qualified to speak as the mob of Rome or even the Praetorians. There were not many places outside Italy, and few within it outside Rome, where it was possible for 35,000 Roman citizens to voice any, let alone a united, opinion. If ancestry were still a criterion of fitness to rule, Vitellius could point to a father who had achieved in the reigns of Tiberius and Claudius the high distinction of three consulships; and as consul in 48 and governor of Africa thereafter, he could at the age of fifty-four look back to a career if not of distinction yet of moderate success. He felt himself to be popular with his men, and he was undoubtedly easy-going, unpretentious, open-handed. Without vaulting ambition, he was willing to accept a leadership strongly pressed upon him by his subordinates. In any event Galba could not last long, and his death looked like bringing a new coup d'état. If the armed forces serving outside Italy were now to appoint their commander-in-chief, no army group had a better right to nominate one than that of the Rhine.

The attitude of the legionaries was more positive and self-interested. Though recruited primarily from Italy and highly Romanized areas, they had acquired from long service in one place a cohesion among themselves and a sort of local loyalty. A soldier had two countries: Italy and his camp. In theory and in law Roman legions were subordinate to their commander-in-chief, the emperor acting as the executive arm of the Roman Senate and People. They could be moved from one part of the wide empire to the other as he decided. In fact, none of the formations then under the command of Flaccus and Vitellius had been in Germany for less than twenty-eight years, and one—the Fifteenth —had occupied the same headquarters for fifty-nine years. As the term of legionary service was of twenty years, this implies—all allowance made for cross-postings—that many of the men, young and old, had served all their lives in the same legion and the same area of Germany. They had formed local attachments of every kind. But the policy of Galba, who had already moved the Tenth Legion from Pannonia to Spain after a stay of only five years, might well herald a threat to this comfortable immobility. Indeed common prudence was bound to suggest to Galba that troops prepared to make an emperor of Verginius Rufus should not be allowed a second chance of demonstrating their power: the legions in Germany were faced with the near certainty that the friend of Vindex would gradually avenge him by scattering them to the four corners of the world. If, however, Vitellius were to become emperor at the cost of a walk to Rome, there would be prospects of pickings—promotion, for example, to the Praetorian Guard at vastly greater rates of pay; or failing this, the assurance of returning to one's old locality under an easy master. And the local population of civilians, among whom time-expired veterans formed a noticeable element in the garrison towns, were equally enthusiastic for Vitellius; the Treviri and the Lingones, Galba's victims, equally friendly.

The enthusiasm translated itself into practical forms. Both troops and civilians offered contributions to the cause, the former their savings lying in the military chests of the legions, their sword-belts, medals and silver parade equipment; the latter money, equipment, horses. The metal was used to mint a coinage which we may plausibly identify with the so-called military issues of 69—coins showing, for instance, clasped hands symbolizing union and loyalty with the hopeful legend FIDES EXERCITVVM or the even more buoyant FIDES PRAETORIANORVM, but containing no mention of Vitellius, whose constitutional scruples apparently forbade the assumption upon the coinage of the recognition of the Senate and People of Rome formally to be accorded to him in April. But the troops gave him the title 'Germanicus', something less than an imperial one, yet with happy associations. (It was of the type applied to the commander successful in a military campaign on the frontier, like 'Africanus' or 'Dacicus', though there had been no campaign as yet.) 'Augustus' he was less anxious to assume, and 'Caesar' he became only in the last desperate days of his reign.[18]

A strategy was quickly formulated, or revealed. While token forces were left in the headquarters establishments along the Rhine, something between a third and a half of the legionary strength, plus a large number of auxiliary units of infantry and cavalry, were to move on Rome and displace Galba—or, as it was soon known, Otho. The need to maintain and strengthen communication between the Rhine and Rome, the difficulty of feeding large numbers of marching men and the strategy of invasion dictated a two-pronged advance. One would be led by Caecina, the other by Valens, with units drawn respectively from the Upper and Lower Military Districts. In due course Vitellius would follow with the remainder of the forces available.

The prospects for the campaign were good. The governors of Britain, of Belgian and Central Gaul, and of Raetia declared their adherence. The first of these provinces provided drafts of legionaries. Thus Spain with its single legion—the Sixth, the formation which had acclaimed Galba in April 68—presented only a slight threat. A key legionary garrison, that of Pannonia, nearest to Italy, seemed no problem, for L. Tampius Flavianus, its governor, was a relative of Vitellius. In Syria Mucianus was hardly a military menace, and had little in common with Vespasian in Judaea, himself tied down by the Jewish War. In Italy itself there was a hotch-potch of fragmented forces, none deeply attached to Galba. Apart from this, the Roman legionary order of battle comprised only the three formations widely spaced along the lower Danube against a continual threat of incursion from the north, two legions in far-off Egypt, and a single one in the province of Africa. Vitellius seemed to himself to dispose of an overwhelming military superiority. Nevertheless, it was decided to strike at once and to begin the long march southwards in order to cross the Alps at the earliest possible opportunity.

Fabius Valens was to take the longer route from the Rhineland via Lyon to the Mt Genèvre Pass, which, though not the lowest of the Alpine passes, is comparatively sheltered and easy. Its choice might well surprise an enemy guarding against an invasion which in the winter months seemed most probable by the easiest route of all, the Ligurian coast road. Caecina was allotted the shorter but much more strenuous passage by the Great St Bernard, which in any event would have to be controlled sooner or later since in summer it provided the quickest communication between Rome and Rhine. The two forces could effect a junction at Pavia or Milan. The exact numerical strengths of these forces it is difficult to determine. Tacitus' account, not readily explicable on our information, assigns to Valens about 40,000 men and to Caecina 30,000. Both figures are probably exaggerated and look suspiciously like an approximate estimate of the total strength of the Rhine garrisons: 5,000 to a legion, with auxiliaries roughly as numerous. But Vitellius did not contemplate stripping the long and vital Rhine frontier of all its troops. On the other hand we may accept the historian's statement that Valens received drafts of legionaries drawn from the formations of the Lower District, together with the main body of the Fifth at Vetera and with auxiliary cavalry; to Caecina was given the Twenty-First from Windisch together with corresponding supporting troops. Each commander was also to be allotted some of the amphibious Batavian cavalry skilled in crossing their native and all other rivers, and with them a few German cohorts recruited east of the Rhine and possessing similar training. After all it might be necessary to force a defended Po.

A fortnight's hard staff work enabled both commanders to be on the road by the second half of January. Valens' route lay through Trier, the capital of the friendly Treviri. At Metz their neighbours the Mediomatrici were predictably less friendly, and though the townsfolk showed every civility to a dangerous guest, the nervous troops were involved in a panicky outbreak which hostile propaganda alleged to have cost 4,000 lives. After this—whatever the true figure—the provincials were so alarmed that on the approach of the marching column (as later at Vienne, under suspicion for its connection with Vindex) whole communities went out to meet the Vitellian force with white flags and pleas for mercy. Women and children prostrated themselves along the highways, and every conceivable concession was made which could speed the irascible visitor upon his way.[19]

News of Galba's assassination and Otho's accession reached Valens about 23 January, when he was at Toul. The information signified little, except that the Vitellians now had the moral advantage of confronting an adversary whose title to empire was considerably worse than their own. For the Gauls, and indeed for the Roman world at large, the future seemed even more sinister and unpredictable than it was already: the Vitellians were not turning back.

At Langres the army was joined by a portion of the eight Batavian cohorts, others travelling via Besançon to reinforce Caecina's men; what the local Lingones chiefly remembered afterwards was a squabble between the Batavians and the legionaries, typical of many. At Chalon-sur-Saône one reached the valley of that river, and at its confluence with the Rhône lay the capital of the Three Gauls, Lyon. The city offered the warm welcome to be expected. The First (Italian) Legion, commanded by Manlius Valens and consisting of Italians six-foot tall—chosen by Nero and given the grandiose title of 'The Phalanx of Alexander the Great'—and an auxiliary cavalry regiment were pressed into Fabius Valens' service, though the Eighteenth (Urban) Cohort was left at Lyon, where it was normally stationed to police the largest city on the west. Vienne, on the other hand, paid for its past activities by losing its right to possess a local militia and by handing out heavy protection money to Valens. At Luc-en-Diois, in the Drôme valley, it is alleged that he threatened to set fire to the town, one of the two capitals of the Vocontii, unless the tribute demanded was paid.

The long catalogue of woes may be plausibly attributed to stories retailed to Pliny the Elder, an important source for Tacitus and others. In 70, when he was perhaps an imperial agent in Gaul, one can well imagine the eagerness with which local magnates would have apprised a financial official of the havoc they had suffered at the hands of a faction against which Pliny's master Vespasian had rebelled and, equally well, the ready credence given by that official to allegations providing most acceptable propaganda material.

At Gap, in early March, it was necessary to detach some 2,600 men to meet an Othonian naval invasion of the Ligurian coast. In the latter part of the month Valens and his army were crossing the Mt Genèvre into Italy (the winter was mild, or spring early), and at its end they were in Turin. The march had gone well. A truculent attitude and a good choice of time and route had secured them an uninterrupted passage. Otho's maritime expedition had had little influence upon the advance, and though the detachment diverted to deal with it had been largely unsuccessful and a cry for further help met Valens at Turin, he refused to fritter away any more men on what proved in the end a blind alley. Indeed his troops wanted no diminution of their strength now that they were almost in sight of the enemy.

Caecina's progress was more strenuous. In the first half of January he left Mainz in advance of his troops, and travelling on horseback up the bank of the Rhine arrived at the low plateau near the confluence of the Aare and the Reuss, upon which lay the permanent camp of the Twenty-First Legion at Windisch near Brugg in the Aargau. The situation he found there was one of some confusion, and he was faced by a task involving more than a winter crossing of the Alps.

The fortress lies towards the north-east end of the long and wide strath that runs from the Lake of Geneva to that of Constance between the Jura and the Bernese Oberland. This corridor leading from the Rhineland to Italy was inhabited by the Helvetians, once famous as a populous warrior-tribe whose emigrants had presented a severe challenge to Julius Caesar 126 years before as he trailed them to central France and fought hard with them in the Saône-et-Loire. In 69 they had long enjoyed the benefits of the Roman peace, and their industry, productive soil and position upon a main highway of travel and trade had brought a prosperity destined soon to be increased under the Flavian régime. As a gesture to their warlike past, the Romans allowed them the privilege—it was not an onerous one—of manning some of the forts along the Rhine towards Baden. Of these Zurzach was one of the most important. The garrisons of these forts were raised and paid by the Helvetians and formed no part of the regular Roman army: honour was satisfied and money saved.

The events of these days are narrated by Tacitus in some detail. No less than three prominent Helvetians are named. This attentiveness is explicable by the use of Flavian sources concerned to honour the régime. In his later years, Vespasian's father had carried on a banking business in the Helvetian capital Avenches, and the future emperor had spent some part of his childhood here with his parents and elder brother Sabinus. A commemorative stone that has survived was dedicated by two ladies called Primula and Isias, proudly described as the 'nurses of our emperor' (*educatrices Augusti nostri*). Indeed the upsurge of building in Flavian times seems to attest the favour of Vespasian towards his youthful home and a desire to offer recompense for the hard times of early 69.[20]

The trouble at Windisch initially involved an act of looting. The pay for the men garrisoning the Helvetian frontier forts was sent down at regular intervals from Avenches. The route followed by the paymasters crossed the bridge over the Aare that lay a little to the north-west of the legionary camp. Early in January, discipline being unsettled by the news from Cologne and Mainz, some rowdies of the Twenty-First held up the paymasters on their way and stole the pay. The Helvetians were not prepared to put up with this sort of treatment. Feelings ran high, and about a week later an opportunity for revenge occurred. Somewhere on the main road west or east of Windisch their militia arrested a centurion with a small escort of legionary soldiers: they were carrying an appeal for support from the Rhine armies to the garrison of Pannonia, east of Raetia and Noricum. This smelt like treason. The messengers were kept in confinement, perhaps in the hope of obtaining restitution for the loss of the money. Such tactics were not well advised, and the Helvetians were foolish to take a revenge which was not only of doubtful legality but presented a direct challenge to a powerful army.

The resulting tension that confronted Caecina as he arrived constituted a threat to his line of communications. He immediately moved out the Twenty-First Legion in an exercise of systematic devastation of the lowlands. This even included an attack on the nearby spa of Baden, which the troops knew well and which, in the sheltered valley of the lower Limmat, had developed from a village to a holiday town and watering-place where you could bathe and take the sulphur waters in the comfort and scenic beauties typical of this and all other spas. Archaeology reveals a burnt stratum attesting a conflagration, perhaps of this year. The Helvetians now sounded a general tocsin and called up men long unused to war. Caecina replied by summoning to his assistance auxiliary units stationed not far to the east in Raetia (probably at Bregenz), and caught the motley Helvetian levy between two fires. There seems to have been no set battle, but a series of skirmishes lacking all firm military direction by the inexperienced Helvetian leaders. The case was hopeless, and illustrates the nature of Roman imperialism: beneficial if you worked with it, and what else could you do? Even if competent as soldiers, the people could not then have found refuge behind the long-disused and crumbling walls of the hill forts they had maintained before the Romans came. Towards the end of January, after a few days of chaos, the Helvetian conscripts threw away their arms and made for the fastnesses of the Mons Vocetius, sometimes— though without great probability—identified with the Bözberg between Basel and Brugg. A cohort of Thracians was promptly ordered to drive them down from the height, and other auxiliaries, from Germany and Raetia, beat the forested area and killed the skulkers in their hiding-places. Casualties were heavy among the Helvetians.[21]

By the time this mopping up was completed, the drafts allotted from the Fourth and Twenty-Second Legions had arrived in Windisch from Mainz, and in the first week of February Caecina moved towards the Helvetian capital, eighty miles away, with a substantial army of some 9,000 legionaries and perhaps twice that number of auxiliaries. Further resistance was not to be contemplated. The Helvetian leaders sent out plenipotentiaries to negotiate a surrender. Despite the vigour of the repression, understandable without positing any particular venom on Caecina's part, the Roman was sensible enough to avoid vindictive terms that might implant an enduring resentment and present a renewed peril. One Helvetian leader regarded as particularly responsible for the call to arms was executed forthwith. The fate of the rest was left to Vitellius, still at Cologne. A representative party of Helvetians were sent there under Roman escort. At the audience, the Rhineland troops breathed out fire and slaughter, and thrust their weapons and fists under the noses of the unfortunates. Even Vitellius made a show of verbal severity. But he was quite prepared to deal gently with them. In any case there were mitigating circumstances, and the Helvetians had already paid a heavy price for trying to ride the high horse. No further executions were exacted, nor did Avenches suffer.

It was about 23 February before the party returned from Cologne. Caecina had employed the interval in very necessary preparations for the rigours of an Alpine crossing made before the date at which the passes are normally open. Whether the higher parts of the Great St Bernard route were or were not capable of taking wheeled traffic—in Augustus' time they were not, and the evidence of Roman paving at the top may be later than A.D. 69—it would have been madness to rely upon the normal legionary transport. Horses and mules had to be requisitioned and the baggage of the waggons redistributed.[22]

Amid these preoccupations good news came to reward Caecina for his determination. A unit stationed in the Po valley had declared for Vitellius. It was the Silian cavalry regiment which had served in Africa during Vitellius' popular period of office there as governor, had been earmarked by Nero for his Eastern campaign sent to Alexandria and then recalled in view of the threat from Vindex in Gaul. At the moment it was marking time in the Eleventh Region of Italy, which contained the important towns of Milan, Novara, Ivrea and Vercelli. Towards 22 January the officers of this unit, on hearing first of the revolt of Vitellius and then of the death of Galba, had to decide their attitude to the usurper and assassin Otho. They were not acquainted with him personally, and finally decided that they preferred the devil whom they knew, perhaps also calculating that a timely change of front might win them considerable prizes in a contest in which the odds seemed heavily weighted in favour of Vitellius' seven legions. These considerations they put to their men, who agreed. Some elements of the unit were sent to bring the news to Caecina and await instructions.

Caecina gave them a hearty welcome, and immediately sent off some auxiliary infantry from Gaul, Lusitania and Britain, as well as cavalry from Germany and the unit called the 'Petra's Horse' to consolidate the position in the Eleventh Region, where the turncoat regiment seems at this moment to have been the sole unit.

Less reassuring was the attitude of Noricum, where the pro-Othonian governor, Petronius Urbicus, had mustered his auxiliary forces and cut the bridges over the Inn at Innsbruck-Wilten and Rosenheim. It was clear that the Vitellians were not going to have it all their own way. Upon reflection Caecina decided that any attempt to deal with this danger from the flank—and after all Urbicus had no legions, and the cutting of the bridges was essentially a defensive act—must be postponed. The vital thing was to exploit the mild weather and the lucky situation in northern Italy.

Towards the end of February he set his heavy column in motion. The legionaries toiled up the long slopes from Martigny towards the promised land. The weather held, and the long ascent went without a hitch. Early in March Caecina stood in Italy: he had stolen the race from his rival and colleague Valens by almost four weeks and found himself master of the north-western portion of the Po valley, the storehouse of Italy, famous for its millet, pigs, wool, and wine stored in pitched jars larger than houses.[23]

The months of January and February, during which Valens and Caecina were known to be making their several ways towards northern Italy with the evident intention of displacing Otho, saw signs throughout the empire of the growing unease which sprang from the apparently inevitable return of civil war, the ultimate disaster which the principate was instituted to prevent. In Rome the foreboding was heightened by the feeling that the capital, above all other places, would lie at the mercy either of an Otho or of a Vitellius exasperated by war and elated by victory.

In the East similar, if less urgent, doubts and fears existed. Galba had been promptly recognized by Vespasian when the news of his accession reached Judaea in late June 68. Military operations against the Jews were suspended. In December, after notifying Galba of his intentions, he sent off his son Titus, now twenty-nine years old and a competent commander of the Fifteenth (Apollinarian) Legion in Judaea, to pay his respects to the new emperor in Rome, where it was known that Galba had finally arrived.

Titus was a man of charm and talent. Though short and tubby, he enjoyed good looks and great strength. He had an unusually retentive memory, and a capacity for learning all the skills of peace and war. He handled arms and rode a horse like an expert, and had a ready knack for composing poetry and speeches both in Latin and Greek, whether extempore or not. He was something of a musician, too, having a pleasant competence as a singer and harpist. A minor accomplishment was that he was good at shorthand: he had achieved a high speed and would compete with his secretaries for fun. He could imitate any man's handwriting and often claimed that he might have made a first-rate forger. His affability and generosity are best illustrated by a dictum of his dating from the time when he was emperor: at dinner one evening he realized that he had conferred no favour in the last twelve hours and exclaimed, 'My friends, I have wasted a day!' Such varied talents and virtues could hardly fail to win admirers. On his December journey he was accompanied by one of them, King Agrippa II, ten years his senior, ruler of Golan and a large area east and north-east of the Sea of Galilee. Agrippa was a typical figure in the organization of Roman rule: a client-king, controlling a small border state with some degree of independent action, and suffered to keep his little court so long as he preserved order and maintained friendly relations with Rome. Agrippa had every inducement to hope that Titus would one day be emperor, or at least a member of the governing élite.

As it was winter they avoided the open sea and coasted along the southern flank of Anatolia in warships. Towards the end of January they had reached Corinth, where one transhipped to the western Gulf. Here they heard the disturbing news of Galba's assassination and the near-certainty of an invasion of Italy by Vitellius. Titus reviewed the difficult position anxiously with Agrippa and some advisers. Finally he decided against putting himself in a false and possibly dangerous situation: he would return at speed to Vespasian for further consultation. Agrippa, however, continued on his way to the capital, where he remained the eyes and ears of the Flavians until secretly summoned home on the proclamation of Vespasian as emperor in July. He at any rate was safe enough in Rome under Otho: he had come in the irreproachable guise of a client-king, a friend and ally of the Roman people, owing allegiance to whatever emperor destiny—or the Roman people—should select.

Titus traversed once more the Aegean and coasted along the south-west seaboard of Anatolia and across the mouths of the Gulfs of Cos and Syme until he came to Loryma on the Carpathian Sea, where improving weather encouraged him to make the short crossing of twenty miles to the city of Rhodes. From here he pressed on eastwards to Andriace (the port of Myra), where St Paul had transhipped ten years earlier; thence, with continuing good weather and perhaps increasing impatience, he risked the longer open passages of 170 miles to Paphos in Cyprus (two days and one night at sea with luck) and the 250 miles from Paphos to Caesarea. At Paphos he paid a quick visit to the famous Temple of Venus with its vast riches and strange aniconic cult emblem, a truncated cone. Titus did his duty as a sightseer and then asked the oracle of the shrine if the weather would hold and make a continuation of the direct passage possible. Yes, it seemed it would. Then, offering a more lavish sacrifice, he enquired of his own future in veiled language: 'Shall I succeed in what I am hoping and planning?' The priest

Sostratus was discreet and well-informed. The omens offered by the livers were favourable: but would Titus be pleased to see him in private? The two conferred, and Titus emerged from the interview reassured and confident. What kind of optimism this was we do not know, but at least the open crossing was performed without incident. When he reached Caesarea, the Roman capital of Judaea, he found that the armies of Syria and Judaea had recognized Otho as emperor.

The purpose and implications of Titus' journey have been long debated. The account survives in a number of allusions; and the fullest version, that of Tacitus, is, as usual, the best. But even his account is obscure in some particulars, and the abortive trip seems hardly worth a mention. But it must have figured prominently in the accounts of the Flavian historians, no doubt because it seemed to demonstrate the loyalty of Vespasian and his faction to the last respectable emperor, Galba, and perhaps hinted that they were the chosen instruments of a mysterious providence revealing its purposes soon after Galba's death. But we are entitled to ask whether it was really necessary for Vespasian to send his son—admittedly in a lull in the fighting—on a potentially dangerous winter voyage merely to pay personally those respects which he must have offered to Galba in Spain months before by letter. A second reason is produced by Tacitus: Titus was of the right age to seek office—an allusion to the fact that on 30 September 68 he had entered on his twenty-ninth year, and could consequently stand for the praetorship. It was quite legitimate for army officers serving abroad to return to Rome with their general's permission to sue for civil offices. Titus could therefore plead this as a publicly acceptable reason for the journey. But the fundamental cause must be sought in the rumours of an impending adoption which developed in Rome after Galba's arrival and which could have reached the ears of Vespasian by December. Certainly, as Titus travelled westwards, public opinion on his route believed that here was a possible heir for Galba. Crowds met him at his landfalls. Clearly, one should be polite to a potential emperor. After this, the sudden disappointment of Corinth must have been a considerable blow even to a sanguine nature accustomed to easy success. He could expect no gratitude either from Otho or from Vitellius for a journey ostensibly undertaken in the first place as a tribute to Galba; and it might be dangerous to put himself as a hostage into the hands of the new master, whoever he was to be.

If the reasons for the journey, and its commemoration, are not quite clear, Titus' second enquiry of the oracle makes us wonder whether he was already contemplating the possibility of a Flavian bid for the principate. If this were so, it would explode the claim advanced by some of the Flavian historians that only in June did Vespasian reluctantly accede to the pressures of his followers. No clear answer to this

problem is possible. Under Nero prominence was dangerous. Since the
death of Corbulo at Nero's jealous insistence in October 66—shortly
before Vespasian's appointment to Judaea in February 67—every important governor and commander must have felt himself to be balancing
on a knife-edge. In such years inactivity was a virtue, as Galba had
believed. But a man charged with repressing a Jewish insurrection
could hardly be inactive. Unless the campaign—incredibly—failed,
success must bring danger. The war must not be prosecuted too
quickly. Nevertheless, Vespasian's reputation grew steadily. The initial
jealousies between the governors of Judaea and Syria soon turned to
consultation and mutual confidence. In this process Titus was credited
with a considerable part, and already in October 67 he had paid a visit
to Mucianus, though we know nothing of the motive for it. From July 68
onwards a degree of positive collaboration was achieved, which, since it
was not disloyal to Galba, must have envisaged the day, surely not far
distant, when his successor would be chosen. It is therefore likely that
in February or March 69, on the return of Titus to Judaea, the fears and
ambitions of the Flavian faction had crystallized into a decision to await
the outcome of the imminent conflict between Otho and Vitellius, with
possibly some forward planning for either of the two possibilities: the
defeat of Otho, the defeat of Valens and Caecina. Only with the news
of the First Battle of Cremona at the end of April could firm decisions
be taken; and these were based on the interaction of the attitudes of the
legionaries and of the Flavian leaders. These attitudes seem broadly to
have coincided: Vitellius and his people were incompetent and intolerable; and the chances of a successful Flavian intervention were
manifestly good. It was not possible for contemporary Roman historians to write a detailed account of these transactions unless the confidential memoirs of Vespasian, Mucianus, Titus and Tiberius Alexander
were accessible to them, which is highly unlikely, and we can hardly
blame Tacitus if, writing thirty years after the events, he leaves many
things in obscurity. With a good deal of obscurity we must ourselves be
content. Only one thing is certain: the final decision of Vespasian to
claim the empire was not taken until May or June 69.

Some alarm was caused by the appearance of the first in a series of
false Neros. Nero had died in a small villa four miles from Rome in
circumstances not entirely clear, and since the Senate declared him a
public enemy he cannot have received the honour of a state burial in the
glare of publicity. In Greece his appearances at games and competitions
in person in 67, eccentric and fantastic as they were, his declaration of
the freedom of Greece, his attempt to dig a canal through the Isthmus
of Corinth and his lavish concessions gave him a degree of publicity
accorded to few, if any, of his predecessors. After June 68 rumours circulated that he was still alive. Pretenders claiming to be Nero arose in

68, in the reign of Titus and in 88, and three and a half centuries later St Augustine asserts that many people of his day thought that Nero never died, but that he lived on in the age and vigour in which he was supposed to have been slain, until the time should come when he would be revealed and restored to his kingdom. Such a depth of credulity explains the flutter of excitement surrounding the present impersonation. In the autumn of 68 Nonius Calpurnius Asprenas, appointed governor of Galatia and Pamphylia by Galba, who in uniting these two provinces reverted to Augustus' arrangement which Claudius had abandoned, was proceeding with two triremes across the Aegean to Ephesus. He put in at Kythnos, a minor island of the Cyclades group famous chiefly for its cheeses and hot springs, but lying on the Athens–Delos route and used as a port of refuge in the not infrequent event, even in summer, of squally Aegean weather. While Asprenas was in harbour, the captains of his two ships were approached and invited to meet a man who claimed to be Nero. They agreed. There was certainly a facial resemblance, and the impostor shared Nero's singing and lyre-playing abilities. In fact he appears to have been a slave from the Pontus, or, according to other versions, a freedman from Italy. From merchants' slaves, deserters and soldiers on leave or posting, who happened to pass to and from the East, he had gathered a band of followers, some armed. There was talk of him in Corinth and Ephesus. His request to the trierarchs, made with a pathetic appeal to their 'loyalty', was that they should take him to Syria or Egypt. In their perplexity, the captains diplomatically replied that they would have to win over their men, and would return when all was ready. But they faithfully reported the whole story to Asprenas. The governor had no hesitations: whether the man was Nero or not, he must be got rid of. The unknown individual was killed at his orders, and his head, notable for its glance, hair and ferocious expression, was carried away by the party when they left for Ephesus, and from there sent to Rome. The removal of this claimant did not preclude a number of successors, and in Trajan's reign Dio Chrysostom, and about the same time the author of the Apocalypse, seem to attest contemporary rumours concerning a surviving Nero.[24]

A more impressive story came from Moesia. In January, stimulated, if stimulus were necessary, by rumours of impending civil war in the empire, 9,000 wild and exulting horsemen of the Rhoxolani, an ever westward-pressing Sarmatian tribe now probably roaming the area north of the delta of the Danube, moved upstream, crossed the frozen river between Gigen and Svištov, and in a sudden incursion cut to pieces the local garrison of two auxiliary cohorts. After this easy victory the invaders loaded themselves with the loot for which they had come and prepared to re-cross the river. But now their luck turned. The early spring which facilitated Caecina's crossing of the Great St Bernard melted the ice of the Danube. The snow turned to slush, the tracks became slippery and the furious gallop of the Rhoxolani declined to the pace of a plodding caravan. On a rainy day they were caught by the seasoned Third Legion, moving eastwards from its headquarters at Gigen. This formation could look back to many battle honours dating to the late republic, and a few years before had exchanged the burning suns of Syria for the bleak mountains of Armenia and a toughening-up under a hard commander, Corbulo. In 68 they had been transferred to the Danube area. Now, a few months after their arrival, they were to show that they knew how to cope with wintry conditions and the cavalry of the steppes. Moving swiftly they fell upon the encumbered barbarians. *Pilum*-discharge was followed by the sword, according to the drill-book. The mass of the Sarmatians had little or no defensive armour, for they relied on their horses' speed; and the chiefs, though formidable in the charge with lances and enormous four-foot-long swords, double-handed and twice the length of the Roman weapon, were helpless when bogged down and dismounted: they floundered about like rhinoceroses in cuirasses of iron-plating or toughened leather far more cumbrous than the flexible *loricae segmentatae* of the Romans. Most of the enemy succumbed to this well-executed assault, a few made their escape to the Dobrogea and the Delta, where they perished of their wounds or of damp and exposure.

This was the kind of police action continually demanded of the defenders of the southern bank of the Danube, but it had been conducted with exemplary speed and effectiveness. By the second half of February all was over. When the news reached Rome, Otho distributed handsome awards to the governor of Moesia, Marcus Aponius Saturninus, and all the three legionary commanders. There was an element of bribery in this; but if Aponius' statue in triumphal guise set up in the hemicycle of the Forum of Augustus was cheaply acquired, Aurelius Fulvus, the commander of the Third, certainly deserved the award of an ivory ceremonial stool and the right to wear an embroidered toga. In any case, the victory delighted Otho. and though he had no part in it personally, it seemed to give him an added prestige. On 1 March, when according to an immemorial annual custom the Vestal Virgins renewed the sacred fire that symbolized Rome's eternity, a laurel wreath was placed over the palace entrance in a ceremony itself commemorated by the assiduous Brethren of the Fields, led by their vice-president, Otho's brother Titianus. Such lavish self-congratulation seems to betray a lack of confidence, but the necessity for the operation demonstrated the importance of the watch on the Danube.

In Corsica the governor Decumus Picarius rashly declared for Vitellius and was at first followed by the ignorant and sheep-like populace, especially after he executed two Romans (one a naval officer) who had disagreed with this venture. But when the natives discovered that the governor's new allegiance involved their own conscription and military training, it became less popular. A conspiracy was formed and the governor was assassinated when helpless—in the bath. His immediate staff were also disposed of. Their heads, like those of outlaws or false Neros, were taken to Rome by the conspirators in person, optimistically hoping for a reward. But they got neither thanks from Otho nor punishment from Vitellius, neither of whom had the time or inclination to bother about such little people. Indeed, in the worldwide upheaval, the smaller units of the empire counted for little: they could only look helplessly on at the struggle of the giants.

In the neighbouring island of Sardinia no such reckless coups and counter-coups were attempted; but the chance survival of a first-hand piece of evidence gives us perhaps a better impression of the day-to-day work of a provincial governor even in a year of crisis. In 1866 a bronze inscribed tablet, now in the museum at Sassari, was found by peasants near the village of Esterzili in the south-east central portion of the island east of the upper Flumendosa. Boundary disputes are endemic in Mediterranean civilizations, and on high bare ground such as this there was a standing tendency for the poorer mountaineers to attempt to trespass on richer land below. The inscription runs:

18 March in the consulship of the emperor Otho Caesar Augustus, verified copy of an entry in the portable volume of statutes of L. Helvius Agrippa proconsul exhibited by the quaestorial secretary Cn. Egnatius Fuscus, the said entry being document number 5, heads 8, 9 and 10 as follows:

On 13 March L. Helvius Agrippa proconsul reviewed the case and pronounced sentence:
WHEREAS for the public good it is desirable to abide by judicial decisions once made, and in the matter of the Patulcenses the highly respected imperial procurator M. Juventius Rixa [A.D. 66/67] more than once pronounced that the territory of the Patulcenses should remain unchanged according to the delimitation published by M. Marcellus on a bronze tablet [in 115 B.C.] and on the last occasion pronounced that because the Galillenses frequently reopened the issue and disobeyed his decree, he had wished to punish them, but in consideration of the clemency of the emperor best and greatest had been content to admonish them in an edict that they should be still and abide by judicial decisions once made and at latest by 1 October next [A.D. 66] should evacuate the farm-lands belonging to the Patulcenses and should surrender them with vacant possession; and that if they persevered in their disobedience, he would severely punish the ring-leaders of rebellion
AND WHEREAS afterwards the highly distinguished senator Caecilius Simplex [proconsul A.D. 67/68] when approached by the Galillenses in connexion with the same dispute with the assurance that they would produce a document referring to the matter from the imperial chancellery pronounced

a

b

c

PLATE I   Coins of Galba (*a* and *b*) and Otho (*c*)

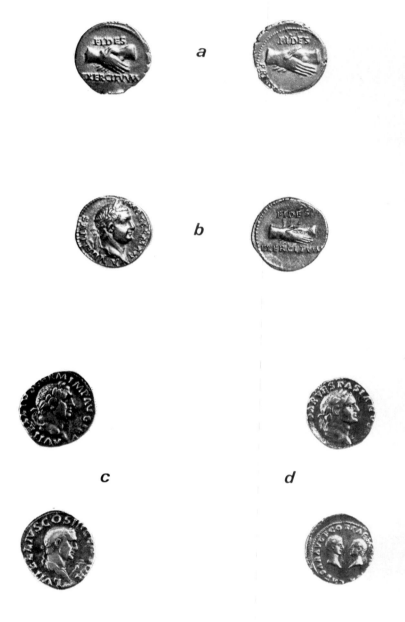

PLATE 2   Coins of Vitellius (*a*, *b* and *c*) and Vespasian (*d*)

that it was a humane action that postponement should be granted to the petitioners to prove their case and in fact granted them the space of three months up to 1 December [A.D. 67] on the understanding that unless a constitution had been produced by that date he would follow that which existed in the province
NOW THEREFORE having myself been approached by the Galillenses excusing themselves for the fact that the constitution had not yet arrived and having granted respite until 1 February next [A.D. 69] and understanding that a delay is desired by the farmers in occupation of the lands in dispute I HEREBY ORDAIN AND PRONOUNCE that the Galilenses [*sic*] shall by 1 April next [A.D. 69] depart from the lands of the Patulcenses Campani upon which they some time ago trespassed. If they do not obey this ordinance and pronouncement, let them know that they will incur punishment for their longstanding disobedience which has already been repeatedly denounced.
PRESENT IN COUNCIL
M. Julius Romulus, Vice-Governor; T. Atilius Sabinus, Financial Secretary; M. Stertinius Rufus junior; Sex. Aelius Modestus; P. Lucretius Clemens; M. Domitius Vitalis; M. Justus Fidus; M. Stertinius Rufus
IN WITNESS WHEREOF THE FOLLOWING HAVE AFFIXED THEIR SEALS: [eleven names][25]

Here are some instructive insights into Roman documentation and above all into the relations between a Roman administration and the provincials: the obstinate occupation of neighbours' land, the official care to refer to and abide by decisions delivered many years previously, the weakness of the system of annually changing senatorial governors, the ineffective repetition of threats of punishment not clearly specified and not applied. In the eyes of a senatorial Roman governor (and the province had in 67 become senatorial instead of imperial, although an imperial decree ('constitution')—if previously or now existing—would be valid) such little squabbles over land were matters of slight importance, and delay was encouraged by the troubles of 68 and 69. It was, of course, inconceivable that Nero, Galba, Otho or their civil service would have either the time or the interest to deal with petty matters in a remote and only partly Romanized country. Similar disputes occurred continually in every corner of the Mediterranean world. We may compare, for instance, the appointment of arbitrators by Pompeius Silvanus, governor of Dalmatia, made in this very year or shortly before—officials whose thankless task it was to sort out longstanding boundary arguments between small communities behind Zadar, in one of the few fruitful areas of the Dalmatian coast. Nevertheless we should perhaps praise the patient and careful legalism of the Romans rather than condemn the ease with which trespassers—if such they were—could cock a snook at the authorities. Incidentally, if it is true, as seems likely, that the Sardinian governor's legal draughtsmen were not ignorant in March of the consular arrangements made by

C

Otho at least a month earlier, we learn from the inscription that Otho
had not, as is generally believed, resigned the consulship at the end of
February 69. Like Vitellius, he may have declared himself *consul
perpetuus*.[26]

While Corsica was murdering its ambitious governor and Sardinia
disputing on tribal boundaries, to their north the Ligurian campaign
was in full swing—if that is not too grandiose a title for the rather
tentative fighting caused by the Othonian amphibious expedition along
the coast of Liguria. The course of this fighting illustrates another
aspect of civil war: the impact upon civilians of troops whose discipline
and sense of responsibility to a firmly constituted authority have
evaporated.

In February, on hearing that Valens and Caecina were on the way,
Otho decided that, despite his lack of legionary troops near at hand, some
attempt would have to be made to bar the most obvious point of entry
into Italy from the north-west. Snow could reasonably be expected
to block most of the Alpine passes until April; but the Aurelian Way
(Arles–Aix–Fréjus–Antibes–Cimiez–Ventimiglia–Genoa–Pisa–Rome)
presented an easy route even in winter. Only a few months before,
when Otho had marched along it from Spain, he was reminded,
by inscriptions upon milestones, of the extensive work carried out on it
by Nero in 58. The highway was in good repair and near sea-level. He
would now use what resources he had to dominate the coast road into
the Var and possibly enter Gaul. And whatever his shortage of
legionaries, he felt he could rely on his Praetorians and the fleet—
especially those naval personnel set upon by Galba when he entered
Rome and since then enrolled in a legion by himself, even though the
formation had not yet been formally constituted and given a name,
number and eagle. To these men were added some Urban Cohorts,
admittedly of slight military value, and drafts from the Praetorians.
The mixed force was to be commanded by two senior centurions,
Antonius Novellus and Suedius Clemens, together with Aemilius
Pacensis, to whom—perhaps for services rendered in January—Otho
had restored the rank of tribune of the Urban Cohort, of which Galba
had deprived him. The outset of the expedition was scarcely propitious.
When it got under way on about 10 February, the weather being kindly,
Aemilius Pacensis was for reasons unknown put under arrest by his own
troops, while Antonius Novellus proved to be a nonentity. In this three-
cornered rivalry, Titus Suedius Clemens came clearly out on top. Even
Tacitus gives him grudging praise for his determination, and he was to
continue his career under the Flavians: in 81 he turns up again as camp
commandant of the Third (Cyrenaican) and Twenty-Second Legions
stationed in Egypt. It was perhaps a good thing that there seemed to be
no sign of the appearance of Valens' army on the coast, and if Clemens'

intelligence was good and he had learned that the Vitellian commander had turned off the Rhône valley into that of the Drôme with the evident intention of using the Mt Genèvre Pass, he may well have reported this immediately to Otho, whose plan of campaign it obviously affected. By the beginning of March, having sorted out its command structure, the expedition was approaching the little province of the Maritime Alps, whose chief towns were Cimiez (behind Nice) and Vence, and whose hinterland embraced the valleys of the Var, the Vésubie and the Tinée. The local governor, Marius Maturus, was vigorous and pro-Vitellian, and did his best to keep out the unwelcome intruders. He called up the mountaineers of his province, but this amateur militia (he had nothing else, it seems) was quite unable to face even third-rate Roman troops. In a brush east of Cimiez it was scattered to its remote hillsides, where the Othonians had neither the will nor the knowledge to follow. There was no booty to be had from men who lived by herding sheep in the mountains, their diet mutton, milk and a drink made from barley.[27]

But this attempt at resistance, however ineffectual, induced an ugly temper and the Othonians turned (somewhat illogically, surely) against the Italian district around Ventimiglia immediately to the east. The disorderly troops proceeded to burn and plunder with a brutality rendered even more frightful by the total lack of precautions everywhere against such an unforeseen emergency. The men were away in the fields, the farmhouses were open and defenceless. As the farmers and their wives and children ran out, they met their end, victims of war in what they thought was peace. Among these victims was Julia Procilla, the mother of Agricola, Tacitus' father-in-law. A rich lady from Fréjus, she had estates outside Ventimiglia. When the news of the fatal disaster reached Rome, where Agricola was perhaps still continuing the temple inventory assigned him by Galba, he set out north to pay his last respects and settle up the family affairs. His presence in the area of Ventimiglia and Fréjus during the summer months of 69 stimulated the historian's knowledge of, and interest in, events in that quarter.

The news of this Othonian activity on the coast had been reported to Valens at Gap in early March by messengers sent no doubt by Marius Maturus over the mountains via Digne. In response, Valens detached two auxiliary cohorts, four troops of unidentified cavalry and a whole regiment of Treviran horse under its commander Julius Classicus, a name fated to recur. The total effective can hardly have exceeded 2,600 and may have been less. These troops, with some additional forces of little value, proceeded to Fréjus, where a proportion was left as a rearguard. About 22 March, perhaps between Menton and Ventimiglia, contact was made with the Othonians, who had less cavalry, but more infantry—and above all a fleet. While the land forces were engaged, the fleet sailed past behind the Vitellians and completed a discomfiture begun by a failed cavalry charge. Only dusk, if we are to believe Tacitus, saved the small Vitellian force from annihilation. A few days later, they were reinforced from Fréjus and suddenly attacked the Othonian camp, with initial success; but their opponents rallied and once more inflicted and also suffered some losses. In this last encounter there was no clear victory for either side and by tacit consent a truce was called, the Vitellians going back as far as Antibes and the Othonians as far as Albenga. Eighty miles now separated the opponents. The long withdrawal by the Vitellians is understandable: they desired proximity to their reserves at Fréjus and a gap between themselves and the victors; as for the Othonians, who had proved superior, the move may be explained by a desire to keep an eye on the passes through the Apennines from the plain of Piedmont where Valens had now arrived. An appeal to him by the Vitellian coastal force at the end of March was, after some hesitations, rejected.

The Ligurian campaign has been dismissed by historians as a pointless and ill-conducted foray, or elevated into a totally incredible attempt at a grandiose Othonian pincers movement. The truth lies somewhere between these views. Though Otho may have been a knave, he was not a fool. The wish to close an obviously open door in the face of an invader believed likely to enter by it is not folly; nor was it folly on the part of Suedius Clemens to move back to Albenga. Thus, though Otho's expedition failed to secure a footing in Southern Gaul or to detach substantial portions of the southern Vitellian army, it did, along with other factors, direct Valens' thrust towards Pavia and Cremona, and destroy any thought of turning the Othonian position on the Po by the use of the coast road to Rome. It was in the plains of northern Italy that the campaign would be won and lost.

In the first week of March Caecina Alienus led the Twenty-First Legion and his other heavy troops through Aosta down the valley of the Dora Baltea to Ivrea and the other cities of the Eleventh Region, already occupied by his light forces. He encountered no resistance, and discipline was good: it was vital to make a favourable impression upon Italy. However, when Caecina had occasion to address reception committees properly dressed in togas, eyebrows were raised when he appeared in the military dress (breeches, a practical garment in the north now being adopted by the army, and a general's bright cloak) normally laid aside in a civilian context. His wife, too, made tongues wag: instead of preserving a decent decorum, she paraded in public on horseback in a loud purple dress. Women had no business to flaunt themselves in this brazen manner.

Before Caecina reached the Po, his auxiliaries had already approached it at various points on its upper course. They found that it was defended by light Othonian forces of no great military value. They had mopped up a few troops of cavalry and 1,000 sailors of the Ravenna fleet between Pavia and Piacenza. Opposite the latter city, the amphibious Batavian and German cavalry used their special skills to cross the River Po and make prisoners of a few Othonian reconnaissance parties sent out from the city, whose centre lay more than a kilometre south of the bank; while north of the river and downstream, the invaders actually captured a cohort of Pannonians near Cremona, and may already at this early date have occupied the town. By this advance they had crossed the River Adda, moving from the Eleventh to the Tenth Region, which was otherwise in Othonian hands. Cremona now, or a little later, gave the Vitellians a warm welcome, and continued to do so for most of the year.

By 20 March Caecina and his legionaries were on the Po. Elated by the easy successes of his auxiliaries, the general now tried a head-on attack upon Piacenza. For some ten days this key town had been held by a spirited Othonian commander, Titus Vestricius Spurinna, now in his forties, known many years later to the Younger Pliny as a lively old man with a fund of anecdotes relating to his long and distinguished career and his many acquaintances. The commander's enterprise and discretion supplied the deficiencies of his troops. These were only some 2,700 in number, of which 1,500 were provided by three Praetorian cohorts more accustomed to ceremonial duties in Rome than to marching, digging and fighting. In addition he had 1,000 men drawn from the various infantry vexillations in Rome and a few cavalry. Prudence dictated strengthening the defences of Piacenza, but the men were truculent and suspicious of the command, scented treachery to Otho, and after hearing on their arrival of the behaviour of the Silian cavalry regiment and the reverses near Pavia and at Cremona, demanded some sort of offensive. Unable to control these would-be heroes, Spurinna determined to teach them a lesson. If they desired to venture out against the enemy, well and good: he would be their leader. About 11 March, he quietly moved the Praetorians out on a long route-march westwards, but on the south side of the river, using the Via Postumia and ostensibly making towards Pavia. There was, he knew, little real risk in this, for Caecina's legionaries were still some 120 miles away in the neighbourhood of Novara, and Valens had not even reached the Alps. Towards evening, he turned off the Via Postumia down a side road leading to a minor crossing point, and ordered his men to encamp for the night at Pievetta. The long day's march of seventeen miles was followed by digging rendered more onerous by the smallness of the force. Blistered feet and hands, weariness and muscle-ache worked marvels. The hotheads began to take a different view of the grandeur of war. The next morning, the older and less excitable men pointed out to

their subdued comrades the danger involved in the exposure in open
country of 1,500 Praetorians to many times that number of hardened
legionaries. The centurions and tribunes made use of the changed
attitude, and the troops had to agree that there was much to be said for
Spurinna's policy of resisting the enemy behind the walls of the well-
stocked city of Piacenza. Finally Spurinna explained his proposals
without indulging in recriminations, and the whole force trooped back
to the fortress, a small reconnaissance party being left at the river crossing. A week was available for reinforcing the city walls, neglected, like
those of the Helvetians' forts, in a century of peace, for heightening the
parapets and for providing arms and some training in the technique of
defence. By the time Caecina did arrive, the Othonian force at Piacenza
was in better heart and improved form; but Spurinna immediately
reported the arrival of the enemy, and their apparent strength, to his
colleague Annius Gallus. Gallus had left Rome together with Spurinna
but had turned off the Aemilian Way. No authority gives us a clear
account of Gallus' movement at this time, but probability suggests that
he first of all occupied the crossing points of the Po below Cremona,
those at Brescello and Ostiglia—the bridges here would have to be
guarded, and their possession enabled Gallus to face westwards on both
banks of the Po. At the moment of receiving Spurinna's warning he
seems to have been operating in the area of Verona with the slightly
optimistic idea of welcoming the inflowing Danube troops. He now
decided that his presence at Piacenza was vital, and set off south-
westwards.[28]

At Piacenza, the two-day encounter began with a few verbal exchanges that led to nothing. Then the Vitellian commander launched a
vigorous but careless assault. The men approached the walls with
bibulous bravado, after the main meal of the day, well washed down.
Their use of slingshots and inflammatory missiles proved a failure, the
only effective result being the destruction of the amphitheatre outside
the walls, the biggest in Italy, and apparently now used as a strong-
point in the defensive scheme. Afterwards, gossip attributed the loss,
quite unrealistically, to a few jealous Cremonese camp followers in
Caecina's army: Cremona had no such splendid building.

Soon after first light on the following day a much more determined
attack was mounted. Admittedly not much could be achieved by the
wild assaults of the German auxiliaries who with bared bodies and
native battle songs clashed their shields over their heads in a preliminary war dance. Such primitive warriors could not stand up to the
rain of javelins and stones from the walls. The Vitellian legionaries
understood their business better. Heavy fire was directed at the ramparts to keep the defenders as far as possible behind the merlons and
provide cover for the attack below, where the standard techniques of

tortoise, mound and mantlet were employed to pierce the wall; and
men wielding crowbars attacked the gates. At suitable points the
Othonians hurled down millstones collected for the purpose, and many
of the attackers beneath were crushed to death. Finally, after a hard
struggle, the attack had to be called off, and Caecina retired in discomfiture across the Po to his base at Cremona, less than two days'
march (30 Roman miles) distant.

The failure at Piacenza was a regrettable check for Caecina, but perhaps hardly the disaster that the admirers of Spurinna may have
represented it to be. Clearly, at some time or other the defences along
the Po had to be probed, and if Piacenza proved too strong there were
plenty of other crossings. As the Vitellians marched away, they were
joined by naval personnel detached from the Ravenna fleet under a
centurion who knew Caecina and by Julius Briganticus, the commander
of a cavalry regiment, nephew—and enemy—of the Batavian leader
Civilis, and now a lone wolf far from his territory with only a few
followers.

As for Spurinna, on discovering that the enemy had stolen away to
the north-east he wrote to his colleague Annius Gallus countermanding
any reinforcement of Piacenza. The danger point was now Cremona.
On receiving the news, Gallus halted his force, consisting of the First
(Support) Legion, two Praetorian cohorts and a cavalry element
(totalling perhaps 6,500), at a small village on the Postumian Way
called Bedriacum. It lay north of the Po and roughly midway between
Cremona and Mantua, commanding a road junction. The name of this
tiny spot, as insignificant as its modern successor Tornata, was to be
famous—and ill-omened—in Roman history.

4

Otho's Reaction

On the evening of 15 January an obsequious Senate had promptly awarded Otho the imperial titles. It was in no position to do anything else. But public opinion had to be won over into accepting an assassin as an emperor, and it is not surprising that in this Otho failed. He was regarded with apprehension by all except those who had given him his position: the Praetorian Guard. However, he scored a political success on the following day. At a thanksgiving sacrifice on the Capitol, he summoned the consul designate Marius Celsus, a close confidant of Galba and destined by him to hold office in July and August of 69. On the day before Celsus had been saved from the hostility of the troops by being taken into protective custody. He had now agreed with Otho that the public interest demanded some sort of reconciliation. He appeared and made a speech asserting his fidelity to Galba up to the last and, indeed, claiming credit for it: but now that Galba was dead and Otho recognized, he was prepared to cooperate. Otho asserted tha the bore no grudge. He immediately treated Celsus as an intimate friend, and shortly appointed him to joint command of the forces.[29]

This act of policy (principle hardly entered into the situation) was welcomed by the leading members of society, and was a nine days' wonder in popular talk: it seemed to augur something better than had been feared. But death by execution, public or private, awaited the ex-Praetorian prefect Laco, Galba's confidential freedman Icelus, and Nero's disreputable commander of the Praetorian Guard, Ofonius Tigellinus. No tears were shed for these. And Tigellinus, whose supporter Maevius Pudens had been privy to the Othonian plans for a coup d'état, might well have been inconveniently well-informed about the backstairs intrigues of 10–15 January. Four new consuls were fitted into the programme for 69, among whom Verginius Rufus stands out as a man of reputation whose selection for a second consulship was meant as a sop to the legions of Germany.

More than this was needed to stop Vitellius, the extent of whose support and ambitions only became clear as Otho examined Galba's confidential correspondence. As the month wore on and brought more and more sinister reports of troop movements, Otho began to realize that he

had put his head into a hornet's nest and that the inheritance he had
snatched from Piso was likely to prove fatal to himself. But he concealed his fears and tried to behave as if the sky were without a cloud.
He wrote a succession of letters to Vitellius, attempting to buy him off
—a prospect not entirely chimerical, had the decision rested with
Vitellius alone—with offers of money, influence and a life of pleasure in
any place of his choice. Vitellius at first responded with similarly unreal
and diplomatic offers. But as the confidence of both parties grew, the
tone of their correspondence became more peremptory. The moment
for bribery was past. The embassy which with great difficulty Galba had
managed to get together to approach Vitellius was recalled, and a fresh
one, ostensibly representing the Senate, was dispatched to both armies
in Germany and to the garrison of Lyon. Inevitably the move was
abortive and the escort of Praetorians was hurriedly brought back
when it became obvious that the ambassadors were going over to the
Vitellian side.

But these were temporizing exchanges. It was difficult for Otho to
take a strong line until he knew what support he commanded throughout the empire. The news gradually trickled in, and it was favourable.
By 7 February he had heard from the Thirteenth Legion at Ptuj, by the
14th from the Galbian VII at Petronell or the Danube, whose commander Antonius Primus repeatedly communicated to Otho his will-
ingness to move immediately to northern Italy to forestall the Vitellian
invasion which could not be long delayed, and whose vigour communicated itself to the governor of the neighbouring province of Noricum.
At the end of the month came welcome tidings from Moesia. In the
west the situation was less good. The proximity of the Rhine troops
automatically induced the falling away of the Iberian peninsula (despite
a momentary recognition from the pliable historian-governor Cluvius
Rufus) and of the whole of the Gallic world. Nothing else could be
expected from virtually defenceless provinces. But Britain also declared
for Vitellius, though it had troubles of its own which prevented much
active participation. Yet the adhesion to Otho of Pannonia, Dalmatia
and Moesia brought him a legionary potential exactly matching that of
Vitellius: four legions in Pannonia and Dalmatia, three in Moesia. To
these were added the legion and other garrison troops in Rome. Moreover, by mid-March, before Otho left Rome, it was known that the
eight legions of the East (3 in Syria, 3 in Judaea, 2 in Egypt) had sworn
allegiance to him. The ultimate prospects, then, if it came to civil war,
were not unfavourable. But Otho's initial caution is perhaps illustrated
by the slowness of the legislative action by which the emperor assumed
power. Though the Senate had granted him full recognition on 15
January, it was only on 26 January that his consulship was voted by the
people; and his tribunician power, always the main constituent of the

position of princeps and granted by a law passed by the nominally sovereign people, was only voted on 28 February. By this time, it seems, Otho had decided that no retreat was necessary or desirable.

Hence the increasing acrimony of the exchange between the two rivals. The change of mood induced attempts at assassination or at least the belief that such attempts were being planned. Vitellius' agents in Rome went undetected in that great capital where so many men were strangers one to another, but they were unable to penetrate the Praetorian hedge. The Othonian agents sent to Germany were for their part conspicuous, and were arrested. The danger is more than once alluded to in our sources: after all, Gaius and Galba himself offered recent precedents. Then there were the relatives. Vitellius' mother, daughter and infant son were in Rome, and might seem valuable hostages. At the end of March, therefore, when Otho was known to have appointed Titianus as regent during his absence from Rome, Vitellius wrote threatening him and his son with death if anything happened to his own family. Nothing, in fact, did happen, and in due course the young child was allowed by Sabinus, after Titianus' own departure, to leave and meet his father at Lyon.

But throughout January, February and March the atmosphere was strained, heavy with suspicion. The Praetorians suspected senatorial plots against Otho's life where none existed. Some of them insinuated themselves into the great houses disguised as civilians, and the privacy of the home was scarcely secure. A striking instance of jealous fear was provided by a ludicrous yet potentially dangerous incident. As part of the general mobilization Otho had ordered the Seventeenth (Urban) Cohort to move from Ostia to Rome, where it was to pick up its active-service baggage, arms and equipment from the arsenal in the Praetorian barracks before proceeding on its way. The Praetorian tribune charged with the issue, one Varius Crispinus, decided that the cohort's vehicles should be loaded at night, when the barracks were quiet and there would be greater freedom from distraction. The move was misinterpreted by some of the Praetorians who observed it. The issue of arms was taken to be part of a plot—obviously a senatorial plot —upon the life of Otho. Under this misapprehension a group of drunken Praetorians themselves seized the arms, killed Crispinus and two of their own centurions, and rushed off in what was meant to be a rescue operation. As this disorderly throng burst through the palace gates, Otho was entertaining a large party of eighty senators, many with their wives. The clamour outside increased. Otho and his guests, equally mystified and equally afraid, viewed one another with a wild surmise. Was this a coup organized against the senators or against the emperor? But Otho did not lose his presence of mind. To gain a few moments' respite, he told his Praetorian prefects, who were present, to address the mutineers, and at the same time hurried the company away by another door. Seconds later, the soldiers burst into the dining room and asked what had become of the enemies of Caesar. The tribune Julius Martialis, and a legionary prefect Vitellius Saturninus, were wounded as they attempted to stem the surge of bodies. In desperation Otho got up on a dining couch in order to be seen and heard, and succeeded with some difficulty in persuading his hearers that he was alive and well, and that there was no plot against his life. Meanwhile the guests threw senatorial and magisterial dignity to the winds; concealing their insignia and avoiding their waiting link-boys, they vanished down the dark streets of the capital in all directions. One or two made for their mansions, the vast majority for the homes of friends and faithful retainers where they could lie low. The next morning Rome resembled a captured city. The houses were shuttered. The streets were empty. The troops involved were sullen rather than regretful. After they had been addressed by their prefects and promised a douceur of 5,000 sesterces each, Otho entered the barracks. He was immediately surrounded by the officers, who stripped off their badges of rank and asked to be retired from the army. Theatrical gestures of this sort were often surprisingly effective, especially if they appealed to honour and esprit de corps. The men were sensitive to this reflection upon themselves. They returned to duty in an orderly way and, without any prompting, demanded the punishment of the ringleaders. Otho responded with a strong and tactful speech, partly of reproof, partly of encouragement. Only two men were punished.

This suspicion and uncertainty were also displayed at meetings of the Senate, less dramatically but more informatively. Here the feeling of individual members that they were under suspicion, and the even chance that the public enemy of today would be the emperor of tomorrow undermined any real and frank expression of opinion. Silence might seem dumb rebellion; criticism was as dangerous as support, whether of Otho or of Vitellius. Wary politicians confined themselves to perfunctory rebukes of Vitellius, and certain of them, while not mincing matters, timed their denunciations for moments of uproar when everyone was on his feet, or else blurted them out in an incoherent torrent of words which nobody could quite catch. The spectacle was degrading, and illustrated the essential powerlessness of the Senate and the cowardice of its leading members.

Otho's reign in Rome lasted, in effect, for two months, and from the very slight record that we possess of a period overshadowed by military preoccupations it is impossible to deduce what political qualities Otho might have deployed in a longer reign. It is clear that once in power he tried to be conciliatory. His manner was affable, he was a good talker and was able to keep his head in a crisis. To judge from the speeches put into his mouth by Tacitus, he was eager that the Senate should play its full part in government. But there were fears that these favourable displays would yield in time. Some concessions were made to the Senate in the matter of the pardoning of certain members under sentence. In Spain, where Otho was known, additional families—and presumably their land—were included in the territory of Seville and Merida, the latter being the capital of the province of Lusitania which Otho had governed, and the former the second or third town in Southern Spain, to which province the emperor also assigned some parts of Morocco—presumably Tangier among them on the south side of the strait. New but short-lived constitutions were devised for Cappadocia and Africa. From such slight activities no trend of policy emerges, nor indeed do the disputes of 69 arise from the conflict of policies: they issue purely from groups or individuals contending for power.

Before leaving Rome, Otho removed a member of a prominent noble family, Cornelius Dolabella, to a mild banishment in the Augustan colony on the Via Latina under the ancient town of Aquino, where he remained until an evil destiny prompted him to leave it without permission. Dolabella was a distant relative of Galba's and his name had been mentioned during public discussion of the adoption.

In attempting to win over the Roman and Italian public, Otho suffered from two heavy handicaps. The manner in which he had gained the principate could not be, and was not, forgiven. The murder of his predecessor, responsibility for which Otho at no time denied, was an unparalleled and inexcusable crime that made nonsense of Rome's claim to be a civilized and civilizing power. It was also, in the circumstances of Vitellius' revolt, an act of consummate and suicidal folly, which Otho soon came to regret. Two of our sources refer to a saying of his: 'What need had I to play the long pipes?' Secondly, his close connection with Nero, stressed by Otho himself by his restoration of the overturned statues of Nero and Poppaea, and by his acceptance of the unofficial title 'Otho Nero', rendered him deeply suspect in the eyes of the great majority of Romans, however moderate an attitude he sought to adopt. Sooner or later, it was felt, the old Adam would reassert himself and Rome would be saddled with another expensive and irresponsible playboy.

Towards the middle of February, assured of the allegiance of Pannonia, he dispatched Suedius Clemens with his naval force to bar the coast road in Liguria, and at the same time Annius Gallus and Vestricius Spurinna were sent north ahead of the emperor. Their forces, as we have seen, were not considerable.

But in the first week of March Otho took an irrevocable step that proved his will to fight it out in northern Italy. By this time he was assured of the support not only of the Danube troops, but of those of the

East. It was also the latest possible moment at which the intervention of these troops could be effective against an invading force expected over the Alps in the course of April. Otho, therefore, on or about 3 March, issued urgent movement orders to the legions of Pannonia, Dalmatia and Moesia. Within forty-eight hours of receipt of the order, 2,000 men of each formation were to be despatched, and the remainder of the legionary effectives within a week. Their place, as garrisons arranged along the frontiers, was to be taken by the auxiliary infantry and cavalry. The first of these troops, the advance party of XIII, the nearest legion, could be expected on the Po in the first week of April. But only when six of the seven legions had arrived could the Othonian forces equal in number the combined armies of Caecina and Valens, and this moment would not arrive until 23 May or thereabouts. This implies a determination to hold the Po line and keep communications with the north-east open in the interval.

The supreme commanders, Suetonius Paulinus and Marius Celsus, do not seem to have left Rome until about 10 March, since there is no evidence in our sources of their presence in the north until the occurrence of events datable to the end of the month and contemporary with Caecina's abortive attack on Piacenza; and the Othonian order of battle reveals no troops that could have travelled with them, and thereby limited their speed of travel to that of infantry or cavalry formations. Whether or not the Ostiglia bridge continued to be occupied is uncertain. But what is clear is that the more westerly crossings at Piacenza, Cremona and Brescello must have taken precedence in the claim for defence.

When Otho himself left for the front on 14 or 15 March he took with him the remainder of the Praetorian cohorts (that is, 12 less the 5 already dispatched and less those, perhaps 2 in number, assigned to Suedius Clemens), some time-expired Praetorians called up for the emergency, a large number of naval aspirants to legionary service, and a bodyguard of picked men. The total strength of the imperial retinue can hardly have exceeded 9,000 soldiers. Their objective was Brescello, and the distance involved, 350 miles, would take a marching column at least twenty-three days.

Shortly before Otho's departure, the unusually early spring melted the snows of the Apennines and caused severe flooding in Rome, where the Tiber was notorious for the suddenness and frequency of its inundations. A very considerable rise in its level caused the collapse of the old Pile Bridge, the Pons Sublicius, which spanned the river below the Island. Now that the stone Aemilian Bridge provided adequate communication between the western bank and the Forum Boarium, this relic of the earliest history of Rome was, strictly speaking, unnecessary; but however often destroyed, it was restored—as it had been by

Augustus a century earlier—as a link with the heroic days of Horatius. And religious scruple decreed that the reconstruction should be in wood, and that from it, as heretofore, on every fourteenth day of May, the pontiffs, the Vestals and the magistrates should (in a ritual no longer understood) throw down into the water puppets of rush, cheaper than a human sacrifice, to placate the indignation of the river spirit whom the bridge had defied. In 69 its timbers fell once more and dammed the Tiber, which flooded not only the low-lying parts of the cattle market and the Vatican area, but also districts in the Campus Martius normally immune. Many Romans were trapped at night in the lock-up shops in which they slept or in ground-floor flats. Unemployment and food shortages, encouraged no doubt by the dislocation of the Ostia–Rome freighter service, caused famine among the poorer classes, and the standing water sapped the foundations of jerry-built tenements, which collapsed as the river retreated. Even the Flaminian Way, the road to the north and to the front, was blocked; and the superstitious shook their heads over the evident anger of the gods. But preparations went ahead for the expedition. Otho's distrust of the Senate was such that he felt bound to order that a large proportion of the members and many of the magistrates should accompany him, ostensibly as a travelling council of state, in reality as hostages. The unmilitary men were much put about. Some scarcely knew what war meant, except on paper, for the soil of Italy had known no fighting since the civil wars of the Second Triumvirate a century before; and under the Roman peace, many provincial governors had hardly seen a sword drawn in anger. The more the nobility strove to hide their anxieties, the more obvious they became. On the other hand there were fools who thought that war was a picnic, and tried to cut a dash by purchasing showy arms and equipment, fine horses and even, in some instances, canteens of lavish tableware recalling the senatorial spreads discovered by Julius Caesar in the tents of the republicans after Pharsalia. The sudden demand for both necessities and luxuries led to a general increase in prices, particularly of food, the main concern of the poor.

Among those senators who, willingly or unwillingly, followed Otho were the consul L. Verginius Rufus, the consul designate for May and June T. Flavius Sabinus, Lucius Vitellius the brother of Otho's rival, the prosecutor Eprius Marcellus, Licinius Caecina, Mestrius Florus (Plutarch's friend), and many more. The minutes of the meetings of the Brethren of the Fields are eloquent: from 14 March onwards the college, normally represented at any one ceremony by four or five of its twelve members, display a single name, the young deputy-president L. Maecius Postumus. Missing are regular attenders like M. Raecius Taurus, as friend of Galba—and later of Vespasian—a desirable hostage, Q. Tillius Sassius, the mild Publius Valerius Marinus and Lucius Salvius

Otho Titianus—the last, however, not because he had left Rome on 14 March but because he was then made imperial regent by his brother to deal with day-to-day administration. At the same time (if we believe Plutarch and accept a plausible supplement in the text of Tacitus), Otho committed the policing of the capital to the man who in any case bore nominal responsibility for it—Vespasian's elder brother, Flavius Sabinus.[30]

Before leaving Rome, Otho addressed a mass meeting in the Forum, stressing the factors that told in favour of his cause and blaming the Vitellian legions not so much for rebellion as for ignorance—ignorance, that is, concerning a coup that took place a fortnight after they had declared their allegiance to Vitellius. This diplomatic approach was attributed by some critics to the caution of Otho's supposed speech-writer, Galerius Trachalus. Connoisseurs of rhetoric, indeed, professed to detect the authorship of the harangue from its style, familiar from Trachalus' position as consul in 68 and his frequent appearances in the courts, where his ample and sonorous Latin, fine diction and impressive appearance—he would have adorned any stage—exercised a magic appeal upon popular taste. Anyway, the crowds cheered. But whether the applause was sincere or hollow, who could tell? The support which the common people of Rome had voiced for Galba, and were in the future to accord Vitellius and the Flavians, was not denied to Otho.[31]

Despite the floods, the emperor, Senate and army crossed the Milvian Bridge, climbed the ridge by Grotta Rossa and disappeared north-wards. Rome could only wait helplessly and perhaps indifferently for the issue of the struggle: defeat, victory or compromise. Ten days later, as Otho came down from the Passo del Furlo towards Fano, he received a letter from his Praetorians at Brescello containing wild allegations of treachery against Suetonius Paulinus, Annius Gallus and Marius Celsus. He did not believe these stories, but as something had to be done to pacify those who were his most enthusiastic supporters, he transferred the supreme command to his brother Titianus, who was called from Rome to the front and joined the rest by the time Otho himself arrived on the Po. As his assistant it was tactful to appoint the troublemaker Licinius Proculus, a man as loud as he was ignorant, but one of the two Praetorian prefects. The accused commanders were not displaced: they were merely submerged in a larger council of war in which he, the emperor, would in any case now have the last word. Then, moving on through Rimini over Augustus' bridge (as the traffic does today) and along the Aemilian Way, he left the senators behind him at Modena and hastened with his troops to Brescello and Bedriacum. But before he arrived the old commanders had redeemed themselves by a successful action.

About 24 March, while Valens was still beginning the easy descent from the Mt Genèvre Pass, Caecina was, as we have observed, retiring from Piacenza to his base at Cremona. On his arrival he found that the auxiliaries left to guard the area had been roughly handled in a raid carried out by an enthusiastic Othonian general called Martius Macer, who, as the road bridge was cut, had ferried across the Po his force of 2,000 gladiators, skilled swordsmen not normally employed in war. This was another blow. Caecina felt strongly that it was high time to refresh his fading laurels by some sort of victorious initiative, or his troops would become restless and he himself lose face with Vitellius in competition with Valens. Small though his army was, it was larger than the Othonian force at Bedriacum; and Caecina was fertile in bright ideas, even if vanity and ambition frequently led him to underestimate his opponents.

The landscape east of Cremona offers few surprises. An immense and almost level plain, tilted insensibly towards the south-east and the Po, it was in its central part occupied by the triumviral settlements of 41–40 B.C., when the land had been requisitioned as a punishment and allotted in regular quadrangular plots, delimited by survey, to the de-mobilized soldiers of Octavian. The evidence of this is still visible in the grid with which modern roads, tracks, field boundaries and streams conform over many miles. The sides of the major divisions of this cen-turiation are some 700 or 710 metres in length. Across this grid, and only in part conforming with it, runs the Postumian Way, now a minor though useful country road, in the first century the main highway connecting Piacenza, Cremona and Verona. It is laid down upon straight lines determined by the surveyor's square, the *groma*, with occasional turns into a new reach. In 69 the land was as fruitful with millet and barley as now with maize, and well-watered by small but numerous watercourses, ditches rather than streams, meandering to-wards the Po. Here and there were patches of woodland and screens of trees along the roads, occasional vineyards, and, studding the plots, the dwelling places and barns of the farmers, a sylvan fenland more attrac-tive in summer than those of the Wash or the Low Countries. Bleak and muddy in winter, the land flourished and clothed itself in spring, hot and moist and productive, the source of men and wealth for the expand-ing cities of the plain. Here in peacetime slow ox teams creaked along the dusty lanes or paved highways, the vine trimmers sang at their work, audible from afar in the quiet, the ploughman pressed on his heavy plough, carrying on the old struggle with Nature, dominating, improving, nourishing. When the shadows of the tall trees lengthened, the smoke rose everywhere from the house-tops as the evening meal was prepared on the open hearth by the housewife. But in war this flat-ness, scarcely interrupted by the irrigation channels and little streams, provided an open field for the manoeuvre of great masses. The element

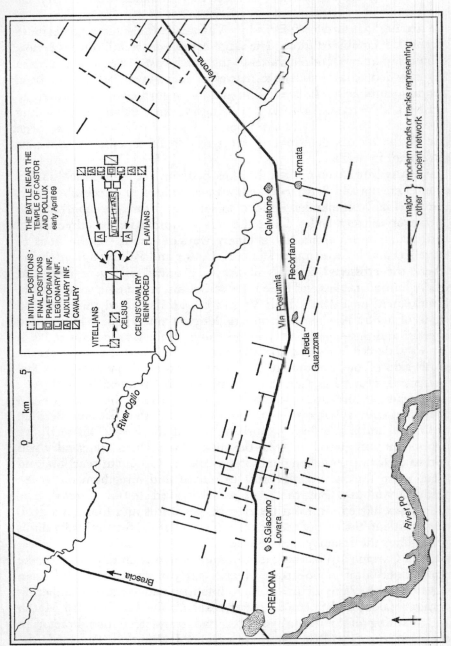

Fig. 2 Parts of the territory of Cremona and Mantua with (inset) the battle near the Temple of Castor and Pollux, early April 69

of surprise was scarcely to be achieved, luxuriant though the foliage might be. In the legionary scrum, the heavier packs would carry the day.

Caecina, soon to be reinforced by Valens, had selected a good site to receive the combined force. The large camp, whose building was now begun, lay a few hundred yards to the north-east of Cremona, a town too crowded to accommodate masses of men, even if this had been desirable militarily. It lay within the angle formed by the roads to Brescia and Verona. Through it or alongside flowed a stream providing water and access for small boats from the Po—a facility which had been one of the factors determining the selection of the site for the new settlement in 218 B.C.

In early April, after a few brushes between reconnaissance parties from Cremona and Bedriacum, not always decided in Caecina's favour, the Vitellian commander decided to set a trap for the enemy. Some twelve or thirteen miles along the Via Postumia in the direction of Bedriacum and Verona lay a lonely wayside chapel of the gods of travellers and horsemen, the Dioscuri, Castor and Pollux: a little shrine where the crossroad festivals of simple country folk were held and where humble tablets and little ivory sculptures commemorated a boon, a retirement or a death. In it Virgil's carrier dedicated the reins and comb of his trade when his mules no longer trotted briskly by, pulling luggage and passengers on the long straight road. Its successor today is the wayside cemetery and its little chapel, filled with ex-votos, on the south side of the Postumian Way close to the village of Ronca de' Golférami, rather less than thirteen miles from Cremona.[32]

It was near this shrine, roughly half way between the Vitellian and Othonian camps, but rather closer to the latter, that Caecina decided to lay his ambush. About 5 April he placed the best of his auxiliary infantry in some woods close to the road, along which the cavalry was told to go forward challengingly to provoke an Othonian reaction, and then, when the enemy appeared, to retreat and lure them on to the point of ambush. But the plan was betrayed to the enemy. The Othonians moved out from Bedriacum westwards and took up a position a little to the east of the Temple of the Castors, Suetonius Paulinus controlling the infantry and Marius Celsus the cavalry. Since the repulse of Caecina at Piacenza, their resources had been improved by the appearance of the 2,000-strong advance party of the Thirteenth Legion together with Pannonian auxiliary infantry and cavalry numbering perhaps 3,000; and Suetonius, after reaching the Po about 19 March and learning of Spurinna's success, had transferred one Praetorian cohort at least from Piacenza to Brescello or Bedriacum. This made the total Othonian force east of Cremona up to some 15,000. A skeleton force was left at Brescello and in the camp at Bedriacum, for the opportunity demanded that every possible man should be used to profit by a situation in which the numerically inferior Othonian force could deal with a portion of the enemy detached far from its camp. The Othonian array was orderly. Three Praetorian cohorts (1,500 men) held the high-road in depth six men abreast and ready to deploy. On the left was posted the advance party of the Thirteenth Legion with four cohorts of auxiliary infantry and 500 horse. The right front consisted of the First (Support) Legion, two cohorts of auxiliary infantry and 500 cavalry-men. The line was therefore carefully balanced about the fulcrum of the Via Postumia, and upon this, in reserve behind the infantry, lay 1,000 cavalry drawn from the Praetorian and auxiliary units. Celsus himself seems to have had under his command a small cavalry force, perhaps of legionary horse, on the road in front of the Othonian line, where he could direct the manoeuvre with the fine timing necessary for success. Screening the infantry behind him, he was to act the gullible victim of Caecina's cunning and himself to spring the trap. As the Othonians moved forwards in formation, but before the cavalry forces of Caecina and Celsus made contact, the advancing Vitellians turned round and made a feint of retreat. Celsus realized that this was the trick he had been expecting and moved cautiously after Caecina, keeping his troops under strict control. The enemy were not so disciplined. Too soon their cohorts jumped out from their place of concealment in the trees. This suited Celsus admirably. He immediately halted his men short of the wood and began to retreat slowly, followed by the unwary Vitellians, who fell headlong into the kind of trap they had themselves set for others. Suddenly they found themselves confronting a solid mass of Praetorian infantry. Hemming them in on right and left appeared the enemy auxiliary and legionary infantry. As for Celsus, at the last moment he had caused his small cavalry force to divide and wheel apart, each party returning in a loop, reinforced now by the two bodies of 500 cavalry and the reserve of 1,000. Their task was to close the ring about the Vitellians. When encirclement was complete, Suetonius was to launch his infantry attack from the east; but it seems possible that the move-ment was carried out slightly late, or the cavalry were slightly too slow. Through a gap in the box the Vitellians, or some of them, had time to retreat to the rows of a vineyard whose heavy props connected by over-head trellises impeded movement and offered shelter. Nearby, too, was a piece of woodland where they re-formed and whence they had the spirit to counter-attack and inflict casualties on the first arrivals among the Othonian cavalry. One of the wounded on the Othonian side was Prince Epiphanes of Commagene, a spirited young man commanding an auxiliary regiment recruited from his people.

Finally the Othonian infantry charged. The enemy were crushed and the rout communicated itself to their reinforcements as they arrived piecemeal from the Vitellian camp far to the west. The collision between those seeking to advance and those attempting to retreat led to total confusion and defeat. Casualties were heavy. A year or so later Plutarch passed this way in the company of his friend the senator Mestrius Florus —the same who had followed Otho unwillingly to the north—who pointed out the ancient Temple of the Castors and told him that on passing by after the fighting was over he had seen a pile of corpses so huge that those on the top were level with the gable-ends of the building.

There is no doubt that, despite some slight mistiming, this was a very considerable success for the Othonians. Good intelligence, a carefully worked out plan, numerical superiority and a lively fighting spirit cannot fail as recipes for military success. Armchair critics—and perhaps some of the rank and file among the troops—complained, of course, wise after the event: Suetonius, by preventing his men from pursuing the beaten enemy to Cremona, had deprived the Othonians of the chance of smashing Caecina's army completely. Perhaps they did not know, or conveniently forgot, that the camp of the Vitellians lay twelve miles away, and was manned by a sizeable force of fresh troops who might well have done great execution if the Othonians, tired by a battle and a pursuit, had appeared before their defences. Caecina, though guilty of many mistakes, had not committed anything like all his forces near the Castors, and he seems to have realized pretty soon that it was useless to reinforce failure. Despite the indignation of his men, he had not allowed the legionary element to be thrown in to save a hopeless situation. They would fight another day. The decision of Suetonius Paulinus to break off the battle and be content with the losses already inflicted was perfectly correct, and the disparity between the numbers available to him—about 15,000, nearly all committed— and the total effectives of Caecina—about 18,000, of whom only a few thousand had been thrown in—tends to justify his caution. A second complaint, probably equally misconceived, survives in the historical tradition as a memory of after-dinner arguments and table-top diagrams sketched in wine upon the marble. Suetonius, it was said—an odd criticism to pass upon the man who had conquered Boudicca only eight years before—was too old and too slow: he had insisted on filling up ditches to make sure of the lateral contact stressed by the textbooks, and had so wasted valuable time. This is an echo of Paulinus' perfectly proper concern to bridge the watercourses of the area represented now-adays by the Delmona and the Fossa Bonetta or the Roggia Offredi in the close vicinity of the Castors; but it may be questioned whether this was a lengthy procedure or would still have had to be prolonged when the moment for advance arrived. Such stories are inflated and exploited when generals fight their battles again on paper and when politicians and pamphleteers are concerned with whitewashing themselves and

blackening the rest. But the genuine victory came too late to allow Otho
to brush off previous complaints, and in any case the emperor had already
appointed Titianus and Proculus at the end of March some days before.

As a result of the fiasco near the Temple of Castor and Pollux,
Caecina had to face a certain amount of restiveness among his own men
in the camp outside Cremona. His answer was two-fold. He pointed out
that the trap devised by himself had only failed because the auxiliary
infantry had disclosed themselves prematurely, and that once surprise
had been lost it would have been folly to waste the legionaries in an
effort to retrieve a minor check sustained by auxiliaries. This was not
perhaps the whole truth, but he had other points to make. It is not unlikely that he gave the impression that if the numerically superior force
of Valens had not loitered on the way to Italy, the rendezvous of the
two armies would have taken place much earlier and given their side a
vast advantage over the foe. As it was, they—Caecina and his men—
had with small forces occupied a whole Italian region including five
important towns before Valens had ever set foot in Italy. They had
borne the brunt of the fighting, indeed, on both sides of the Alps. The
arguments were specious but plausible, and by diverting the anger of
the troops from himself to Valens, Caecina was securing his credit with
Vitellius. Besides, he was generally popular—a tall well-built figure
possessing a certain charm of manner and panache in speech. No one
could accuse him of lack of enterprise. The second answer to the criticism was of a different kind. Soon after the battle, he set them to work
on the building of a bridge south of Cremona to replace that which
normally carried the Via Postumia across the Po south-westwards in the
direction of Piacenza. The river is wide, with sandbanks here and there,
shallow in summer, brimming and dangerous after rain. It had indeed
been possible to improvise a crossing opposite Piacenza, where
Spurinna's garrison was too weak and preoccupied to interrupt an
operation conducted some little way from the walls of the city. But the
raid by the gladiators of Macer in the opposite direction at Cremona
called for a more effective response. Rome, the objective, lay to the
south and if checked at Piacenza and towards Bedriacum, they, the
Vitellians, must force a crossing at Cremona. A permanent bridge must
be built to facilitate quick and continuous transit, and to remove any
threat of interference by the units of the Ravenna fleet patrolling the Po.

Caecina chose a form of bridge not only quick to build in wartime and
catered for in the Roman military manuals, but so well adapted to local
conditions that it is still used today at various points in the Po valley.
A line of pontoons was arranged, facing upstream, each boat equally
spaced from its neighbours, and secured to them by heavy timbers. The
structure was held in place by anchors at the prows, with sufficient
slack on the cables to allow these to be paid out if the water-level should

suddenly rise, as it so often does in spring. This would prevent the rupture or dislocation of the bridge. The outermost pontoon carried an artillery tower which, with the addition of each successive pontoon, was transferred accordingly. On the tower were mounted various types of catapults, discharging stone balls, arrows and firebrands. The Othonian answer was to erect their own tower on the south bank and reply in kind. When this proved ineffective, they hit on another device and about 12 April prepared fireships loaded with pinewood primed with sulphur and pitch, which were floated downstream against the bridge. A breeze sprang up at the crucial moment and secured a heavy impact with the pontoons. At first clouds of smoke were visible. Then the structure burst into flames along its length and the bridge engineers were forced to jump for it, exposing themselves to the attack and jeers of the Othonians. Soon after this, Macer's gladiators were reinforced, and it looked as if Caecina's bridging operations were doomed to failure. Yet the threat existed and would have to be dealt with decisively by Otho if the river line was to be held.

The issue was far from being closed, however. There was an island in the river near the bridge, one of those gravelly, ever-changing deposits that in summer split the waters of the Po. It was a no-man's-land, perpetually changing hands. To reach it the gladiators had to row hard, but the more skilled Batavians and Germans were in their element: launching themselves into the river west of Cremona, they swam downstream to the upper tip of the island. It happened on one occasion during the fighting in these days that the amphibious auxiliaries got across to the island in strength. In reply, Macer manned some galleys of the Ravenna fleet and attacked, using his toughest gladiators. But the latter found it harder to aim from the heaving decks than did the northerners from the firm footing of the island. The Othonian rowers and fighters fell over each other in the boats, which the Batavians and Germans, plunging into the water, held back by the sterns, or else climbed on board and drowned their opponents in hand-to-hand mêlées. Only a few of the vessels managed to escape and return to the base. From the two banks their fellow-soldiers looked on, cheering and booing like spectators at the games.

News of the battle at Castors had reached Valens just after he arrived at Pavia on 6 April. His troops, in controlling whom he too had had difficulties, were anxious to hurry on in the role of rescuers, and their general was content to give them their heads. He joined Caecina at Cremona on the evening of 8 April after a march of fifty miles covered at a smart speed in two days.

The army of Caecina regarded Valens coolly. Had he come a week earlier, he would have been more welcome. His lateness had blunted the advance and slowed the momentum of the Vitellian cause. Rumours of riot and rapine in the western force were contrasted with their own achievements, which, despite the late check, were considerable. And the two commanders themselves nourished the secret jealousy of rival contenders for Vitellius' ear and favour. Valens, thought Caecina, was interested only in feathering his nest with money and loot; Caecina was regarded by his colleague as a conceited poseur. But the pot and the kettle refrained from open abuse. The generals applied themselves to the problems of their trade. The Vitellian intelligence was good. The area to the east was scoured by daily reconnaissance, and a trickle of deserters brought in interesting news. As Caecina and Valens saw it, they themselves disposed of an army of almost 50,000 men, considerably outnumbering—at any rate for the moment—the scattered forces of the enemy along the Po. However, this numerical superiority was a wasting asset. They could expect nothing more of substance from Germany, whereas Otho was near at hand with a considerable force from the south and the Danubian legions were not far away in the north-east. The balance of advantage would soon swing against them. They decided to wait for any false move on the Othonians' part while maintaining their troops on continuous alert. No offensive action would be risked, but the construction of the bridge would be pushed on despite difficulties. Its completion or near-completion might well lure the enemy forward in an attempt to halt the opening of a passage to the south. But if not, they would cross the Po in a day or so and leave the Othonians behind them. Either way, the decision would come quickly, and this was what was necessary.

As the Vitellian commanders laid their plans, the emperor arrived at Brescello. After quickly reviewing the latest situation, in which the arrival in Bedriacum of the main party of the Thirteenth Legion constituted the major change, Otho gave notice of a council of war, to be held two days later in the camp. On 12 April the momentous meeting occurred at Bedriacum. It was attended by the emperor, his brother Titianus, the Praetorian prefect Proculus, Suetonius Paulinus and Marius Celsus, together, presumably, with the legionary commanders. Annius Gallus had been injured a few days before by a fall from his horse, but messengers had been sent to seek his views and report back. Another possible member is Flavius Sabinus, the consul designate, but Spurinna was far away at Piacenza. If he had been present, our information concerning the deliberations would have been less one-sided than it is.

The forces of which the Othonians now disposed in the vicinity of the Po were the small garrison of Spurinna, the band of gladiators opposite Cremona, and the army at Bedriacum which, at the time of the Castors engagement, numbered 15,000, but which now, since the appearance of the main body of the Thirteenth Legion on 7 April, could be put at 20,000 or more. To these forces we must add the 9,000 men accompanying Otho from Rome. Still, the total of the land forces scarcely exceeded 30,000, supported perhaps by a few naval details from Ravenna. Confronting them was an army approaching 50,000. But the Othonians were even better aware than the Vitellians that this discrepancy would soon narrow. How soon would the gap close? There is good reason to think that on the present date, 12 April, the Fourteenth Legion, a formation highly regarded, had passed Este, and that VII Galbiana under Antonius Primus had cleared Concordia, between Aquileia and Oderzo; while XI from Dalmatia, however dilatory the governor of that province, must soon put in an appearance. Some auxiliary forces from Moesia had arrived, but the advance and main parties of the nearest Moesian legion were still far away. However by 15 April two of the Pannonian/Dalmatian legions should be available. There was therefore a strong case, said Suetonius Paulinus, for waiting at least until 16 or 17 April before joining battle. Indeed the longer wait might be better still. There was no immediate danger of further forces coming from Germany: as far as one knew, Vitellius was still at Cologne, scraping an auxiliary barrel of third-rate units, since the rump of the legions could not be taken from such a potentially dangerous frontier. The Gallic provinces were with reason ill-disposed to the invader, the Helvetians had actually rebelled, the British legions were entangled in their own problems. The passage of time would make the supply position of the Vitellians in the Eleventh Region more difficult, and northerners usually found the malarial climate of Italy trying as summer approached. Suetonius gave it as his considered opinion that battle should not be offered immediately, but postponed for one or more weeks.

Paulinus' views were shared by Marius Celsus and Annius Gallus. The case for immediate action has not been preserved in our sources, but it can be easily reconstructed. The Othonians ought to strike, it was claimed by Titianus and Proculus, while the troops still retained the elation and momentum of victory. As to numbers, if the enemy had three legions—XXI, I Italica and V—the Othonians for their part could show I Adiutrix, XIII and a portion of XIV, to say nothing of Praetorians equivalent to at least one legion. Suetonius' argument about numbers was therefore hardly convincing. But the bridge-building of Caecina, though hampered by their own attacks, was still proceeding and before long might be complete. The enemy would then be in a position to by-pass the Othonians on the river in a sudden dash to the south. If the Vitellians occupied the capital, they could claim the psychological and material advantages which the Othonians so far retained by its possession. Moreover, the senators at Modena could not be relied on: they would throw in their lot with any apparently victorious army. It was obvious that many senators distrusted Otho personally and remembered the death of Galba.

Above all, Titianus and Proculus continued, it was important not to
fob off the Praetorians who constituted Otho's most devoted adherents,
and who disliked the professional legionary commanders and all their
views. At this point it was worth noting that not all Otho's troops, not
all his Praetorian tribunes even, were opposed to a compromise solution.
If time were allowed to pass, and desertions, fraternization and secret
negotiations occurred, the most likely outcome would be that both
Vitellius and Otho would be jettisoned and the principate once more
offered to Verginius Rufus. Even his punctilious principles might not
stand up to a third temptation, especially if it had the backing of the
Senate, or a portion thereof. The only safe policy was to act at once.
Otho must bring the bridge-building to a halt by planting near it an
advanced base from which daily attacks could be safely launched.
Meantime Bedriacum, Brescello and Piacenza would be held; and it
would be advisable to strengthen the gladiators opposite Cremona.
Once the escape route here was closed, the Pannonian and Dalmatian
legions could be used to enforce a capitulation on Otho's terms.

The case for immediate action was accepted by Otho, who may well
have been swayed especially by the well-founded suspicion that a
number of prominent Romans would have been glad to rid themselves
of the incubus of a civil war between two rivals who desired personal
power but had no public policy. Indeed he had little stomach for such a
war himself, and it was not for this that he had plotted against Galba.
Titianus' plan at any rate promised an almost bloodless Vitellian surrender. He gave orders that the main portion of the army at Bedriacum
should advance on the afternoon of 13 April with maximum secrecy and
after a rapid march entrench camp near the bridge on the day following. A strong reserve would be maintained in Bedriacum under Annius
Gallus, who would probably be fit enough for this post, and he, Otho,
would hold Brescello with the Praetorians he had brought from Rome.
From this position he could head off any Vitellians who might somehow get away southwards, and maintain the defence of a bridge vital to
the advancing legions from the north-east. Spurinna was urgently
ordered to bring up his two Praetorian cohorts from Piacenza to reinforce the gladiators, who were placed under the command of the
consul designate Flavius Sabinus, an appointment which represented
Otho's answer to complaints, ill-justified indeed, about Macer. These
troops, ready for action on 14 April, were to stage a diversionary raid
on that afternoon across the river while the main Othonian army was
planting its advance camp in the vicinity of the bridge.

Characteristically, the emperor left the exact working out of the
march distances and encampment to his field commanders. In so doing
he sealed his doom.

5

The First Battle of Cremona

The task confronting the Othonian commanders was no easy one. To construct a camp in close proximity to a hostile force was a difficult operation, though it was not infrequently done in battle with undisciplined barbarians, and Roman troops were trained in the necessary drill. But as the cumbrous army moved off, an observer might have been forgiven for supposing that it was setting out for a distant campaign, not for an imminent engagement. On the narrow road was a large part of the Othonian army, laden with all the equipment, including timber ready cut, necessary for constructing the advanced camp, to be sited some four miles only from that of the enemy, close to Caecina's bridge over the Po, which was also defended. The distance involved, twenty miles, was decidedly in excess of what could be covered in one day if massive digging operations were necessary on arrival. A start was therefore made on 13 April, and in order to achieve such secrecy as was attainable in a manoeuvre extending over two days, it was decided that on the first of these they should not venture within the probable range of enemy reconnaissance, about a dozen miles.[33]

On the afternoon of 13 April the army moved out of camp westward, and having covered four miles only encamped between the modern villages of Voltido and Recórfano, at the apex of the triangle whose long sides are formed by the Via Postumia and the grid track through Recórfano, and upon whose hypotenuse lies the village of Tornata. The command selected a site which, as peevish critics remarked, managed to be without water in a countryside full of streams in spring spate. The complaint is trivial, for water cannot have been far away, but it well illustrates the childish recriminations with which military men sometimes stud their memoirs. The important aim, secrecy, was achieved, for it was not on the evening of 13 April but only on the morning of the following day that the Vitellian scouts reported the advance of the Othonians, now very much nearer Cremona. For the same reason the first day's camp, like that which they had just left, lay slightly off the line of the highroad. Brief as the distance from Bedriacum was, it was worth covering on the 13th; it enabled the next day's march to fall slightly short of the normal infantry prescription. Given an early start,

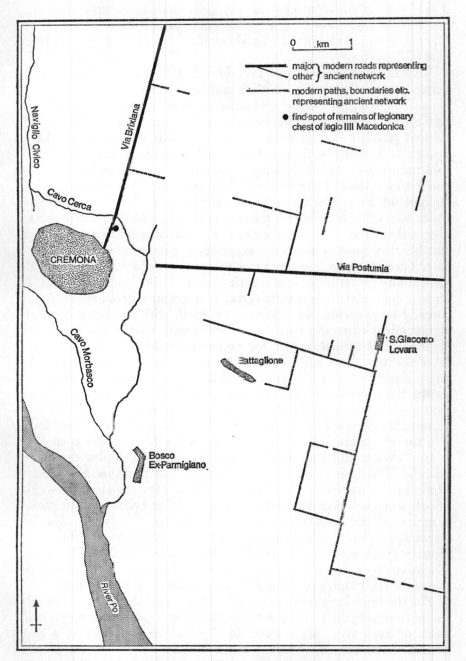

Fig. 3   The site of the First Battle of Cremona

they could march sixteen miles in five hours and still have plenty of time for digging. Roman practice suggests that the camp construction would have been done by one legion while the rest stood on guard, and several hours' work with the spade would be necessary in view of the size of the army.

That evening Titianus and the generals debated the following day's route. They had to decide whether, and how far, to follow the main road on 14 April. The use of the centuriation *limites*, paths or tracks parallel and at right angles to the highroad, would eventually bring them to the desired position. But these dirt tracks and baulk paths were muddy in spring, and would inevitably slow the advance of the baggage vehicles and therefore of the whole army to two miles an hour or less. This was intolerable. Most of the day would be consumed by such a slow and painful advance. On the other hand, the use of the metalled Via Postumia, while speeding up the rate of march, would also increase the risk of detection, for wherever else the Vitellian scouts might or might not be, they must certainly be expected to patrol the main thorough-fare. Tacitus, however, seems to conceive of the debate as hinging on the desirability or otherwise of waiting until Otho appeared with his Praetorian escort. This is quite certainly a serious misconception. It had already been decided by Otho on 12 April, with the consent of Sue-tonius and Celsus and therefore *a fortiori* with that of the obsequious Titianus and Proculus, that the emperor would hold Brescello: that issue at least cannot have arisen at this point, though it no doubt did in many a post-mortem afterwards. And the historian uses language which could be understood (and usually is understood) to mean: 'They hesitated whether to fight'—as if that decision, too, had not been thoroughly thrashed out and settled at the council of war at Bedriacum. But the words are also capable of bearing a different, and preferable, sense: 'Doubt arose as to the chances of a battle developing during the march.' This is intelligible. The difficulty was to know how best to compromise between the two alternatives. How soon or how late should the advantage of speed on the highway be exchanged for greater security on the by-way? Should they take the turn to S. Giacomo Lovara, less than four miles from the Cremona camp, but leading by the shortest route to the bridge area? Or should they travel via Sóspiro and Farisengo by safe, slow tracks? Suetonius Paulinus characteristically voted for the latter, even though it would involve a late arrival.

But the historian cannot always read the secret thoughts of men. We cannot exclude the possibility that caution and patriotism may, at the back of Suetonius' mind, have toyed with the possibility of a com-promise between the generals on both sides before the fatal battle started. For this, time was necessary. There are a number of hints in our sources that there was a widespread fear on the Othonian side of 'treachery'—a fear not diminished by the calculation that such a solution would avoid the shame and loss involved in warfare between Roman and Roman.

The debate on the evening of 13 April was indecisive. It was continued on the next morning and had not reached a conclusion when a Numidian horseman brought an urgent message from Otho, pressing for speed at all costs. But what event had occurred since 12 April to render this curious hastener necessary? There are two possibilities. Titianus and Proculus, neither of them experienced in active warfare, may have felt unable to come to a decision without consulting Otho; and if so, the exchange of messages could have been made between Voltido and Brescello during the night of 13/14 April. Alternatively, Otho himself may have received news which increased his anxiety. Had Flavius Sabinus discovered the absence of his two Praetorian tribunes on the errand described below, and had he believed that his whole force, to whom he had just come as a stranger, was unreliable? Whatever the cause of Otho's desire for haste—and the phenomenon was debated at length by contemporaries—it tilted the balance of decision. Titianus and Proculus, outvoted though they were by Suetonius, Celsus and others, used their rank to overrule all further opposition: the army would keep to the Via Postumia and take the more dangerous S. Giacomo turn. The van was to consist of two auxiliary cavalry regiments, whose task it would be to ward off an attack or create a diversion beyond the road junction which constituted the danger point of closest approach to the enemy. Then the sequence was to be the First (Support) Legion, the Praetorians, the Thirteenth Legion and the 2,000-strong advance party of the Fourteenth Legion, the baggage being interspersed between the formations. The whole column would be supplemented by auxiliaries.

A little later on the same morning, Caecina was supervising the construction, or rather the reconstruction, of the bridge near the confluence of the Cavo Morbasco and the Po, when the commanders of two Othonian Praetorian cohorts came up to him. They asked for an interview. As things turned out, the interview never took place, and on these men and their proposals the historical tradition seems to have derived no information from the memoirs or recollections of Caecina, who had no reason to speculate on the hypothetical proposals of a defeated enemy. Consequently, Tacitus, too, is silent on their identity and intention. Their démarche invites surmise. The disposition of the Praetorian cohorts is known. Of the three originally assigned to Spurinna in March, one had been taken away from him by the time of the Castors engagement: at this, three—clearly Gallus' two and Spurinna's one—were present. The remainder—apart from the drafts given to Suedius Clemens—accompanied Otho from Rome and were now mostly with him at Brescello, while one or two may have been left with the Bedriacum army. The obvious answer to our question on the identity of the two cohort commanders is that the units concerned are those which Spurinna was ordered to bring eastwards to reinforce the gladiators south of Cremona, a movement which must have taken place on 13 April. Otho's transfer of the command at this point from Macer to Flavius Sabinus is described as welcome to the gladiators; but we have no information concerning the reaction of the two Praetorian cohorts when they found that Spurinna had been ordered to move them from the city which they had defended so successfully and brigade them with gladiators under a new general. They—or their officers—may have decided that Otho's cause, now guided or misguided by Titianus and Proculus, stood little chance against the combination of Caecina's and Valens' armies if conclusions were to be tried immediately. So far speculation. What is certain, and consistent with the theory, is that the attack launched on 14 April by the gladiators (there is no mention precisely of the Praetorians) was a failure, and that after the battle violent language was used about the treason of certain Praetorians. Since this charge cannot be levelled against the main body of the Praetorians at the First Battle of Cremona, it must relate to the only other Praetorian force in the offing: the two cohorts on the south bank. The intention of the interview sought with Caecina by the commanders was almost certainly to explore the possibility of avoiding a head-on collision of the legions by some sort of political compromise, almost certainly a protest against the futility of civil war. Whether this attempt should be described, to use Tacitus' terms, as 'treachery' or as 'some honourable plan' designed to avoid pointless bloodshed is an academic, if not a philosophical, question. In the event, the interview fell through, and the battle was fought.

Scarcely had the tribunes begun to speak to Caecina than their words were cut short by the arrival of scouts who told the Vitellian general that the enemy army was at hand. Dismissing the officers, Caecina mounted his horse and made at full gallop the ten- or fifteen-minute ride to the main camp three miles away. Here he found that the legions had already been alerted, and arms issued to them. They were now drawing lots to determine the order of march and of array. The First Battle of Cremona was about to begin.

All warfare and all battles are to a degree enveloped in chaos and confusion. The somewhat conflicting and unsatisfactory evidence for the course of the First Battle of Cremona (as it should be called) attests the piecemeal impressions left upon observers by the various aspects of a loosely and untidily fought engagement. Both the nature of the terrain and the character of the Othonian marching column divided the battle into a series of almost independent encounters. What is quite clear is that the Vitellians were more firmly led and enjoyed better intelligence, a higher degree of preparedness and coordination, and above all superior numbers. No one who studies the circumstances can be in the least surprised by the upshot.

While the legions of Caecina and Valens were drawing lots, the Vitellian cavalry galloped out of the camp eastwards towards the enemy. Despite numerical superiority, they were repulsed by the Othonian vanguard, consisting of two cavalry regiments, one from Pannonia and one from Moesia, the latter a very early arrival from that area. In the interval since the Vitellian scouts warned Caecina (and no doubt Valens, too, at approximately the same time) of the Othonian advance, the forces of Titianus and Proculus had approached the turn to S. Giacomo Lovara. While the infantry and interspersed baggage began to turn left towards the Po and the bridge, the two cavalry units had continued onward along the Via Postumia with the intention of engaging, or at any rate distracting, the Vitellians, who, if one considered the obstacles to sight presented by the dense vineyards on the east of the town, might be expected not to know precisely what was afoot. It is evident that this supposition was unduly optimistic. But the Othonian cavalry did their work well, and it is perhaps not too venturesome to see here the competence that Marius Celsus had already demonstrated at the Castors. So effective were they that the Vitellian auxiliary cavalry would have been pushed right back to the walls of the camp, had not their vanguard legion, the First (Italian), emerged to stem the rout. Drawing their swords, they compelled the retreating horsemen to face about and resume the fight.

By this time the leading Othonian legion, the First (Support), had moved on to the branch road and made its way about a mile from the junction, emerging into more open country as it drew nearer to the Po. But behind it, and along the Via Postumia in the direction of Bedriacum, there was considerable disorder and confusion. The formations were divided and slowed up by the baggage trains, and there seems to have been little cavalry to provide a screen. Visibility was poor. The solid supports upon which the vines were trained and trellised impeded both the visual tactical signals upon which a Roman army heavily depended, and the movements themselves which those signals were designed to control. While the Praetorians in the middle of the marching column seem to have remained on and around the main road, the Thirteenth and the vexillation of the Fourteenth had to deploy to the right to form some kind of line no doubt parallel with the north-south lines of the centuriation grid at that point. Some men were able to see and rally round their legionary and manipular standards, others were looking for them. There was a confused hubbub of rushing and shouting troops—an evil augury in any force representative of an army which prided itself upon its discipline, its clear chain of command and its coherence in battle. An unfortunate rumour added to the disarray. For some reason or other—treachery was afterwards alleged, or else a rumour intentionally spread by Vitellian agents—the men of I (Support) got it into their heads that their Vitellian opponents had decided to desert to their side. The cheers and greetings of the Othonians were answered by fierce yells and abuse. This incident was doubly unfortunate for the Othonians. It convinced the Vitellians that they had no fight in them, and I (Support) sapped the morale of its fellow formations by creating the suspicion that it meant to desert. A further difficulty was the presence in and around the Via Postumia of minor watercourses, obstacles sufficient to slow up infantry. Even the highroad presented a problem by its relative narrowness. It was not raised on an embankment above the surrounding countryside as Tacitus, perhaps misled by the word *agger* in his sources, seems to imply and as some modern historians confidently assert; but the term is justified by the presence of drainage ditches on either side, which still survive in an attenuated—or sometimes an amplified—form, spanned occasionally by culverts giving access to the fields. But the main impediment to the orderly deployment was probably the watercourses whose modern descendants bear the names of the Roggia Gambara and the Dugale Dossolo, flowing south, and the Roggia Emilia and Dugale Gambalone, flowing east. This was not the kind of land envisaged in the training manuals of the Roman army.

As one approached the Po, the landscape opened up. Neither ditches nor vineyards troubled the inexperienced but spirited First (Support) as it faced the Vitellian Twenty-First (Hurricane) Legion. The latter, like its fellows, had marched out from the camp in good order, knowing where to go and what to do. The Othonian formation, raised by Nero from naval personnel and formally embodied by Galba, probably in the preceding December, had never fought a legionary battle before. But it was well-led, in high spirits and eager to win its spurs. In an initial dash —after recovering from the effects of the misunderstanding—it overran the front ranks of its opponents and carried off their eagle. This was the ultimate disgrace for a Roman legion. Smarting under it, the Vitellians charged the attackers in return, killing the commander Orfidius Benignus and capturing not indeed the eagle, but a number of standards and flags. The effect on the First (Support) Legion of this severe counter-attack, and especially of the loss of its commander, seems to have been that it fell back and left the troops on its right in an exposed position.

At the other end of the Othonian line, at or north of S. Savino, the Thirteenth and the advance party of the Fourteenth, apparently unprotected by auxiliary and cavalry forces and infantry, faced the

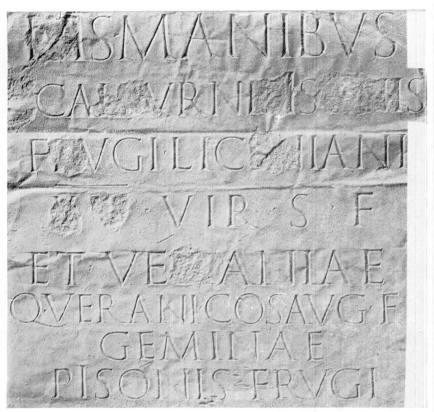

PLATE 3   An inscription commemorating Piso and his widow Verania

PLATE 4   The text of a decree by Lucius Helvius Agrippa, Governor of Sardinia

PLATE 5　Otho as Pharaoh of Egypt

PLATE 6　Papyrus Fouad 8

Vitellian Fifth Legion. While some details are not clear here, the 2,000-strong vexillation apparently found itself enveloped. It was rolled up from the north, while the Thirteenth under Vedius Aquila (who seems to have lost his head) could not hold the attack of the Fifth, led by the popular Fabius Fabullus. It was here that the unpreparedness of the Othonians for battle was most marked, and here that the obstacles of vine and ditch were most prominent. Lateral contact seems to have been lost, in Roman eyes a cardinal error. The Othonian right wing began to yield ground as the left had done.

The heaviest fighting was in the centre where along and alongside the Via Postumia the Othonian Praetorian cohorts, who cannot have been more than five in number with a strength of 2,500 men, faced the First (Italian) Legion. The latter had already shown its determination by quelling the panic of the Vitellian cavalry. It faced equally determined adversaries in the Othonian Praetorians, than whom nobody had more to lose by defeat. Here, as it turned out, the issue of the whole campaign was decided. The two sides fought hand to hand, throwing against each other the weight of their bodies and bossed shields. The usual discharge of javelins had been discarded, and swords and axes were used to pierce helmets and armour. It was a measure of the desperate folly of this war that these opponents often knew each other personally. Whereas the navy men of the First (Support) Legion had never seen troops long stationed in Windisch, and whereas the Thirteenth (in Pannonia from A.D. 46) and the draft of the itinerant Fourteenth (in Britain from 43 to 67) had nothing in common with the Fifth, in which, cross-postings excepted, there served no single individual who could remember any other station than Vetera in Lower Germany, the contestants in the centre had probably trained side by side. The Othonian Praetorians—substantially the Praetorians of Galba and Nero—must surely have met or worked alongside the men of the First (Italian) when both formations were training for Nero's campaign in the East in 67, perhaps already in 66. Many will have recognized a comrade in the enemy ranks. A battle between such evenly matched enemies was inevitably bitter and for long undecided; high praise must be given to those numerically and in other ways at a disadvantage—the Othonians. But when the left and right wings of their army yielded, even the devotion of the Praetorians to their emperor availed no more.

The final blow to any chance of an Othonian recovery was one which no one on their side could have anticipated. On the afternoon of 14 April, in accordance with Otho's instructions, Flavius Sabinus had placed his gladiators in the Ravenna galleys and got them across the Po to deliver the diversionary attack on the Vitellians from the south. This, together with the advance of the cavalry from Pannonia and Moesia, was designed to prevent the Vitellians from interfering with the

D

Othonian advance and the proposed construction of the forward camp. In our sources there is no mention of the two Praetorian cohorts brought up from Piacenza on the previous day. We may guess the reason. It was an incident which Spurinna, whatever his penchant for dinner-table reminiscences in after days, can scarcely have been pleased to remember, still less to relate. Flavius Sabinus had noticed early in the day that the commanders of the two cohorts had disappeared. Officers do not disappear unless they mean treachery, especially on the eve of a battle. Sabinus had concluded that, if the tribunes were traitors, it would be best to keep the troops they commanded out of the way. They took no part in the foray or the battle, and it is their absence or their treason whose condemnation is obscurely voiced in our sources. Without Praetorian support, the small band of gladiators succeeded in crossing the river. In view of the near certainty that the Vitellians were well-informed of the situation, they were probably allowed to do so. When they had proceeded some way from the bank, they were suddenly attacked by the Batavians under Alfenus Varus. Most of them fled back to the Po, where they were cut to pieces by other Batavian cohorts stationed there to block the retreat. The victors, having disposed of the would-be diversionary attack, marched rapidly north-eastwards to join in the main battle. Since the First (Support) Legion had retired, they made contact with the reeling Praetorians and made doubly certain their collapse.

The battle was now decisively won by the Vitellians. The surviving Othonians, left, right and centre, streamed back to the distant camp fourteen miles away. On the retreat, too, losses were heavy. The roads —the Via Postumia and the *limites* parallel to it—were choked with dead. Few prisoners were taken. The two Roman armies had fought well in an evil cause, and the Othonians had no reason to feel ashamed of their performance. Their ranks had been broken, but not their spirit. It was some consolation to them to reflect that a large part of their forces had not been committed, and that more were arriving from the Danube. Those who had fought at the First Battle of Cremona had been heavily outnumbered, the victims, they felt, of incompetent leadership and treachery. There was no reason why the tables should not be turned.

Once the Othonian front had collapsed, Caecina and Valens marshalled their forces and moved cautiously forward towards Bedriacum. But dusk was now near. Although they had no tools to dig a proper textbook camp, having come straight from battle, lightly laden, an attack with tired troops upon the strongly-held enemy camp was quite out of the question. Besides, there was a hope that a night's delay and reflection might induce an Othonian capitulation. Of the morale of the defenders of Bedriacum little was known, and the nearness of their

Danubian reinforcements constituted yet another hazard. Every consideration prompted the Vitellians to keep a respectful distance between
themselves and Bedriacum. In fact, they bivouacked under arms at a
point five miles short of the enemy camp, a little to the west of Voltido.

Meanwhile, what of the Othonian leaders? They knew the facts, and
were guided by the hard logic of the event, not by emotion. Indeed,
when the tide of battle turned irreversibly against them, Proculus and
Paulinus displayed a prudent disregard for honour. They abandoned
their retreating troops and fled westwards from the area of Cremona,
making their way by devious and different routes towards their new
master from the Rhineland. Of their movements, until they turned up
to eat humble pie before Vitellius at Lyon less than ten days later, we
know nothing. But dates and distances suppose a hasty journey to
secure the audience grudgingly and contemptuously granted. The first
Othonian commander to regain Bedriacum, Vedius Aquila, was
greeted with jeers and catcalls: it seems that the commander of the
Thirteenth (Gemina) was incautious enough to return before nightfall
and was immediately surrounded by a noisy mob of troublemakers and
runaways, eager to find a scapegoat for defeat. Titianus and Celsus
were luckier—or more cautious: by dusk, sentries had been posted and
some sort of discipline imposed by Annius Gallus, who, still con-
valescent from his fall, had been moved to Bedriacum since the council
of war and left in charge of the camp during the battle. He appealed for
unity, and was listened to with respect. Titianus and Celsus entered
unseen and unmolested.

Early on the next morning (15 April), Marius Celsus called together
the senior officers to decide between resistance and capitulation. With
good reason or by a convenient fiction, he claimed the knowledge that
Otho would not wish them to prolong a civil war when the initial contact had been so much in his disfavour. Indeed, Otho would never have
plotted against Galba had he known that civil dissension would follow.
What good had Cato and Scipio done by prolonging futile fighting in
Africa after Caesar had won at Pharsalia? And at that time, in 46 B.C.,
the struggle had been for liberty versus autocracy, not in favour of this
or that emperor. Even in defeat men should employ cool reason in
preference to desperate courage. Celsus' arguments were effective.
Since Otho, still alive at Brescello, might have been, but was not,
consulted, we must assume that Celsus' version of the emperor's attitude
was believed. Even his brother did not dissent from it.

It was therefore decided to send Celsus himself to the enemy as a
plenipotentiary, offering recognition of Vitellius and a reconciliation of
the armies. Before he returned, some time elapsed, longer than that
required by a ten-mile journey and by the negotiation of such simple
terms. Titianus began to have second thoughts, and manned the walls

more heavily in the fear that Celsus had been refused a hearing; and perhaps this last flicker of defiance had been stirred by fresh news of the approach of the Fourteenth Legion from the north-east. If Valens and Caecina had proved difficult, the Othonians could still give a good account of themselves. But soon the watchmen saw Caecina as he rode up on horseback, raising his right hand in a conciliatory salute; soon Celsus himself returned unharmed, though a rough reception from the victims of the Castors battle had had to be checked by their centurions and by the intervention of Caecina. Agreement had been reached, and all was well. The gates of the camp swung open, and the two armies fraternized as passionately as they had fought. The bitterness of some individuals had been swamped by a wider tide of relief: the frightful *revenant* of civil war had departed, it seemed, and the men of the usurper Marcus Otho swore allegiance to the usurper Aulus Vitellius.

At Brescello Otho and his Praetorians awaited the issue of the battle. Otho was ready to exploit victory or take the consequences of defeat. Whichever way things went, he knew what he would do. Late on the evening of 14 April the ill rumours that travel fast had covered the forty miles from Cremona. Then, during the night and the next morning, wounded men straggled in from the battlefield, telling the full extent of the disaster.

The reaction of the Praetorians was not perhaps surprising. As the men who owed most to Otho and had most to lose by his fall, they had an interest in encouraging him to stand fast and fight another day. But self-interest was reinforced by personal devotion. Since January Otho had grown to the stature of his office, inspiring a loyalty and affection hardly paralleled in the Long Year. The parasite and dilettante had become a leader. On the morning of 15 April there was an emotional scene. The troops gathered in a mass to hear him speak, to offer their own appeals. Distant onlookers saluted Otho, the nearer bystanders threw themselves at his feet, some even clutched his hands. Plotius Firmus, the prefect, expressed the general feeling, and urged Otho not to give up. His appeal was reinforced by a message brought by Moesian mounted elements who had arrived at Bedriacum on 13 April just in time to participate in the battle. After the defeat they had ridden hard to Brescello, forseeing the necessity of offsetting the bad news by providing the latest information of the advance from the Danube. They reported that when, on 9 April, they had left Aquileia, the frontier town of Italy on the north-east, the main party of the Seventh (Galbian) Legion from Petronell had just entered the town: it might be expected in Bedriacum in the course of the next five days. The legionary commander, Antonius Primus, was full of enthusiasm. What was more, the Fourteenth with its great fighting reputation was much nearer: it should arrive at any moment. Behind both came the larger forces of

Moesia. There could be no question but that the campaign could be carried on with good prospects of success.

None of these arguments had much effect upon Otho's resolution: he had no intention of being the cause of further Roman bloodshed. Having failed in the first encounter, it was his duty to renounce his position. Thanking the troops in a dignified speech, he blamed Vitellius for the outbreak of the civil war, and said that he wished to be judged by posterity on the example he had set in preventing its prolongation. Peace demanded his death, and upon this he was irrevocably decided.

He then summoned his staff in order of seniority and paid them his farewells: they were to get away quickly and avoid attracting Vitellius' annoyance by procrastination. When his followers wept, he restrained their emotional displays with calmness and intrepidity. To those departing up- or downstream along the Po he allocated the available units of the Ravenna fleet, and gave to land travellers horses and *diplomata*. Any potentially incriminating documents were destroyed. Such loose money as was available he distributed carefully and systematically to each according to his rank and needs. The approach of death had turned the gambler into a man of charity and prudence.

Among his suite was his nephew, the son of Otho Titianus, the young lad Salvius Cocceianus, who had accompanied his father and uncle to see what war was like. The boy was frightened by the sinister turn of events, broken-hearted by the reality of defeat and death. Otho took care to comfort him, saying that Vitellius was not after all an ogre: in return for the immunity accorded to his own mother, wife and children in Rome, he would undoubtedly spare Cocceianus and his father. 'I had intended,' he went on, 'to make you my heir, but thought it best to wait until the position was clear. Now it cannot be. But you must face life with head erect. My last word is this: don't forget that your uncle was an emperor—and don't remember it too often either.' Otho's estimate of Vitellius' character was shrewd enough. The boy lived to celebrate his uncle's birthday for many years. But his memory was too good. In the end devotion helped to secure his death at the whim of Domitian.

After this, Otho dismissed everyone from his presence and rested for a while. Then, in privacy, he wrote two farewell messages. One was to his sister, the other to Statilia Messallina, Nero's talented and beautiful widow, whom he had planned to marry. While he was so busied, he was distracted by a sudden disturbance. In the streets of Brescello the Praetorians were threatening the departing senators, especially Verginius Rufus, whom they were holding prisoner within the walls of his lodging. If Otho had renounced the principate, better Verginius than Vitellius! Such hopes were vain. Verginius was even more reluctant in 69 than he had been in 68. Otho reprimanded the ringleaders of the riot in no uncertain terms, secured an end to the disturbances, and personally bade farewell to each of the grandees as they left, making sure that none was molested. Apart from the Praetorian cohorts there was soon no one left except a personal confidential freedman and some servants. From Bedriacum there was no word. One blow at least Otho was spared.

Towards evening he quenched his thirst with a draught of cold water, called for two daggers, carefully tested the blade of each, and placed the sharper one beneath his pillow. Then he went to bed, passing a quiet night and by all accounts enjoying some sleep. At daybreak on 16 April he called his freedman, satisfied himself once more that none of his entourage was left, and told the man: 'Go and show yourself to the Praetorians, unless you wish to die at their hands: otherwise they will suspect you of having assisted me to die.' When the man had gone, Otho held the dagger upright with both hands, and fell upon it with the full weight of his body. One groan, and all was over. As the servants accompanied by the Praetorian prefect forced their way in, they found, half concealed and half revealed by his hands, one single wound, in the heart.

The funeral took place immediately. This was what Otho himself had requested, fearing the treatment meted out to Galba three months before. Those Praetorians who were chosen to bear him to the pyre were proud to perform this last service. Emotion ran high. As the cortège passed, the troops crowded around, kissed the wound and hand and feet of the dead man. Those further off knelt. Some indeed committed suicide beside the pyre, not because they were beholden to him for any favour except the privilege of Praetorian service, nor from any fear of the vengeance of Vitellius, but because they were devoted to Otho and wished to share his moment of glory. Afterwards, at Bedriacum, Piacenza, at the camp of the Seventh (Galbian) Legion and that opposite Cremona, there were some officers and men who performed the same frightening act of self-immolation. It is hard to think of any Roman leader who had received such tributes of adoration and despair.

The Praetorian prefect Plotius Firmus acted sensibly. He assembled the troops as soon as possible after the funeral and administered the oath of allegiance to Vitellius. Some of the men refused, and tried to storm Verginius' billet, but the latter slipped away by a back door and foiled the untimely and unwelcome compulsion. The oath was then sworn by all, and the tribune Rubrius Gallus conveyed to Caecina their adherence, which was accepted. Hostilities now ceased everywhere, and the scattered Othonian formations were told to stand fast pending orders from Vitellius.

The situation was less straightforward for the members of the Senate who had been compelled to follow Otho northwards. They were in a serious predicament. Left behind at Modena, they will have received the news of the defeat at Cremona by the afternoon or evening of 15 April. The troops escorting them—in theory a guard of honour, in fact gaolers—refused to credit the report. Distrusting the fidelity of the senators to Otho, they spied on their every movement and word. Proper deliberation became impossible. Whether Otho intended to fight on, whether indeed he was still alive, was not known. To delay recognition of Vitellius was imprudent: it might be fatal to accord it. Between their fears of future disfavour or immediate death, only evasive and temporizing attitudes could be adopted. Divided in space from their fellow-senators, internally riven by dissension and jealousy, hamstrung by fear of the Praetorians, they could do nothing. Ambitious little men sought to make capital out of the indecision of the prominent, who had to walk with extreme care; and unfortunately the local town council, forgetting the rump in Rome, had put them in an even falser position by addressing them as 'Conscript Fathers', as if they possessed or had themselves claimed a constitutional status. The least objectionable decision would be to retire a little towards Rome, an action which could perhaps be explained away whatever happened. The move of twenty-five miles to Bologna providentially occupied most of 16 April. Perhaps the situation would become clearer. At their new headquarters, desperate for reliable news, they went to the length of posting pickets on the Aemilian Way, the road from Ostiglia and all the minor tracks leading in from the north-west. Thus they managed to intercept the freedman of Otho carrying his farewell messages to his sister and Messallina, written on the previous evening. But all he could tell them was that when he left Brescello the emperor was still alive, concerned only to serve those who would outlive him; for Otho himself life held no more attractions. The mention of the firmness of the defeated emperor was a tacit reproach. The hearers were ashamed to probe further. But they could now assume that Otho was by this time dead, and in their own minds they made their peace with Vitellius. His brother Lucius was present when they met to deliberate anew. Tacitus remarks cynically, and perhaps truly, that he was already courting the attention of the flatterers. Suddenly a new arrival threw the Senate into fresh consternation. Coenus, another of Otho's freedmen, had turned up. Leaving Brescello later than his colleague and bound equally for Rome, he found that, by the time he had reached Bologna, rumours of Otho's death had overtaken him. These rumours automatically invalidated warrants signed by an emperor who was, it seemed, no longer alive. The agents of the imperial post at the *mansiones* were naturally unwilling to supply horses to an Othonian and so court the displeasure of their new master. A bold lie helped Coenus for the moment. The Fourteenth Legion, he asserted, had arrived at Bedriacum on 15 April, joined forces with the garrison there, and defeated the Vitellians bivouacked in the open five miles away to the west. The fabrication was plausible enough. A man well-informed of the military situation might be excused for falling a victim to the deception. At any rate, Coenus achieved his aim, and got away to Rome with his refreshed *diplomata*. It was true that retribution was shortly to overtake him when the truth was known in the capital, for the authorities there could not afford to be seen to have connived at an act so dangerous to the new régime.

Meanwhile this new development made things even more impossible for the senators at Bologna. Their departure from Modena might after all be interpreted as disloyalty to Otho—if Otho still lived. It would be best to hold no more meetings. It was only on 17 April that the miserable men were put out of their agony. A dispatch from Valens gave details of the Battle of Cremona and confirmed Otho's death. The forlorn politicians made their own ways back to Rome, keen now to be present at the first official expression of new-found loyalty.

Before the pickets were posted on the roads leading into Bologna, dispatch riders carrying official news of Otho's death—certified presumably by Plotius Firmus and Otho's secretary Secundus—had already passed through, not bothering about the Othonian senators who at that moment were installing themselves in the town. Their instructions were to travel at maximum speed to the capital, for it was vital that the rump of the Senate in Rome should be prevented from taking in ignorance any action tending to demonstrate loyalty to an emperor now dead and a cause now lost. A desperately hard ride took them the 344 miles to Rome in less than three days. On 18 April, the penultimate day of the Festival of Ceres, the Senate was hurriedly convoked to hear the fatal and auspicious news. The city prefect, Flavius Sabinus, forthwith administered the oath to the garrison of Rome, substantially now the cohorts of the City and the Watch. The news was brought to the theatre, where there were performances from the 12th to the 18th, and there the audience applauded when the new emperor was named. There was indeed little else that they could do—except for one spontaneous gesture. Adorned with laurel leaves and flowers, they made the round of the temples of Rome, carrying in procession busts of Galba hurriedly removed on 15 January, and, as it seems, since then piously preserved. As a climax to the procession the garlands were heaped in a great mound around the Basin of Curtius, the place stained with the blood of the emperor who had died before their eyes and whom they had been powerless to save. Only by such symbolic acts could the common people of Rome protest against military powers over whom they could exercise no control.

The Senate, however, had to look to the future. It met on the following day to recognize Vitellius. Policy prompted messages of congratulation and thanks to him and the armies of Germany, conveying intimations of

the grant to Aulus Vitellius of all the imperial prerogatives—the post
of commander-in-chief, the annually renewable power of a tribune of
the people, the title of Augustus, together with all the other powers and
privileges as granted to Augustus, Tiberius and Claudius. Soon a letter
from Fabius Valens addressed to the Senate via the consuls gave details
of what had happened as seen from the side of the victors. It was framed
in moderate and decent terms; but there were some sticklers for protocol
who felt that Caecina Alienus had observed the proprieties better by
reporting, as convention prescribed, only to his superior officer Aulus
Vitellius. It seemed that already it was possible to detect a slight
difference between the blunt professional soldier and his more pliable
and politically-minded colleague.

Thus ended the three months' rule of the usurper Marcus Otho, begun
by an act of murderous treachery, ended with a deed of patriotic self-
sacrifice. The emperor retains a small but permanent niche in the record
provided by Roman historians and poets. Nothing, of course, could
excuse in their or our eyes the brutality of the January assassinations,
though there were those who sought to find mitigating circumstances in
an alleged intention to restore the republic. The time was long past for
any such ambition. Whether Piso or Otho, enjoying similar support
from those who are faithful servants of any régime, would have made
the better ruler, it would be interesting—and most idle—to speculate.
What Rome needed was a period of prudent and economical government, and collaboration between emperor and Senate; and it may be
that Vitellius was much less likely than either of the other two to secure
this end. But the view of Mommsen and others that Otho's decision not
to fight on has no merit, since his life was inevitably forfeit to the victor,
is contradicted by a close study of the military situation in April 69. Of
this redeeming credit Otho ought not to be deprived, and young
Martial was echoing the almost unanimous tradition of the historians
when, recalling in Domitian's reign the Long Year of 69, he penned a
prim and simple tribute, whose point, discreetly understated, is that
while Julius Caesar was an autocrat whose life was ended by the hands
of others, and Cato of Utica a life-long champion of the republic who
committed suicide in despair, Otho excelled both; an emperor, he died
of his own free choice to help others:

> When civil war still in the balance lay
> And mincing Otho might have won the day,
> Bloodshed too costly did he spare his land,
> And pierced his heart with an unfaltering hand.
> Caesar to Cato yields, while both drew breath:
> Greater than both is Otho in his death.

6

Vitellius' March to Rome

From Trabzon to Tangier, and from Brough-on-Humber to Berenice on the Red Sea, a web of military and civilian seaways and landways held the sprawling empire together. By A.D. 69 the pattern had already reached the obvious boundaries designed by nature for a common-wealth of peoples dwelling around the Inland Sea: the Alps, the Danube, the Euphrates, the Eastern Desert, the First Cataract of the Nile, the Sahara, the Atlantic. In Britain, half-conquered, the boundary ran from Cheshire to Lincolnshire. In the Low Countries it followed the Old Rhine, now a cheerful water-street at Leiden, the Oude Rijn to Utrecht, and the Kromme and Neder-Rijn to Arnhem. East of Nij-megen came the confluence with the broad Waal, which with the Rhine forms the Island of the Batavians, a green low-lying fruitfulness between the branches of the two-horned river. Then, as now, Germany came quickly after the traveller left Nijmegen. All this lower portion of the Rhine frontier was secured by auxiliary troops manning a string of forts: the first legionary fortress, Vetera, lay just inside Germany, keep-ing an eye on the route up the Lippe eastwards. Further south on the southern outskirts of Neuss and straddling the main road of Roman and modern times, lay another fort, measuring 580 by 470 metres, for a single legion, its plan, if not its history, known with notable complete-ness. At Cologne, the capital city of the Lower Rhine District, the saturation bombing of the 1939–45 war opened up the possibility of excavation. It was carefully conducted for many years. We now know the site and shape of the governor's palace by the Rhine, and public-spirited ingenuity has seen to it that the visitor can still, despite rebuild-ing, study something of the impressive remains in a large crypt beneath the Town Hall. Already in 69 a walled city with its municipality, Cologne, the colony of the people of Agrippina, had a permanent bridge over the Rhine, serving to connect it with many Transrhenane Ger-mans and funnel the trade flow in both directions. No legion guarded it; but slightly further on, at Bonn, just before the hills begin, lay the third station (528 by 524 metres) holding another single legion. A little before Koblenz (the confluence of Mosel and Rhine) a humble stream trickles into the latter from the west, flowing from a well-defined side

valley penetrating the wooded hills; its name, the Vinxtbach, suggests
that this was the frontier (*finis*) between Lower and Upper Germany,
and inscriptions found north and south of the tributary make the supposition certain. At Mainz, where the inflowing Main forms a broad
highway to and from the east, the double legionary fort was the main
military site of the Upper District, of which the remaining legion lay
now far to the south at Windisch in the Aargau. Interspersed between
the seven legions were a number of minor forts manned by auxiliaries or
even by local militia, and connecting all these frontier stations, large and
small, ran the main road from the Ocean to Rome. On the waters of the
Rhine the ships of the German fleet gave further protection, and for-
warded a useful riverborne supply of commodities and munitions.

It was this vast and powerful river valley between the North Sea and
Switzerland that had now provided its own pretender and sent out two
armies to claim the principate for him. How much more could be with-
drawn without serious danger to the frontier?

Having dispatched Valens and Caecina in mid-January, Vitellius
made no move to follow them until the end of March, when he had received news of the successful penetration of the Alpine frontier of Italy.
Such caution, left unexplained by Tacitus except by the imputation of
sluggishness to the pretender, was justified. In fact, Valens and Caecina
were lucky, favoured by nature's early spring and Otho's late start; but
the margin between success and disaster was no very large one. In any
event, Vitellius had many tasks to fulfil. Fresh auxiliary and perhaps
legionary troops must be raised to fill the gaps left by the departing
forces. A draft of 8,000 men was exacted from the garrison of Britain,
and allocated to Vitellius' own expeditionary army. The Rhine fleet
was put on alert, and the thinly-manned fortresses and forts given the
appearance, if not the reality, of unimpaired strength by supplementing
a few veterans with a quantity of new recruits. At the moment—though
one never knew what the future might hold—Gaul, source of men,
horses and supplies, presented no problem: the governor of Belgian
Gaul, Valerius Asiaticus, was a supporter whom Vitellius was soon to
select as his son-in-law, and his peer in Central Gaul was the wealthy
and amiable Junius Blaesus. Neither could feel sentimental about Nero
or under any obligation to Nero's friend Otho. In default of a better,
Hordeonius Flaccus was retained and given the overall command of
Upper and Lower Germany.

One of Vitellius' first political measures was to free Julius Civilis.
This Batavian prince, commanding a cohort in the Roman auxiliary
army, had apparently been implicated, with what justice we do not
know, in the Vindex outbreak of March 68. Acquitted of treason by
Galba in the summer, he was rearrested in 69 by the Rhineland troops,
some of whom had fought at Besançon. The release of Civilis was

doubly necessary. It was essential not to leave a fiercely independent and martial race to cause trouble in the Lower Rhine; and the eight Batavian cohorts incorporated by Valens in his army at Langres constituted a strong force which must not be alienated. Another sensible step was to resist the clamour for the removal of the commander of the Rhine fleet, Julius Burdo. Relations with the tribes inhabiting the military districts or bordering thereon had also to be nursed. During the two months, there was no lack of occupation for Vitellius and his staff. In February the envoys of the defeated Helvetians presented themselves, and were treated with consideration by Vitellius. The orator-historian maintains that a bitterly hostile audience was mollified by the artful appeals of Claudius Cossus, one of the deputation, whose appropriate affectation of nervousness commended him to an emotional audience. This may be so; but common sense, in which Vitellius was not entirely deficient, would readily suggest the desirability of playing down an action provoked by the genuine ignorance of the Helvetians and the undoubted riotousness of the Twenty-First.

Britain was certainly in no state to offer more support than the draft of 8,000 legionaries. The natives were restless, and the serious outbreak of Boudicca lay only seven years behind. In addition, the pacific policy of the governor Trebellius Maximus had strained relations between him and his legionary commanders, who looked out from their fortresses upon hills still untamed. Money was diverted to the development of town life. One officer reacted quite strongly: Roscius Coelius, commanding the Twentieth Legion, swung his colleagues and the commanders of the auxiliary army units against Trebellius, who was forced to retire and finally to take refuge with Vitellius, apparently in March. In his absence the administration of the province was carried on by the three legionary commanders jointly under the lead of Coelius. In May, Vitellius, by this time in Turin, found a replacement for Trebellius in the person of Vettius Bolanus, a notable who happened to be present and available, and who had acted as legionary commander and second-in-command to Corbulo during the Armenian campaign of the recent past. The choice was good, and as providential as the return, at any rate temporarily, of the Fourteenth Legion to Britain. Some care was taken to see that the legionary centurions were well disposed to Vitellius. That all this was very necessary was shown by an emergency that arose in the autumn. For some twenty years the client-kingdom of the Brigantians, who occupied northern England from the Humber to the Eden or beyond, had been ruled by a Roman sympathizer, Queen Cartimandua, descendant of kings, rich and—in so far as she had secured the capture of Caratacus in 51—a benefactor of the Romans. Some years before 69, it seems, she had grown tired of her consort Venutius and bestowed her favours on his armour-bearer Vellocatus. The discarded Venutius dis-

covered that the best way of avenging himself was to lead the anti-
Roman party among the Brigantians, and attempt to dislodge
Cartimandua from her throne and from her capital at Stanwick near
Boroughbridge. By August or September, the news that a new pretender to the principate had arisen in Vespasian carried the clear
message that a second internecine struggle between the Romans could
not long be delayed. Venutius decided that his moment had come. He
summoned all the wild men from the north and from the heights, and
put the queen in a critical situation. She appealed to the Romans for
help, which they could not refuse. A force of auxiliaries was supplied,
but the struggle dragged on, Venutius acquiring a throne, and the
Romans a frontier war. It was clear that in this instance the system of
client-kingdoms or buffer-states had broken down, for their proper
function was precisely to save the employment of the Roman army on
peace-keeping duties in remote areas. The inevitable result was the
conversion of a suzerainty over northern England and southern Scotland
into direct rule. The frontier would have to go forward again. But all
this, in the spring of 69, lay in the future. In the Long Year, Britain had
her own worries: she played little or no part in the greater convulsions
of the empire elsewhere.

Towards the end of March Vitellius set out from Cologne towards
Zülpich, Trier and Rome, with a modest force that can scarcely have
exceeded 20,000 men, including the 8,000 legionaries drafted from
Britain. Three weeks and 360 miles later, when he was approaching
Chalon-sur-Saône, he received a laurelled dispatch conveying news of
the victory at Cremona and the death of Otho: Caecina and Valens
would meet him at Lyon. Vitellius' delighted reaction was to assemble
the troops and thank them unstintingly for their support and that of
their fellows. There was other gratifying news from North Africa:
Mauretania Caesariensis (roughly modern Algeria) and Mauretania
Tingitana (roughly Morocco) had gone over to him. The previous
governor, Lucceius Albinus, had been appointed to rule the former
province by Nero and the latter by Galba. When it seemed possible that,
for whatever purpose, Albinus had designs upon southern Spain, a coup
d'état had been staged in the interests of Vitellius. Three officers of the
governor had been assassinated, and on returning by sea from Tingitana, inaccessible by road, Albinus was set upon as he landed in the
larger province and killed. His wife threw herself upon the murderers
and shared his fate. This grim story Vitellius listened to in silence:
what was done could not be undone.

The good news gave him a strong inducement to move more quickly.
Now that the southward-flowing course of the Saône had been reached,
its lively navigation could be used. Telling the infantry to march on by
the highroad, he embarked on a river vessel suitably bedecked to honour

him. Even without the help of the current—and indeed the Saône is notoriously sluggish—it would be easy to cover the eighty miles to Lyon in twenty-four or thirty-six hours. As he approached the capital of the Three Gauls, the hill of Fourvière and the plateau of La Serra rose straight ahead, and immediately beyond was the confluence with the Rhône. The administrative quarter of the city lay upon the dominating heights. As Vitellius disembarked on the right bank, he was greeted by the governor, escorted up to the official residence at the top, and accorded, for the first time, the trappings of power. Junius Blaesus, his host, was a man of birth, wealth and open-handed generosity. He, no less than his guest, enjoyed a banquet, and Vitellius was sensible of his attentions. That beneath the latter's gratitude lurked a resentment that harboured murder is merely one of the improbable stories circulated by Flavian scribblers.

As Aulus looked from the height where the basilica now stands, he had to his right the terraced slope later to be occupied by a handsome theatre flanked by an elegant music hall; looking ahead and steeply down, he observed the three islands where the two rivers met, in modern times joined together to form the tongue of land containing the Place Bellecour and the Gare Perrache. One of these islands, Canabae, 'the Settlement', was a convenient home for those who gained a livelihood from the dense traffic upon the Saône and Rhône. And if Vitellius turned his gaze leftwards across the Saône, he could see on rising ground the suburb of Condate and the monumental area of the amphitheatre and the altar of Rome and Augustus, with its fine sculptured panels of oak foliage in bas-relief and the two 35-foot pillars of Egyptian syenite, which now, cut each in half, provide the four supports for the cupola of St Martin d'Ainay. At the altar delegates gathered annually from the sixty-four communities of Gaul to demonstrate the loyalty to the régime and to the emperor of all those who, while not a nation, felt some corporate identity as speakers of the Gallic tongue. Social, ceremonial and non-political occasions, these assemblies helped Gaul, despite occasional relapses, to forget the vicious rivalries of the age of Julius Caesar and Vercingetorix and to adapt herself more readily to the secure and unheroic advantages of living a settled life in the new towns on the plains. Such local jealousies, such resistance to Rome as remained in the hearts of ambitious men exploiting tribal sentiment still found occasional expression. Thus border warfare had recently flared up under a certain Mariccus of the Boii, a tribe settled on the middle Loire north of its confluence with the Allier. He had raised 8,000 men and gained control of some portions of the land of the Aedui to his east. But when the authorities at Autun called up their militia and requested Vitellius to place some auxiliary cohorts at their disposal, the Boii were scattered and their leader executed. But incidents of this sort are untypical of

Gaul in the first two centuries. It was a land of peace, improved agriculture, developing civic achievement and urbanization, prosperous crafts-
manship, good communications: best of all, a land almost without
history. As for the movement of Vindex, there is no evidence that this
was directed against Rome rather than Nero. During it, Lyon itself had
sustained a brief siege at the hands of Vindex' forces, and now looked
for recompense from an emperor chosen by the victors of Besançon: a
lightening, for instance, of the financial burdens imposed by Galba. But
Lyon was not only the commercial capital and political metropolis of
Gaul: it was also a Roman city. Founded in October 43 B.C. by Muna-
tius Plancus, founder also (as his impressive mausoleum upon the head-
land of Gaeta reminds us) of Augst, it normally maintained a garrison,
if only an Urban Cohort, to protect the Mint; and it was a city through
which Roman soldiers constantly passed on their way to and from the
northern frontier, and where as retired veterans they tended to settle.
Its hills and rivers (scenic attractions to which the Roman was suscep-
tible) were further adorned by elegant and impressive buildings.[34]

By travelling ahead of his army from Chalon, Vitellius had secured
the possibility of a few extra days here without slowing up the rate of
his progress to the capital. In the latter part of April, then, he held
audiences and accustomed himself to the modest but novel pomps of
power. The first occasion was pleasant indeed—a detailed account
of the victory at Cremona and of the death of Otho from the lips of
Caecina and Valens. For their services they received a glowing tribute
at a military parade, at which they were stationed immediately behind
Vitellius on the saluting platform. Vitellius' wife Galeria had arrived in
Lyon with their children. The daughter was now of marriageable age.
Her fate was the traditional one in noble Roman families: to serve as a
political instrument, offered in marriage to Valerius Asiaticus, as she
was later to be offered to Antonius Primus. But the son and heir, a young
child some six years old, who unfortunately suffered from a serious impediment of speech, was his father's darling. The doting Vitellius now
dressed him up in some version of the imperial purple toga, and held
him up to receive the cheers of the troops as 'Germanicus'. The name,
at first hearing grotesque, was not entirely unhappy. It recalled at
once his father's title and the name of Drusus' son, the popular governor
of Gaul and commander-in-chief on the Rhine fifty years before.

Indeed, whatever his shortcomings as a man and a ruler, Vitellius
possessed one notable advantage over his predecessors: he could present
the unusual spectacle of a happy and united imperial family; a mother
—Sextilia—and a wife—Galeria—who provided a pleasing contrast
with many of the women around them; a brother; a daughter; and
above all a son to follow him, if the need arose. On that spring morning
at Lyon no cloud was foreseeable. In the south-east, on the far side of

the flat plain, could be seen the serration of the Alps; beyond the Alps lay Rome, waiting to receive its master and his family.

Meanwhile, two crestfallen Othonian generals were kicking their heels in Vitellius' anteroom. The excuses to which Paulinus and Proculus were reduced did them little credit, for they actually claimed that the long march of the Othonians before the battle, the exhaustion, the chaotic confusion, and a number of other purely fortuitous incidents were so many stratagems of their own designed to favour what they had come to believe was the righteous cause. The story was incredible, the hypocrisy revolting. But Vitellius contemptuously took them at their word in the matter of treachery, and acquitted them of the serious imputation of loyalty. They survived to be saddled with an ignominy which in Suetonius' case at least was regrettable, for in his day he had served his country well in the Atlas mountains and in rebellious Britain. It seems that Titianus and Celsus were also present. No action was taken against them either; for Titianus had acted out of loyalty to his brother, and Celsus was transparently an honest man. Also pardoned was Galerius Trachalus the orator, confidant of Otho, but friend also of Galeria and a popular figure in Rome. No severe measures were taken against individual Othonian leaders or their property. Effect was given to the wills of the enemy troops who had fallen in battle, or else the law of intestacy was applied. It is clear that neither vindictiveness nor cupidity were characteristic of the new emperor, though some felt that there was a hardening of attitude on the arrival from Bologna of Lucius Vitellius, a man as determined and obdurate as his brother was easy-going.

After nearly a week at Lyon, Vitellius moved down the Rhône and held court at Vienne on the eastern bank, the first town in Southern Gaul and one whose Roman remains are as impressive today as those of its rival Lyon. It was probably here that Vitellius received news of his recognition on 19 April in Rome. In acknowledging the dispatch, he postponed—if only for a few weeks—the acceptance of the title 'Augustus' and steadfastly rejected the name 'Caesar' until the last desperate days in December.

Vitellius left Vienne in late April. The Alpine passes were now open. We have no information as to the choice the emperor made between the two available routes, by Mont Genèvre and the Little St Bernard. Considerations of supplies, which would not be so plentiful where Valens had passed a month before, and of the route prescribed for the return of the Fourteenth Legion are among the reasons which suggest that from Vienne he made for the more northerly pass via the valley of the Isère. At some point between Lyon and Italy he was joined by Cluvius Rufus, governor of Nearer Spain.

Rufus had promptly recognized Otho in January and as promptly

gone over to Vitellius' faction. Such rapid changes of allegiance sound
ill; and Tacitus speaks rather patronizingly of Cluvius. But the literary
commander had vigorously confronted the threat posed by Albinus
from Morocco by moving the Tenth Legion down to the Gibraltar area
to repel any invasion. The death of Albinus and the adhesion of north-
west Africa to Vitellius removed the danger, and we must suppose that
Vitellius now thought that Cluvius would be better employed at court,
while still remaining theoretically governor of Nearer Spain and
exercising his powers by proxy. What is clear is that as late as December
Cluvius was still on terms of friendship with Vitellius, and it seems
possible that he fulfilled for him the functions performed by Trachalus
for Otho.

The most pressing problem facing Vitellius when he reached Italy
was the dispersal of the Othonian formations. After what they regarded
rather as a deception practised upon them than a defeat inflicted, their
morale was high. The reasons that had made them enthusiastic supporters of Otho—if Spain and Germany could create emperors, why not
they?—were still operative so long as potential emperors, *capaces imperii*,
were available. Numerically the Othonians were scarcely inferior to the
Vitellian forces, and the issue had been evenly balanced when they were
not so numerous. Luckily for Vitellius, the three legions from Moesia
posed no problem. They had been still a little way east of Aquileia when
the fatal news of battle and suicide reached them. Incredulously they,
or at least their advance parties, or that of the leading formation VII
Claudia, pressed on into the frontier town, and it is alleged by the biographer Suetonius, though not entirely convincingly, that they there
proclaimed as their new candidate Vespasian, governor of Judaea, and
placed his name upon their flags. But this is almost certainly an anticipation of events. In any case, the movement, whatever its exact
nature, failed, and the Moesian troops discreetly returned to their
various fortresses upon the Danube without penetrating further into
Italy. No action was, or could be, taken against them in the confused
circumstances of the time. Their moment to intervene in the game
was still to come.

The participants in the First Battle of Cremona, both Othonian and
Vitellian, still lay in the Bedriacum–Cremona–Piacenza area. At Veleia,
south of Piacenza in the foothills of the Apennines, a 25-year-old soldier
who had served two years in the Fourth (Macedonian) Legion was
buried by his comrades at this time: he is described as belonging to the
drafts from the three legions of Upper Germany, that is, from Caecina's
force. Of the Othonians, VII Galbiana and XI were probably in the
neighbourhood of Este: Vitellius ordered them to return to their respective stations in Pannonia and Dalmatia. XIII was punished for its
prominent part in the battle by being allotted the unenviable task of

building amphitheatres at Cremona and Bologna, where Valens and
Caecina proposed to put on competing shows. Civil engineering work
was of course regularly performed by Roman legionaries in peaceful
conditions, but the motive here was partisan and peevish. The assign-
ment was carried out, sometimes amid the stupid jeers of the local youth;
their behaviour was to cost Cremona very dear. The First (Support)
Legion was sent off to cool down in Spain as a complement to X and
VI, though the beaten legion did not forget its hostility to Vitellius.[35]

But the most truculent formation among the Othonians was the
fighting Fourteenth, which considered itself ill-used. Its recent movements had been indeed bewildering. In Britain since Claudius' invasion,
it had been recalled in 67 by Nero for service in the East, and was still
in central Europe (either Pannonia or less probably Dalmatia) when
Otho summoned it to Italy in March 69. Its advance party was committed in the battle outside Cremona; but the main body had arrived
just too late to take part in a confrontation which the legionaries
reasonably thought had been unnecessarily hurried and in which, but
for their absence, the issue might have been different. Recriminations
flew backwards and forwards. This vexation, to say nothing of the
existence of three successive emperors since January, had sapped morale
and discipline. Already in the interval of a month since the battle, it had
been thought desirable to move the Fourteenth westwards from Bedriacum to Turin with a view to its return to Britain, which would be
popular. At Turin however (it is not clear whether Vitellius or his
marshals were present) trouble arose. An unhappy calculation had
decided that the restive legion should be kept in check by sharing a
camp with the Batavian cohorts with whom it had been inharmoniously
brigaded before. The two formations were birds of a feather, but hardly
turtle-doves. One day a local workman was abused by a Batavian
soldier for cheating him, and a legionary who was billeted upon the
townsman came to the man's defence. The squabble spread as the two
opponents were joined by their comrades, and the consequences of the
riot might have been serious but for the intervention of two Praetorian
cohorts on the side of the legion. When the matter was reported, Vitellius wisely separated the Batavians from the Fourteenth, adding the
former to his army and ordering the latter to cross the Alps via the Little
St Bernard, avoid Vienne (and presumably Lyon also) and march
straight across Gaul to Boulogne, where it would embark for Britain.
This movement was carried out without further trouble, with one
notable exception. As a parting gesture of defiance, the Fourteenth left
fires alight everywhere in Turin on the night of their departure, and a
portion of the city was burnt down. The memory of this havoc, like
those of many calamities in this year, was effaced by the more dreadful
fate of Cremona.

The presence of two Praetorian cohorts in Turin needs some explanation. The most probable is that these were part of the three units commanded by Spurinna at Piacenza; later they had been moved to the site opposite Caecina's bridge, involved in what appeared to be an attempt at an armistice before the battle, and then, it seems, moved westwards by the victors to form a suitable escort for Vitellius, who was expected to enter Italy by Turin. The two cohorts could well have formed the basis of a reconstituted Praetorian Guard; the fate of the others was different. Vitellius decided that the elements at Cremona, Bedriacum, Brescello and Bologna should be offered honourable discharge from the forces. This would preserve their right to an allocation of land or a money payment in lieu, while making way for the promotion of ambitious Vitellian legionaries to the better-paid formation. The Othonians handed in their arms and equipment to their commanding officers, and some of them at least settled in the district around Fréjus or possibly at Aquileia. This process had hardly been completed when in August new possibilities opened up for them.

The Batavians had had almost as chequered a career. In addition to the uncertainties caused by repeated changes of allegiance, they were swayed by a more lasting duty—that to their own people on the Island at the mouth of the Rhine. After their brief stay at Langres, they had apparently been divided between the forces of Valens and Caecina, for they are mentioned as fighting in both. Reunited by Vitellius for a few days in northern Italy, they were soon on the road again, this time once more to Upper Germany. It is hardly surprising that all these complicated moves are not always clearly reported in our sources. But they symbolize well enough the fevered convulsions of the Long Year. Together with the Batavians went a number of Gallic auxiliary units which were to be demobilized to their homes. Now that the fighting seemed over, some serious reduction in the size of the armed forces was imperative merely on financial grounds.

At Pavia, about 18 May, Vitellius received an address of welcome from a deputation of the Senate which had left the capital almost a month before, on the official date of accession. They had already covered the 400 miles by 14 May, but had been told to wait the arrival of the court at Pavia, while the trouble at Turin was sorted out: there was no need to publicize matters unnecessarily. But the Turin turmoil was, as it happened, repeated here. This time the situation was more sinister. While Vitellius was holding a dinner party, Verginius, his potential rival, being present (on the death of Otho on 16 April he had retired from Brescello, presumably to his estate at Como, and had come down to Pavia at Vitellius' invitation), a wrestling match between a soldier of the Fifth and a Gallic auxiliary, staged in a spirit of friendly rivalry, turned sour. The legionary took a fall, and the Gaul was un-

sporting enough to jeer at his opponent. The spectators joined in, and a
general mêlée involved severe injury to two cohorts. The number of
dead in what should have been a trifling dispute was a reminder that
civil war had seriously sapped discipline. Meanwhile, apparently on the
same evening, a slave of Verginius appeared on the scene and for
reasons which escape us was accused of planning to murder Vitellius.
In a manner reminiscent of the trouble over the arming of the Seventeenth (Urban) Cohort in the Castra Praetoria at Rome a few weeks
before, the troops proceeded to invade the officers' mess, clamouring for
Verginius' head. Vitellius had no doubt of his innocence, but it was
with difficulty that he managed to restrain the men who now pressed
for the execution of a senior statesman who had once been their
commander. Indeed, Verginius more than anybody else was the target
of acts of insubordination. The great man retained his aura, but the
troops hated him because they felt he had slighted them; and his
appearance at Vitellius' table was proof that he was no more interested
in becoming princeps than he had been a year before.

From Pavia Vitellius moved eastwards to Cremona, and after attending Caecina's gladiatorial show insisted on walking over the site of the
battle. His officers were only too glad to describe and perhaps magnify
their exploits. But it was a grim scene. With an unRoman and quite
inexplicable disregard for the normal laws of war, the victors and the
Cremonese had done little to clear up the area. It was now the second
half of May. Almost forty days had elapsed since the battle. Yet the
remains of horses and human beings lay unburied everywhere. The
flattened trees and crops bore witness to a devastation whose magnitude
and novelty seem to have blunted the sense of right and wrong. Scarcely
less sinister were the laurel and roses strewn on the Postumian Way by
the misdirected efforts of the Cremonese, a gesture unusually ecstatic
even for a victory over a foreign foe, and macabre and repulsive when
Roman had fought Roman in Italy. In such wars there were no
triumphs.

At Brescello Vitellius was shown his rival's grave, which looked like
any private person's (said Philostratus) and seemed one modest enough
(thought Tacitus) to deserve survival. There were no verses, no appeal
to the passer-by to halt and meditate on mortality. It bore the simplest
of inscriptions: 'To the spirit of Marcus Otho'. Vitellius gazed for a
moment, and then curtly remarked: 'A little grave for a little man!'
Such trifling dicta of the great were treasured, and as time passed became piquant. It is an irony of chance that while Otho's tomb, like that
of Vitellius, has perished, the stone that commemorates Piso and his
wife's devotion still survives.[36]

At Bologna it was Valens' turn to provide a gladiatorial show, for
which he had decorations brought from the capital in an endeavour to

outbid his rival. From now on and with increasing frequency as the
army approached Rome, it was joined by an afflux of actors, musicians
and entertainers who believed, not without reason, that the talents
which had been acceptable to Nero would not be unwelcome to Vitellius. The latter resembled Nero in his passion, despised and deplored by
the old-fashioned, for banquets, musical recitals and plebeian enter-
tainments. 'Give me one of the Maestro's melodies,' remarked Vitellius
one day to a piper, and when the man obliged with a composition by
Nero, Vitellius leapt to his feet and led the applause. But Rome had had
enough of musical emperors.

There were also more serious matters. It was now the very end of
May and decisions would have to be taken on the implementation or
revision of the list of consuls suffect prepared by Galba and modified by
Otho. Nero's original provision had been for two six-monthly periods,
providing four consuls. This had been modified and the number of
magistrates, necessarily only two at a time, increased by a shortening of
their terms of office. The occupants of the April to May (Othonian)
period had, for obvious reasons, been allowed to retain their nominal
position until their term ran out, though it is difficult to imagine what
duties they could have performed. But room must be found to reward
Caecina and Valens. Vitellius reduced the term of the pair due to succeed on 1 July, Arrius Antoninus and Marius Celsus, from three to two
months, and here it is noteworthy that Celsus, though an Othonian
commander, enjoyed sufficient prestige to secure the retention of his
office, even if abbreviated. Caecina and Valens were now to succeed on
1 September, and Caecilius Simplex and Quintius Atticus on 1 November, each pair holding office for two months. The effect of this reshuffle
was to promote three deserving officers—Caecina, Valens and Simplex
—and to demote the relatively unimportant or undesirable ones: the
mild Valerius Marinus, who would swallow any affront, Pedanius
Costa, a supporter of Verginius (though the reasons alleged in public by
Vitellius were different), and finally Martius Macer, who had been a
thorn in the flesh of Caecina and Valens at Cremona. These adjust-
ments were the minimum possible to cater for the situation, and
Vitellius showed sound sense in rewarding good friends without making
notable enemies.

June saw the move southward towards Rome. Providentially the
leguminous and corn harvests were near, and at some cost to the
farmers upon the route, the army could march comfortably upon a
stomach filled by Nature. In the latter part of the month it was at
Grotta Rossa.

As you leave the capital and cross the Tiber by the Ponte Milvio, the
Flaminian Way divides from the Cassian and turns north-eastwards to
traverse the valley bottom for three miles before reaching a line of pink

cliffs that hem in the road between themselves and the Tiber. The pine-crowned bluff at the south end forms an ideal lookout tower from which the sinuous river, the Monte Mario, the Monti Parioli, the Monte Sacro and the north-eastern suburbs north of the Quirinal are clearly visible. The pink cliffs provide the last obvious halting point before Rome. Upon these heights and at their foot a host of unparalleled size lay camped: 60,000 armed men, an even greater number of servants and camp followers, entertainers and shopkeepers, a large crowd of the city populace and a number of grandees who had thought it prudent—and indeed it was customary—to go out to greet the approaching emperor. The atmosphere was almost that of a carnival or fair. Practical jokers managed to hide the belts of some of the troops, and then kept asking them 'whether they were fit for action?' The soldiers were not used to being jeered at, and failing to appreciate childish humour, attacked the unarmed mob, sword in hand. Among the casualties was a father of one of the soldiers, who was killed in the company of his son. When his identity was realized, a sense of shock brought the pointless slaughter to an end.

However, the actual entry was well stage-managed and made a brave show. Vitellius, ever mindful of creature comforts, made sure that the army was properly fed in the morning to prevent the danger of looting. On reaching the Milvian Bridge he himself mounted a white charger and led his army in the full panoply of a general as far as the boundary of the city, which crossed the Flaminian Way a little to the north of the modern Piazza del Popolo. Here he dismounted and correctly assumed the white, bordered toga of a Roman civilian magistrate—theoretically the emperor was such in Rome—and marched at the head of his troops in good order. The front of the column displayed four legionary eagles (those of I Italica from Lyon, V Alaudae from Vetera, XXI Rapax from Windisch and XXII from Mainz: two each from the armies of Caecina and Valens), surrounded by the four *vexilla* (banners) re-presenting the other legions supplying drafts only (XV from Vetera, XVI from Neuss, I from Bonn and IV from Mainz), together with the emblems of twelve cavalry regiments. The main mass of the infantry and cavalry followed, and after them thirty-four auxiliary cohorts grouped according to their recruitment area (Gaul, Batavia, Germany), and variously uniformed. In front of the eagles went the legionary com-manders, camp commandants, staff officers and senior centurions. The legionary centurions marched with their men in full uniform, all wear-ing their decorations. The detailed description that has survived from the newspapers of the time shows what an impression this entry made: an army fit for an emperor, said some; but others wondered if the emperor would be fit for his army.

After parading through the streets—the Via Flaminia (at its southern end, Broad Street) led straight to the Capitol and the old Forum—the men were distributed throughout the city in bivouacs and billets, as Galba's had been. But now the pressure was very much greater. The piazzas, the gardens, the places of resort were full. Once installed, however roughly, the sightseeing troops made mostly for the Forum Romanum to see the exact spot by the fig tree where Galba had been murdered. No doubt Vitellius had presented his men to their own imagination as an army exacting vengeance upon the regicide Otho: it was important that they should appear to themselves and to others as liberators. But in the streets the outlandish uniform of some of the auxiliaries, their shaggy hides and strange lances, were a curiosity. Units which formed the first line of defence on the distant Roman frontiers had seldom or never been seen in the capital. The burly warriors were jostled by the crowd or pushed over; sometimes they slipped on a broken paving stone or neglected cobble. When this happened the answer was abuse, fisticuffs and, finally, resort to arms. The officers, too, added to the confusion by dashing about here, there and everywhere with armed escorts. Rome had sunk from the status of a law-giving capital to that of an overcrowded garrison town.[37]

Vitellius with his immediate entourage walked up to the Capitol. There he embraced Sextilia and honoured her with the title reserved for the mother (or the wife) of an emperor: 'Augusta'. The old lady was no doubt as little impressed by this as she had been when, on learning that her son was now called 'Germanicus', she drily remarked: 'He's still Aulus to me, and I'm his mother.' But it was a proper gesture, and acceptable to the public. A sacrifice to Jupiter Best and Greatest was performed. Not in theory a triumph—for none such could be celebrated in a civil war—the occasion came near to being one in splendour, marking the completion of the progress from Germany to Rome, and the translation of general into emperor. From Brescello Vitellius had sent the dagger with which Otho had killed himself to the Temple of Mars at Cologne, for it was from this temple that in the January days he had been given a sword which had once, they said, belonged to the great Julius. It remained to be seen whether he who had now taken the sword would not also perish by it. The precedents were not entirely encouraging. The fate of Julius and others of his successors may have been in Vitellius' mind later on when, sorting the secret documents in the palace, he came across papers which Otho, despite his precautions at Brescello, had forgotten to destroy: petitions from more than 120 individuals demanding a reward for services rendered on the fatal fifteenth day of January. Vitellius gave instructions that all the petitioners were to be rounded up and put to death. Few tears were wasted on them. The punishment was deserved, however false some of the claims, and precautions were necessary. It was the traditional way in which rulers seek to protect their lives or secure vengeance for their deaths.

But this incident came later. In the evening of the day of entry into Rome, Lucius gave a state banquet for his imperial brother, at which the gossips averred that 2,000 fish and 7,000 game birds were served. On the following day Aulus addressed the Senate and the People. The latter shouted and yelled approval, compelling him to accept the title 'Augustus', so far refused. The other titles (except that of Caesar) he took at intervals, and that of Pontifex Maximus at some date before 18 July. The consular elections were carried out according to the plan already established and with observation of the proper ritual. One of Vitellius' first actions, on getting hold of such money as was available in the treasury, was to send a donative to Hordeonius Flaccus for payment to the troops left in Germany: this had been promised and its discharge was some consolation to them for not enjoying the spoils of victory in Italy.

Vitellius' attitude to the Senate was as conciliatory as Otho's had been, and for the same reason. He made a habit of attending its meetings even when the agenda were trivial. On one occasion the irritating praetor designate Helvidius Priscus proposed a course of action which conflicted with Vitellius' previously expressed wish. This was a direct challenge, and the emperor was at first indignant. Then, thinking better of it, he passed the matter off with an affable snub: 'There's nothing new in a difference of opinion between two senators on politics. I often made it a point of honour to voice my opposition to Thrasea.' The reference was to a much greater man than Priscus—his father-in-law Thrasea Paetus—and neatly suggested the relative importance of the two opposition senators and the fact that Vitellius had no wish to gag debate. And even Helvidius could not find fault when an imperial edict ordered that no astrologer should remain in any part of Italy after 1 October (the victims retorted by prophesying Vitellius' own death). These practitioners had long been a scourge and their predictions in a superstitious age might be feared by authority as self-fulfilling.

Of Vitellius' policy towards the empire as a whole it is difficult to form any opinion. Between the date of his arrival in Rome in late June and the advent in the capital of news of the proclamation of Vespasian at Alexandria only some three weeks intervened, weeks inevitably filled with pressing short-term problems. Thereafter all considerations were overshadowed by the certainty of renewed conflict. But it is obvious that whatever his faults—amplified by the Flavian scribblers—Vitellius retained the favour of many senators and of a numerous section of the city populace almost to the end. What he seems to have lost by August was the agreement of his lieutenants Caecina and Valens in his support. This weakness was to contribute substantially to his defeat. It sprang partly from jealous rivalry between the pair of kingmakers and partly, especially on Caecina's side, from the conviction that, while Vitellius had done well enough as a popular figurehead during the first six or seven months of the year, the prospects for this inexperienced commander were poor in a long struggle with the conqueror of Judaea (for as such Vespasian already appeared), backed by the diplomacy of Mucianus and Titus and the resources of the East. And their own futures, even granted success and harmony, seemed hardly assured when they contemplated the emperor's forceful brother Lucius and his designing wife. What had been a reasonable gamble in January, or even in June, began to appear much less alluring in August.

The financial state of the country can have been no better than it was under Nero or Galba, and in view of the April campaign probably a good deal worse. A tax was imposed upon an unpopular class, the wealthy freedmen, who were made to pay according to the number of their slaves, but this could not have yielded much of a return immediately. In the circumstances it is understandable that Vitellius could do little for the exiles allowed home by Galba and inadequately recompensed by the action of the committee set up by him. However, the emperor was able to make a modest contribution at no expense to himself. He restored to the victims their rights (which had lapsed on exile) over their freedmen, including the right to receive financial support from them in case of need. Some freedmen, however, tried to stultify the concession by hiding money acquired during their own period of servitude and their patrons' absence in disguised banking accounts. Others had joined the imperial civil service in the intervening period. It was felt that, as *liberti Caesaris*, they were likely to be unapproachable by their former masters and in some cases more powerful than they.

To the Roman mob Vitellius was acceptable enough. He knew the importance of keeping himself in the public eye, frequently attended the theatre, and was passionately devoted to racing. Before and after Nero's reign, the Greens (*Prasini*) had enjoyed a long period of success, which had perhaps contributed to Vitellius' financial difficulties. For he himself was an eager partisan of the Blues (*Veneti*) and wore their colour and assisted in grooming their horses, behaviour unusual in an emperor. Despite the depletion of the treasury, he seems to have found money to extend their stables. But it is hard to imagine a more remarkable form of flattery than that which prompted the Brethren of the Fields (according to their minutes for a date in June preceding Vitellius' arrival) to decree a small sacrifice in honour of a victory by the emperor's favourite faction.[38]

From June to September the city of Rome was even more overcrowded with troops than in January, and little seems to have been done —or perhaps could be done in the height of summer—to keep them busy and in training. The problems of discipline that inevitably arise when numbers of soldiers are quartered over wide areas of a large capital were not solved. Many men, in default of better accommodation (though the park of Nero's Golden House, for which Vitellius expressed contempt, must surely have been pressed into service), encamped in the low-lying Vatican district west of the Campus Martius. The northerners were not used to the oppressive climate of a Roman summer, and sought coolness by swimming in the Tiber. But the temperature drops quite severely at night. They suffered from chills, and almost certainly from malaria, endemic in Italy, to which as newcomers they could put up little resistance.[39]

Sickness made many long for a return to the north. But for those who were willing to face the Italian climate, there were rich pickings. Vitellius decided to form sixteen Praetorian and four Urban Cohorts, each of 1,000 (instead of 500) men, with excellent pay and prospects. The vacancies were rapidly taken up; but a process whereby 20,000 men were removed from an army only three times that size was regarded with serious misgivings. These fears were perhaps excessive, for it is clear from subsequent events that by this measure Vitellius bound to himself a large body of totally devoted and desperate men who could be relied on to fight to the last for their emperor and their privileges.

But the good times were drawing quickly to an end. By early August confidential news must have reached Vitellius of the proclamation of Vespasian as emperor made at Alexandria on 1 July and of his acceptance by the legions of Judaea and Syria in the course of the next fortnight. Even before this, Aponius Saturninus, the governor of Moesia, had reported disaffection in the Third Legion, which until recently had served under Mucianus; and the name of Vespasian had perhaps been canvassed by it since the April advance to Aquileia. The governor, his own sympathies not entirely clear, had failed to report the matter as frankly as he might have done, and courtiers played down the danger. Still, Vitellius had to take it seriously and concealment would eventually be out of the question if the grain ships failed to arrive from Egypt. In a speech to the troops the emperor found it prudent to assert that false information was being spread by the dismissed Othonian Praetorians in the north: in fact, he added, there was no danger of a renewed civil war. Any reference to Vespasian was banned, and military police patrolled the capital to break up gatherings of gossipers. The attempt to suppress rumour inevitably stimulated it.

On 7 September Vitellius celebrated his birthday. A public holiday was, of course, declared, and enjoyed with éclat for two days. Gladiatorial shows were put on and festivities organized throughout Rome on an unprecedented scale. To the delight of the rabble and the dismay of sober Romans, the emperor arranged a belated memorial service for

Nero. Altars were set up in the Campus Martius and victims offered at the public expense. Less than four months had elapsed since Vitellius entered Italy and the lavish sequence of shows began, but it was believed that Vitellius' freedman Asiaticus had already outdone the efforts of previous ministers. At such a court, it was asked, who could gain distinction by honesty and hard work?

In these same days the Flavian invasion began, and Antonius Primus led a brisk thrust through Friuli and Veneto.

7

Flavian Hopes

In January, February and March the mild Publius Valerius Marinus, whose consulship Vitellius was to defer, had attended the functions of the Brethren of the Fields with exemplary regularity. He was present at each of their consecutive meetings on 30 January, 26 and 28 February, and 5 and 9 March; and in this he resembled the vice-president, Otho Titianus, and him alone. Such remarkable fidelity might be explained as the result of close friendship or alliance between the two men; and this factor in turn could account for Otho's retaining Marinus, despite his relative unimportance, in the list of consuls. His disappearance from the Arval record after 9 March shows that he was one of the senators who left Rome with Otho six days later. On the day before departure, when there was also a meeting, Marinus was too busy packing to be present, and only one solitary member, Lucius Maecius Postumus, elected vice-president in place of Titianus, now regent, was there to vow a sacrifice, payable if the emperor returned safely from his expedition. After this, the record becomes fragmentary; but if we read the fragments aright, from March to 5 June Marinus was absent; but very shortly thereafter he reappears, at a time when the itinerant senators had scurried back from Bologna to Rome in advance of Vitellius. But it was obvious to Marinus that, as a close supporter of Otho and his brother, he could hope for nothing from Vitellius. When, in late July or early August, news of Vespasian's acclamation in Alexandria reached Rome, the mild man decided that the moment had come to cultivate a new allegiance. He packed once more, and went on board a ship at Pozzuoli bound for Alexandria in ballast. Heaven smiled on the decision. A Nereid sloped the sea towards the East. The etesian winds blew smoothly and steadily. His vessel made the very respectable average speed of 4·6 knots on the thousand-mile voyage. On the night of the eighth day out, or the morning of the ninth, a great fire burning by night or the glint of a mirror by day was seen in the south-east; then successively a radiate statue, and the white tower of three storeys—round, octangular, rectangular—which every mariner knew to be the Pharos of Alexandria.[40]

With many men like Marinus private fears and ambitions were hardly separable from the conviction that they were altruistic patriots. About the time that he decided to leave Rome for a more congenial climate, similar calculations were being made in very different circumstances and in a very different place. Tettius Julianus commanded the westernmost of the three legions of Moesia, VII Claudia stationed at Kostolać at the confluence of the Morava and the Danube. Like the other Moesian commanders, he had been decorated by Otho for his part in the successful repulse of the February invasion, and he could hardly now hope to be *persona grata* to Vitellius also. Moreover, he perhaps felt compromised in Vitellius' eyes by the injudicious behaviour of his troops at Aquileia in April. Finally, he was on bad terms with his superior, Marcus Aponius Saturninus, governor of Moesia. When in June the allegiance of the Danube troops began to waver—and the neighbouring formation, III Gallica at Gigen, took a leading part in swinging opinion in favour of the Flavian cause—Saturninus found himself in an unenviable position, at first outwardly backing Vitellius, in fact desperately playing for time. To give colour to his attitude of proper loyalty and to gratify a private grudge at the same time, he sent a centurion to Kostolać to assassinate Tettiu as a traitor. Warned in time, the legionary commander made his escape across the wild Balkan Range, avoiding the main road that led via Niš to the Bosporus. For the next few months he lay low, awaiting events. After a long and secret journey—purposely loitering, as gossip, and no doubt the incriminated governor, later claimed—he finally hurried forward when the news was favourable, and appeared at Alexandria to court Vespasian. But by that time, in November, he was not alone, or one of two. Many more, risking an autumnal or winter voyage, had made their way to a safe haven in the East.

But that is to anticipate. In the summer, as Marinus sailed into the Great Harbour of Alexandria he could see the simple and proud inscription which the architect of the lighthouse had placed in letters nearly two foot high on the eastern rectangular face of the 400-foot-high Pharos:

SOSTRATOS SON OF DEXIPHANES A CNIDIAN
ON BEHALF OF THOSE WHO SAIL THE SEAS
TO THE GODS WHO GIVE SAFETY

For those who sailed the seas the gods who gave safety were Castor and Pollux: for the storm-tossed ship of state and its troubled navigators might they not be Vespasian and Titus? But here, in the Great Harbour, Marinus' brief and undistinguished appearance in history comes to an end. Whether the favour of Vespasian secured him one of the suffect consulships of 70 or 71 is not recorded. In any case he seems not to have lived long, for when the minutes of the Order resume in 72 there is no mention of the faithful Brother. Yet it is pleasant to conjecture, from the mention of a Publius Valerius Marinus in the consular list for 91, that Domitian remembered to pay to the son the debt for whose settlement the father had had to wait.

The Alexandria that greeted the elder Marinus in the summer of 69 was a splendid city of more than 300,000 inhabitants, the greatest trading centre in the whole world. Two hundred and sixty years before, it had been founded by Alexander the Great himself on a low ridge between the sea and Lake Mariut; and though its greatest days as a centre of civilization and culture had perhaps passed with the disappearance of the Ptolemies who fostered it, yet it remained the capital of Roman Egypt and a wealthy metropolis, an entrepôt between Rome and the Indies, the days of destruction and decay still centuries ahead. Egypt as a whole, moreover, was an exotic jewel in the imperial regalia, the Indian Empire of Rome. The simple phrase in the *Res Gestae* of Augustus, *Aegyptum imperio populi Romani adieci*, 'I added Egypt to the empire of the Roman people', echoes the inscription upon the 78-foot obelisk of Rameses III which Augustus had already set up in 10 B.C. as a reminder to the Roman people of his and their conquest, visible then on the spine of the Circus Maximus and visible today in the Piazza del Popolo. Mindful of his adoptive father's experience (and his own) in Egypt, he had given the country a special status. It was governed, though theoretically a domain of the Roman people, by an equestrian prefect directly responsible in all matters to the emperor.[41]

Senators and the highest class of knights were forbidden to enter the country without the emperor's permission. Since Egypt commands the sea and land routes from the East to the Internal Sea, from Asia to Africa, there was always the fear that a pretender occupying the country, however small his force and however considerable the opposition, might threaten Italy with starvation by withholding Egypt's grain supply, one-third of the home country's import requirement. There was also an internal problem. The country was sprawling, given to strange cults and irresponsible excesses, indifferent to the rule of law —at any rate in Roman eyes—and ignorant of democratic government. The land of age-old autocracy, ossified and stagnant for all the vigour of its trade, Egypt required treatment different from that appropriate to livelier lands now learning for the first time what the Roman peace meant.[42]

Whatever the rules said, in the summer of 69 a senatorial adherent to the Flavian cause must have been welcome indeed in Alexandria, especially if he came from Rome bearing hot news, as Marinus did. He will have been quickly conducted to the nearby royal palace and interviewed by the governor.

Tiberius Julius Alexander, prefect of Egypt, had reached his fifties and the height of his powers and influence. By birth he was a Jew of

Alexandria, by upbringing a Hellenized cosmopolitan, by status a Roman knight, by profession an administrator and general, always a faithful and efficient servant of Rome and of whoever might be Rome's ruler. His father had been inspector-general of the Egyptian customs, his uncle was the distinguished and eloquent philosopher Philo. From an early age, his ambience had been one of wealth, culture, and close contact with the Roman imperial family and with the Herods. In the forties, after some initial military posts in the army of Egypt of which details escape us, he was (as we know from an inscription at Dendera, twenty-five miles north of Thebes) lieutenant-governor of the Thebaid, and from A.D. 46 to 48 procurator of Judaea. As such, he commanded auxiliary cohorts and regiments of the Roman army. Then darkness descends for fifteen years; but in A.D. 63–66 he acted as chief-of-staff to Gnaeus Domitius Corbulo, governor of Syria, at a dangerous and critical time for relations between Parthia, Armenia and Rome. By May 66 Nero had given him the post towards which his previous experience obviously pointed the way: the prefecture of his native Egypt.

On arrival he was welcomed by his relative King Agrippa II, who brought news of unrest in Judaea; and almost at once Alexander's gifts of diplomacy and firmness were put to the test by a serious riot on his own doorstep. Its course is best described in the words of Josephus:

In Alexandria there was perpetual friction between the natives and the Jews, ever since the moment when Alexander the Great had made use of their enthusiastic support against the Egyptians and as a reward given them the right to live in the city on equal terms with the Greeks. This privilege was maintained by the Ptolemies, who indeed allotted them a particular quarter of the city to live in so that they could observe their rituals and way of life with less contact with the gentiles. The Ptolemies even allowed them to call themselves 'Macedonians'; and when the Romans took over Egypt, neither the first Caesar nor his successors allowed any diminution in the privileges granted to the Jews by Alexander the Great. But there were continual clashes with the Greeks, and despite the punishments inflicted on both sides by the governors, trouble grew worse and worse. At the time of which we speak, when there were disturbances in other parts, the situation of the Jews was inflamed. A public meeting, held by the Alexandrians to organize a deputation to be sent to Nero, brought to the amphitheatre not only the Greeks but a number of Jews. When their opponents spotted them, there were immediately loud cries of 'Enemies!' and 'Spies!' Then they jumped up and laid hands on them. Most of the Jews took to their heels and fled in all directions, but three men were arrested and carried off to be burned alive. Then the whole Jewish community rose to exact vengeance. At first they stoned the Greeks, then seized brands, rushed to the amphitheatre and threatened a holocaust of the entire audience. This would have happened had not the governor, who was in Alexandria, bestirred himself to allay the frenzy. At first he refrained from using armed force to bring the people to their senses, but sent some leading Alexandrian notables to them with a warning to calm down and avoid the necessity of the Roman army's intervention. But the rioters replied to the appeal with abuse, and cursed Tiberius.

The latter then realized that only extreme measures would restore order. He therefore sent against them the two Roman legions stationed outside the town and with them 2,000 troops that—unluckily for the Jews—had arrived from the province of Africa. His orders were not only to kill, but to plunder and burn down houses. So the troops attacked the ghetto in the Fourth (Delta) Quarter of Alexandria and carried out their orders, not without some losses: for the Jews had concentrated their forces and put the best-armed men in the front ranks. Their resistance lasted for quite a time. When once they gave way, there was complete havoc. Death overtook them in various forms. Some were caught in the open, others crammed into houses to which the Romans set fire after plundering their contents. They neither took pity on children nor showed reverence for age, but slaughtered indiscriminately until the whole quarter became a blood-bath. Fifty thousand corpses were piled up, and no one would have survived, if the Jews had not appealed for mercy. Alexander took pity on them and ordered the Romans to withdraw. The latter with their usual discipline ceased the killing as soon as they were ordered; but the Alexandrian Greeks, in the excess of their hate, could hardly be recalled from the carnage.[43]

In its barbarity the incident recalls certain events of our own century more closely than anything we know of in Roman history; but it illustrates well enough the problems of maintaining order in a large, motley and virtually unpoliced city of the East. On the whole Alexander emerges with credit. He acted promptly, attempted conciliation, used force as soon as it seemed inevitable, and used it with full effect, calling off his men as soon as resistance collapsed. Josephus' estimate of the loss of life is certainly exaggerated but the best that one can say of this drastic bloodletting is that it mercifully guaranteed a long period of peace which milder methods might have failed to secure.

More prosaic and less emotional sources than the Jewish historian grant us another and more typical aspect of the duties of a prefect of Egypt. In the Khargeh Oasis 100 miles west of Thebes in Upper Egypt, a lengthy inscription, 2·45 metres in height and 2 metres in width, comprising sixty-six long lines, is carved on the east face of the north jamb of the outer gateway to the Temple of Hibis. The text, part of which is also reproduced in a papyrus fragment now at Berlin, is the transcript, crudely but clearly carved by a local mason, of a comprehensive decree relating to abuses in the collection of taxes, issued two and a half months earlier by Tiberius Alexander at Alexandria. Its subscription runs:

In the first year of Lucius Livius Galba Caesar Augustus Imperator, Epiphi 12 [6 July 68].

The main portion of the text is highly technical, concerned as it is with a number of quite different fiscal problems and misdemeanours which had come to light (and perhaps already been dealt with successively and administratively as they occurred) in the first two years of Alexander's tenure of office, much of it inevitably spent in travelling throughout his extensive province. Among other things, we hear of vexatious litigation relating to *res iudicatae* (a favourite sport where governors came and governors went, and reminiscent of the Sardinian dispute), and the practice, in forbidding which Alexander was swimming against the current of history, of compelling individuals to act as tax farmers against their will. But the opening preambles are of more general interest as throwing light upon the character of the governor:

I, Julius Demetrius, strategus of the Thebaid [Khargeh] oasis, have appended for you herewith a copy of the edict sent to me by the Lord Prefect Tiberius Julius Alexander, so that you may know of it and enjoy his benefactions. Year 2 of the emperor Lucius Livius Augustus Sulpicius Galba Imperator, Phaophi 1, Julian-Augustan Day [28 September 68].

Tiberius Julius Alexander says:

Since I am extremely anxious that the city of Alexandria should preserve the status due to it by enjoying the benefactions which it receives from the emperors, and that Egypt, living in tranquillity, should cheerfully contribute to the grain supply and to the supreme felicity of modern times without being oppressed by novel and unlawful actions; and since furthermore, almost from the moment I set foot in the city, I have been assailed by the clamours of petitioners whether in smaller or larger numbers, the same consisting of the most respectable citizens here and of those that are farmers in the country, complaining about abuses very closely affecting them, I lost no opportunity in the past of correcting such abuses as I had authority to deal with; and now, so that you may with greater confidence expect every concession touching both your well-being and your enjoyment at the hands of our benefactor the emperor Galba Augustus, who has risen like the sun to give us light for the good of all mankind, and that you may know that I personally have taken thought for matters touching your relief, I have published in precise terms, in respect of each and every your requests, all that it is lawful for me to decide and to do; and as for more weighty matters requiring the authority and majesty of the emperor, I shall communicate these to him with all truth. For the gods have reserved for this most solemn moment the duty of safeguarding the inhabited world.[44]

Beneath the polysyllabic jargon of flaccid official Greek one senses a genuine attitude of benevolence, some sort of concern for honest government, a desire to do one's duty to emperor and subject. But it was not within the competence, nor congruent with the character, of a Tiberius Julius Alexander to create a new dynasty for Rome. If others gave the

E

word, he would work well for them. In February or March, Otho, and in May, Vitellius were promptly recognized.

The details of the rise of the Flavian cause are hidden in a thick mist. The official view put about after Vespasian's accession was that he reluctantly submitted to pressure from his advisers and friends to break the oath of loyalty to Vitellius sworn so recently as May 69, and that he did so when the new régime showed itself in the colours of an incapable and irresponsible tyranny. Yet it was clear to everybody that the declaration of 1 July must have been preceded by extensive diplomatic activity and forward planning. It could be pointed out by later historians, no friends of the Flavians, that at the moment of decision in late May or early in the following month nothing could have been known of the activities of Vitellius in his capital, since he did not reach it until the end of June. Others might retort that the characters and activities of Aulus Vitellius, Fabius Valens and Caecina Alienus were known to their brother-officers long before June. There were confidential contacts between widely separated armies and officials; and the official couriers sent out by Vitellius to announce his accession adopted an overbearing attitude that went down badly everywhere. Valens, the strong man in the triumvirate, had a dubious past. His implication in the murder of Fonteius Capito, Vitellius' predecessor as governor of Lower Germany, must have caused widespread speculation at the turn of the year. There would be misgivings. Moreover, the senior governors—those of Pannonia, Moesia, Syria and Judaea, in whose hands lay half the legionary strength of the empire—must have looked with dismay at the claim of the German garrisons, rapidly staked and rapidly exploited, to appoint an emperor without reference to them or to the Senate and People. If this was to be the new form of succession to the principate, it was not obvious that the credentials of Vitellius were any better than those of Otho. Then there were two evil precedents set by the Vitellian faction: the execution of certain Othonian centurions, and the massive demobilization of Othonian Praetorians designed to make room for men from the German garrisons.

It is therefore not quite impossible, though it cannot be taken as proven on the strength of a statement in Suetonius, that already in April the Moesian troops, foiled of participation in the spring campaign and looking round at Aquileia for an emperor of their choice, may have thought of Vespasian. After all, Tampius Flavianus and Aponius Saturninus, whom they knew, were old and unpopular, however meritorious their previous careers; Licinius Mucianus, while possessing the gifts and competence of an excellent maker of rulers, lacked the will to be one himself. There remained Vespasian, a no-nonsense professional soldier with two grown-up sons, his efficiency proved by the course of the Jewish War in 67–68.

Titus Flavius Vespasianus, second son of the honest exciseman and banker Flavius Sabinus, was born on the evening of 17 November, A.D. 9 at a tiny village on the Salarian Way near Cittàreale, in the mountains just within the border of the Abruzzi with Umbria. His father was a citizen of Rieti to the south-west, his mother from a good family having property a little to the north, in a most attractive and wild part of the Apennines six miles west of Norcia on the hills above Serravalle and the gorge of the Corno. But as a very young child—presumably while his parents were away on business in Asia—he was brought up by his paternal grandmother on her estate at Cosa on the Tuscan coast. Even after he became emperor he constantly went back to this childhood home which, unchanged, recalled the past and the grandmother to whom he was deeply attached. It was in memory of her that, on high days and holidays, he would drink from a little silver cup which had been hers. Later the parents moved to Avenches, where the father died. It was his mother's ambition for Vespasian's future rather than his own that drove him to embark on the senatorial career upon which his elder brother Sabinus was already engaged. He entered the army and served on the staff of a legion engaged in mopping up unruly mountaineers in Thrace, and later as financial secretary in the joint province of Crete and Cyrene. By Flavia Domitilla he had three children: one daughter who died young, Titus (born on 30 December 39 in a humble home at Rome) and Domitian (born in a slightly better house in the sixth region of the capital on 24 October 51). Both his wife and his daughter were dead before he became emperor, and after Flavia's death he lived with his former mistress Caenis, a freedwoman—secretary of Antonia, daughter of Mark Antony—and treated her virtually as his legal wife. Under Claudius he was given the command of II Augusta which was stationed at Strasbourg in Upper Germany (then governed by Galba), and with his formation crossed to Britain in 43 and took part in the invasion and occupation of the southern part of the country for two or three years. He distinguished himself at the Battle of the Medway, was present at the capture of Colchester, and occupied many sites in south-west Britain, including without doubt Maiden Castle. Vespasian was a born soldier, used to marching at the head of his troops, choosing his camp sites personally, and harrying the enemy day and night and, if occasion required, by personal combat, content with whatever rations were available and dressed much the same as a private soldier. He received the submission of the Belgae of Hampshire and Wiltshire, the Atrebates of Berkshire and the whole of the Isle of Wight. In the last two months of 51 he was consul. After this followed a long period of retirement until his consular appointment as governor of Africa (an annual posting) held around 63 or 64. Here the honest son of the honest tax gatherer proved too puritanical for his motley subjects, if one can take seriously the gossip that he was pelted by the people of Sousse with turnips. Vespasian, however, was the kind of man around whom wits tended to invent good stories. What is certain is that he achieved the considerable feat of returning from a rich province no wealthier than he entered it; and a period of impoverishment followed during which he had to borrow money from Sabinus on the security of his own estates. Worse, he suffered the disgrace of going into business: he became a transport contractor, whence his nickname 'Muledriver', suitable enough, too, for one who, like Galba, brooked no indiscipline from Marius' mules, the legionaries of Rome. However, in 66 he was invited to accompany Nero on his trip to Greece as a member of his suite, but when Nero himself was giving a song recital was tactless enough to leave the room repeatedly or fall asleep. For this stupidity or honesty he was banished from the court, and lay low for a while in Greece until Nero relented and, needing an efficient man without pretensions or great birth to deal with the rebellious Jews, selected Vespasian for the command, which he took over in 67.

Vespasian was the perfect example of the virtues of honesty, frugality and sturdiness which Roman publicists like to attribute to the Sabines. His build was powerful. A hooked nose, tightly-compressed lips and arched eyebrows lent him a strained expression. He enjoyed excellent health apart from occasional gout, but took no medical precautions to ensure it except thorough massaging, a simple life and a tendency to return to his Sabine or Tuscan haunts whenever he could. He frequented the spa at Cutilia between Antrodoco and Rieti, some twenty miles down the Velino valley from his birthplace; and it was here, where the local goddess of prosperity, civil and military, had a shrine by the lake with its prickly water and the floating island, that he was to die. The goddess was named Vacuna, and her worship reached as far as Horace's country, for the poet subscribed one of his letters 'from beyond the crumbling shrine of Vacuna', that is from the villa in the Licenza valley. A century after Horace, Vespasian was to restore this building dedicated to his Sabine Lady of Luck, as we know from an inscription prominently displayed to this day in the village of Rocca-gióvine. Prosperity, victory and success were certainly gifts for which the Sabine emperor ought to have felt grateful.[45]

Vespasian's origins were comparatively humble, and that he fulfilled the Platonic doctrine that rulers should be compelled to rule against their will is clear from his career. Only his mother's persuasiveness caused him to aspire to be a senator, and even in this career, despite good services, promotion was not notably fast, and clearly not anxiously sought. But it was perhaps this very reluctance to advance his own interests that prompted the jealous Nero to appoint him to a position that in 69 gave him the chance, if he would but take it, to become master of the world. Vespasian obediently recognized Galba, Otho and Vitellius, and there was no particular reason why he should now or later give hostages to fortune by rebellion. That the initiative of revolt, or at any rate the overriding pressure for it, came from the governor of Syria is implicit in the account of our most trustworthy and critical source, Tacitus, and with this verdict we are in no position to disagree.

We know much less about Gaius Licinius Mucianus than his importance in the history of the decade 66–76 makes desirable. Thus his early career is obscure, and we owe to a lead pipe, found inscribed with his name at Genzano in 1877, the information that Mucianus had an estate near Ariccia, one of the richest and most desirable suburban areas. Prominent and wealthy, he is alleged to have squandered a fortune in his youth on high living, and earned (no difficult task) the disapproval of Claudius. Under Nero his rise begins. Soon after 57 he was promoted—or relegated—to the governorship of Lycia and Pamphylia, and chance has preserved a dedication to him by a beneficiary at Oenoanda in Lycia and another at Antalya in Pamphylia. He attained the consulship around 65, having taken part in Corbulo's campaigns in the years 58 and onwards; and he then succeeded his superior as governor of Syria, the appointment being roughly contemporary with that of Vespasian to Judaea.[45]

The relations between the aristocratic dilettante and the son of the banker from Avenches, though, or because, they were now governors of adjoining and interdependent provinces, seem to have been cool at the beginning, and indeed both had to tread cautiously in the last years of the suspicious Nero. Once the megalomaniac emperor had disappeared and a measure of republican freedom was restored in the first months of Galba's reign, they communicated more freely, Titus, Vespasian's son, often playing the part of intermediary, his amiable and easy-going character congenial to the childless senator.

An observer delighting in antithesis and paradox saw in Mucianus a compound of self-indulgence and energy, courtesy and arrogance, good and evil. The modern observer cannot deny the Flavians some concern for the welfare of the empire, and Mucianus can hardly be accused of self-seeking. His talent for diplomacy, intrigue and organization was employed to make an emperor of another, not of himself. This indifference to his own advancement coupled with his experience of the East was the reason why Nero had put him in charge of Syria; and though his great services to the Flavian cause earned him two more consulships in 70 and 72, it is noticeable that they, like the first, were suffect and not ordinary: even these distinctions were unobtrusive. He was a fluent orator, in Greek as in Latin, and like many Romans of his class had literary and antiquarian ambitions. After the years of crisis he published a collection of republican historical documents in eleven books, to say nothing of three volumes of an anthology of letters. In a more popular vein his miscellany, the *Mirabilia,* garnered the curiosities of nature which his career had enabled him to hear of, or see at first hand. He is sure that the source of the Euphrates is twelve miles above Zimara, differing from Corbulo, who had another geographical doctrine. An elephant, he records, learned the shapes of the Greek alphabet, and could laboriously trace a sentence in that language, while monkeys have been known to play draughts; and two sagacious goats, meeting on a very narrow bridge, knew how to solve the traffic problem: one lay down and the other walked sure-footed over him. An inhabitant of Samothrace grew a new set of teeth at the age of 104, and between the island of Ruad and the Phoenician coast fresh water is brought up from a spring under the bottom of the sea, which is seventy-five feet deep, by means of a leather pipe. Lycia's governor recalled that while travelling through his province he had been shown a local marvel—a plane tree standing by the roadside near a spring with a hollow cavity inside it eighty-one feet across, and had decided to hold a banquet in it with eighteen members of his suite who reclined upon the soft couch of leaves. Afterwards he had gone to bed in the same tree shielded from every breath of wind and delighted by the agreeable sound of rain pattering through the foliage. It was better than a marble palace. A man whose interests covered both political history and scientific trivia clearly had a lively mind; and his more serious activities as a statesman and a soldier show his practical competence when he chose to exert it.[47]

From July 68, then, if not before, Titus was fully employed as a messenger boy and, potentially, something far greater. We have noticed that in November or December he went off Romewards with King Agrippa, ostensibly to pay his respects to the newly arrived Galba and to begin his candidature for the praetorship, but in fact to explore at the prompting of Mucianus and with the blessing of his father the possibilities opened up by the imminent choice of an heir by the ageing Galba. The news that met Titus and Agrippa at Corinth was crushing. Otho was only seven years older than Titus, so that even if they had been friends, no question of adoption could now arise. But hard on the news of Otho's accession came full knowledge of the claims of Vitellius, then a conviction that an armed confrontation in northern Italy was imminent. Titus returned quickly to his father with fresh hope. Of course it would be well for the Flavians to hold their hand. But by May the situation was clearer. Vitellius had emerged the victor. But the discontent of the Eastern troops and the growing evidence that the new régime was unlikely to be either lasting or acceptable led to the formulation in Mucianus' mind of a second plan: the principate should go to Vespasian, if the latter could be persuaded, with reversion to Titus in due course.

But would Vespasian accept nomination? We have no means of knowing his inner thoughts, but Tacitus cannot be far wrong in his imaginative reconstruction, so far as it goes. The factors that told against acceptance were the hazards of an enterprise from which there could be no going back, the unacceptability of further civil war, and indeed, on a purely personal plane, the danger of assassination. The arguments in favour were patriotism, feasibility without much bloodshed, and the fitness of bowing to a popular demand. The predominant characteristic of Vespasian in 69 was caution. It was necessary to take stock of the military situation in all its aspects. The Jewish War, quiescent for the moment, had to be finished off, and this commitment, together with the safeguarding of the eastern frontier as a whole, meant that a strict limit must be placed upon the extent to which troops were committed to a distant campaign, near or in Italy. Luckily, relations were good with Parthia after the settlement of 66, and she and Rome had a common interest in defending Armenia (and hence their own empires) from the encroachments of the Alans, lasso-throwing horsemen pressing down between the Black and Caspian Seas. This was the threat which had stimulated the projected Eastern campaign of Nero and which was soon to materialize in 72 at the expense of Parthia. In 69, therefore, Volo-gaeses I had every inducement to preserve the peace with Rome—especially a Rome governed by Vespasian, to whom the respect the Parthian had felt for Corbulo seems to have been not unreasonably transferred. Nevertheless, safe though the Roman frontier might be, the prospect of fighting fellow-Romans was as unwelcome to the patriot as it was alarming to the legionary commander and military logician. There was, however, another possibility, sure if slow: that of a blockade of Italy by the interruption of the corn supplies from Egypt and Africa, which together supplied the capital with the bulk of the *annona*. Providing Egypt were secured, Africa could quickly be dominated by an advance along the coast or by a movement engineered in the province itself. The cessation of corn imports would create a shortage in Italy in six months, and it might be possible to secure Vitellius' downfall without striking a blow in anger. It would be necessary to approach Tiberius Julius Alexander, and put out feelers to the commander of the single legion in Africa, Valerius Festus, with whom, rather than with the governor Piso, the decision would lie.[48]

Discreetly sounded, the governor of Egypt approved the plan, but pointed out that the summer convoys would soon be sailing, and could not be retained without revealing one's hand. As for the Danube, by early June it was already clear that the Moesian legions were ready to accept Vespasian, and III Gallica under Titus Aurelius Fulvus (grandfather of the emperor Antoninus Pius) could be relied on to take the initiative in view of its recent service in Syria and its knowledge of

Vespasian. These legions, perhaps with some support from Pannonia, could be used to provide a force to re-occupy Aquileia without necessarily moving more deeply into Italy; nor were the governors of Moesia, Pannonia and Dalmatia likely to stand firm against a movement by their legionary commanders. Perhaps quite a small token force from the East would be sufficient support in this area.

These purely rational considerations may have been reinforced by an element of superstition. Had not the priest at Paphos hinted to Titus that a great future awaited him? That such beliefs had a certain hold on Vespasian is evident from the fact that when he had gained power he kept at his court the astrologer Seleucus and gave special favour to the young renegade Jewish aristocrat, Josephus. In the summer of 67, at Jotapata in Galilee, the latter had been skilled enough to extricate himself from a siege and from a desperate suicide compact among the survivors by going over to the enemy. The incident, confirmed by other witnesses, is told in Josephus' own words in the *Jewish War*:

Vespasian gave orders that he should be kept under strict surveillance, since he intended to send him shortly to Nero. When Josephus heard this, he told Vespasian that he wished to have a private conversation with him. Then the Roman commander cleared the room, allowing only his son Titus and two friends to remain. Josephus then began: 'You imagine, Vespasian, that in Josephus you have merely captured a prisoner, but I bring you greater tidings. If I had not been sent by God, I should have accepted death, for I know well enough the Jewish Law and how generals should die. Are you sending me to Nero? Why? Will those that come after Nero, and before you, keep their inheritance for long? It is you who will be Caesar, Vespasian, and emperor, you and your son here. Shackle me now with greater care and keep me under guard for your own sake, for you, Caesar, will be not only my master, but master over land and sea and every nation of mankind, and I ask for the penalty of still harsher captivity if I prove to speak rashly of God's will.' At the time Vespasian listened with an air of incredulity to the tale and suspected that Josephus had invented the story to save his skin. But gradually he became convinced that God was already inspiring him with the idea of becoming emperor and was manifesting to him his future dominion by this and other signs.[49]

Anyway, Vespasian kept Josephus as a prisoner of war, but under mild conditions, and his attitude was reinforced by Titus' belief. As for the other signs, these were in part old, in part recent. He recalled a moment of his childhood when he was living on his grandmother's farm at Cosa. A violent storm had uprooted a tall cypress, yet on the following morning it sprang up again greener and stronger than before. There were other stories that Vespasian or his courtiers told, when events gave them significance. A stray dog brought in a human hand from the streets while Vespasian was at lunch, and dropped it beneath the table; and a hand is symbolic of power. Again, when he was at dinner, an ox returning from the plough shook off its yoke, entered the room, scattered the servants and fell at his feet as if suddenly exhausted; then it lowered its neck as if recognizing one to whom sacrifice was due. So much for the past. But not far from Jotapata lies Mount Carmel, named after a local Baal having neither image nor temple, but only an altar and the devotion of the local people. When Vespasian offered sacrifice here in the summer of 69, the priest Basilides repeatedly examined the entrails of the victim to foretell the future and finally declared, 'Whatever you are planning, Vespasian—be it the building of a house, an addition to your estate or the acquisition of more servants— this is granted. You shall have a great mansion, wide acres and many people to direct.' Signs and wonders seemed to confirm the arguments of reason. Everything now hinged on the decision of Vespasian himself, between whom and Mucianus a series of private interviews took place on the frontier between Syria and Judaea. Finally, before a rather larger meeting of senior officers, Mucianus made a formal appeal to Vespasian to accept nomination. It cost Vespasian considerable effort to screw his courage to the sticking point. At sixty, one was really too old for adventures of this kind. Gaius and Nero had been in their twenties when the call came, Augustus and Otho in their thirties, Tiberius, Claudius and Vitellius in their fifties. There was, it was true, Galba, who became princeps in his seventies. But the precedent was scarcely encouraging. Two factors finally overcame the modesty or indolence of Vespasian: he had two adult sons ready and willing, in due course, to take the burden from his shoulders; he had also a sense of duty to his country. He accepted nomination.

It was now the very end of May. It was agreed that the safest course would be an initial declaration in Alexandria. If this were well received, it would commit Alexander and Egypt irrevocably to rebellion and blockade, and give a lead to the Judaean and Syrian legions, whose response was not in doubt. A timetable settled, Mucianus returned to his capital Antioch and Vespasian to his, Caesarea. It seemed desirable to stage a short and effective raid into the hills before the fatal date. On 5 June Vespasian marched south-east from his capital and captured the little towns of Bethel and Ephraim, which he garrisoned. Then, with his cavalry, he advanced towards Jerusalem, inflicting some losses on those who expected no such sudden foray. Meanwhile, a lieutenant, Cerialis, dealt with Idumaea in the south, and captured and destroyed the ancient city of Hebron recently vacated by the zealot Simon ben Giora. All the strong places of Judaea were now in Roman hands except four: Jerusalem; Herodium, rising sharply 100 metres above the plateau, Herod the Great's palace, fortress and burial place where seventy-three years before he had been laid to rest amid gold and jewels; and the

twin strongholds giddily placed to east and west of the Dead Sea—
Machaerus, the second strongest place in Judaea (destined with
Herodium to fall in 72 to a Lucilius Bassus who may perhaps be the
naval commander of 69), and Masada, captured in the famous and
desperate siege of 73 by Flavius Silva. By the end of June 69, Vespasian
was back at Caesarea, waiting for news.[50]

On 1 July Tiberius Julius Alexander, prefect of Egypt, addressed a
parade of the two Egyptian legions, III Cyrenaica and XXII Deiotariana, in their camp at Nicopolis three miles east of Alexandria,
reading to them a letter from Vespasian in which he spoke of an
invitation to assume the principate. The troops, together with the
people of Alexandria, enthusiastically acclaimed the new emperor, and
the day was officially reckoned as the date of his accession. This remarkable tribute to the initial support of Tiberius Alexander and
Egypt must reflect Vespasian's realization that his whole strategy had
depended upon it.[51]

Some account of the pronouncement of 1 July has survived in a
papyrus now at Cairo. Its dreadfully mutilated state makes it difficult
to give more than a conjectural version of the document as a whole; but
even so what remains is of capital interest. If we confine ourselves to
what is probable, it seems that the account states that on the day of days
crowds collected and filled the whole hippodrome. Presumably the
largest structure in Alexandria, this lay on the eastern outskirts of the
city, beyond the Canopic Gate and towards Nicopolis, where the
legions had their barracks. No doubt by this time the oath had already
been administered to the troops. Now comes a gathering of the civil
population. In a speech the governor seems to have addressed his 'Lord
Caesar' in his absence, praying for his health and preservation and
describing him, in traditional phraseology as the 'one saviour and benefactor'. Then comes a word or words recalling the description in
Alexander's edict of Galba's 'rising like the sun to shine on mankind'.
The fragment continues: 'Preserve for us our emperor . . . O Augustus,
benefactor, Sarapis . . . son of Ammon.' The crowd thereupon seems to
reply, 'We thank Tiberius Alexander.' Then the governor remarks that
'the divine Caesar prays for your well-being'. His reference to the
emperor is echoed in slightly different terms by the crowd's exclamation
'O Lord Augustus Vespasianus'.

Pitiful as the evidence is and hyperbolic though its language may
seem, the few words do something to fill in the bald statement of our
literary sources that on 1 July 69 Vespasian was proclaimed emperor at
Alexandria. The enthusiasm does not seem wholly fictitious if taken in
conjunction with the literary evidence for the welcome given to Vespasian personally later in the year. That the papyrus fragment does not in
fact allude to that occasion seems clear from the appointment of a

successor to Tiberius Alexander in 69, almost certainly as a result of arrangements made at Beirut and before Vespasian's arrival at Alexandria: thanks expressed by the crowd to Tiberius Alexander exclude a date when the governor of Egypt was Fronto or Peducaeus.[52]

On 3 July, as soon as the news arrived at Caesarea, the army of Judaea (V Macedonica, X Fretensis, XV Apollinaris)—represented, it seems, by the personal guard—greeted Vespasian as Caesar and Augustus; and the formations followed suit in their camps. To the guard and those who gathered round, Vespasian made a short speech of the kind expected of a soldier and an emperor, and was greeted with acclaim and promises of support. A few days later, Mucianus, who had been waiting for this news at Antioch, his capital, immediately administered the oath to his legions, and then went to the theatre, which was regularly used for political meetings, and made a speech to the civilian townsfolk who had flocked there with ready compliance. As we have seen, Mucianus was quite a graceful speaker, even in Greek, and he had the art, denied to the blunter Vespasian, of displaying to advantage all he said or did. One matter in particular he stressed. He asserted —no doubt in advance of certain knowledge, but plausibly enough— that Vitellius had made up his mind to transfer the legions of Germany to Syria, while those in Syria were to be moved to the bases on the Rhine, where the climate was feared as severe and where conditions were believed to be harsh. Neither civilians nor soldiers wanted this. Local ties of every sort made both sides most reluctant to face a change. IIII Scythica had been in Syria since about 56, XII Fulminata since Augustus' time and VI Ferrata since 30 B.C.

The Flavians soon received the support of a number of native rulers, among them Schaemus, sheikh of Homs, a fertile and independent enclave in the province of Syria still ruled by the dynasty of the Sampsigerami—the outlandish name had been applied in derision by Cicero to the 'Nabob' Pompey more than a century before—and also Antiochus IV Epiphanes, ruler of Commagene east of Cilicia. His little state enjoyed an importance and a wealth which derived from its situation: the capital Samsat commanded both the main road from Antioch to Armenia along the Euphrates, and a major route from the west into Mesopotamia.

For some thirty years Antiochus, a Croesus among client-kings, had ruled his country in friendship with Rome. But the fidelity shown during that time and again now in 69 was soon to be ill-rewarded in obedience to higher necessities. In 72, no doubt to strengthen a frontier now in imminent jeopardy from the Alans beyond the Caucasus, an excuse was discovered by Rome (in the person of the then governor of Syria) to tidy up the map and incorporate Commagene in the empire. The dispirited Antiochus retired into private life, first at Sparta and then at Rome, and

Josephus sententiously remarks that despite his riches his latter end illustrated only too well the validity of Solon's maxim, 'Call no man happy until he is dead.' But the chief loser by this adjustment was his son, who at first offered resistance to the takeover, but of course in vain. The prince was none other than Gaius Julius Antiochus Epiphanes, the dashing young warrior wounded at the First Battle of Cremona while fighting for Otho, and later an active supporter of the Romans at the siege of Jerusalem. But at any rate he was given the consolation of Roman citizenship, and in the next generation the grandson of old Antiochus, in formal nomenclature 'Gaius Julius, son of Gaius, Antiochus Philopappus', advanced yet further. In 109 he held the Roman consulship by gift of Trajan, and was in addition citizen and archon of Athens, where he still confronts the visitor in suitably vigorous relief upon the hill and monument named after him. It would be hard to find a better example of the rough and ready Mediterranean amalgam achieved by Rome.[53]

Then Titus' travelling companion, King Agrippa II, sheikh of Anjar and Golan, arrived after a fast voyage from Rome, where secret emissaries from his people had brought him news of Vespasian's proclamation in advance of its becoming known to Vitellius. The winds had been as kind to him as to Marinus. Equal enthusiasm for the cause was shown by his sister Berenice, widow of Herod of Anjar and mistress of Titus. She was now in her forties ('her best years' as Tacitus puts it), but she preserved her looks, her courage and a certain notoriety. Even Vespasian approved of her, or at any rate of her money. After this, we are not surprised to learn that the governors of all the provinces of Asia Minor, though disposing of no legionary garrisons, had promised such support in supplies, facilities and auxiliary forces as they could give and Vespasian might require. Among them were the proconsul of Asia, Gaius Fonteius Agrippa, and the legate of Galatia-with-Pamphylia, Lucius Nonius Calpurnius Asprenas. Both these senators were to be rewarded by new appointments, though their destinies were to prove very different. In addition, there was Cappadocia, still a procuratorial province governed by a knight without the legionary garrison which Vespasian himself was to give it; its governor in 69 is unknown, and equally unknown is the governor of Pontus, added to Bithynia five years before.

In late July Vespasian, Mucianus, Titus and the commanding and senior officers of the legions, together with the potentates who supported the Flavian cause, met to formulate precise plans at Beirut. The spot was suitable. Neither Vespasian's nor Mucianus' provincial capital, it was an agreeable and prosperous town enjoying Latin rights, a mix of East and West, and a suitable starting point for a movement to liberate Rome. The concentration of infantry, cavalry and client-rulers, each outbidding the other in show and protestations, gave the conference the air of a durbar. The setting was imperial.

The strategy of Vespasian must first have been exposed and clarified: it was the blockade of Italy, backed by the eventual appearance on the coast of the Adriatic of an army under Mucianus not inferior in numbers to the force which an optimistic calculation would expect to be forthcoming from the Danube armies. Assuming drafts of 2,000 men from each of the six legions of Moesia, Pannonia and Dalmatia, Vespasian believed that 12,000 might without risk be poised in the spring on the north-eastern frontier of Italy by the Balkan armies, and that for political reasons these numbers should be equalled, and preferably more than equalled, by the contribution of the East threatening Italy from Epirus. The expeditionary force would therefore consist of VI Ferrata from Syria (the longest-serving legion in the province), together with 13,000 legionaries drawn from the remaining formations (for example, 2,000 each from IIII Scythica, V Macedonica, X Fretensis, XV Apollinaris, III Cyrenaica and XXII Deiotariana, with 1,000 from XII Fulminata which had suffered severely in 66). The size, therefore, of the Flavian force available to occupy Italy would be more than 30,000 legionaries, almost exactly equivalent to the nominal effective of the Vitellian legionary force in Italy which it would face. The reason for what appears at first sight the very heavy demands on legions still saddled with the task of ending the Jewish War and capturing Jerusalem now becomes clear. By confronting the Vitellians with an army in good heart, numerically equal or superior to their own and capable of invading Italy if the blockade proved ineffective, Vespasian hoped to offer every inducement to the demoralized enemy to capitulate without a fight. That this highly desirable upshot was not in fact realized is no criticism of the strategy of Vespasian and his officers.

A policy which catered for a possible crossing of the Adriatic demanded the neutralization of the Italian fleets. Vespasian could count on the naval forces based in Egypt and the Black Sea (respectively at Alexandria, and at Trabzon in Pontus), and perhaps on detachments of the Italian fleets in the Sea of Marmara. The Syrian fleet based near the mouth of the Orontes, certainly in existence in Vespasian's reign, may well have owed its creation to the preparation of autumn 69. Later events, as well as the strategy outlined above, strongly suggest that Vespasian had made, or was making, approaches to the commanders at Ravenna and Miseno which were well received.

Next, recruiting arms and supplies. The availability of veterans in the East sprang from the close ties between the long static legions and local communities. Time-expired soldiers were naturally content, whether of Eastern origin themselves or not, to spend their retirement in a familiar setting, where the climate was acceptable, in contact with younger fellow-soldiers still serving; and on the other hand there are indications of local recruiting in the past, though of course Roman citizenship was a prerequisite. No such restriction applied to the auxiliary forces, who would also need to be expanded to make good the drain upon the legions. As for arms, a number of prosperous cities were selected for their manufacture, and at Antioch there was a mint which had duly struck coins of Galba and Otho, though not (owing to the short period between the news of Vitellius' accession known in May and the beginning of the anti-Vitellian movement soon after) of Vitellius. This mint was soon busy striking Vespasianic gold and silver currency to pay for war expenses. The coins showed an emblem already familiar at Antioch, the prow of Astarte's ship, which to a Roman observer might perhaps suggest the comfortable thought that the Eastern Mediterranean was already in Vespasian's control, as indeed it was.

Once the conference was over, all these preparations were rapidly put in hand in the various localities under the supervision of appropriate officials. But Vespasian himself, aware of the value of publicity, personally assumed the task of inspection and encouragement, praising the efficient rather than reproving the idle. As for his courtiers, he preferred to hide their weaknesses and not their merits. A number of promotions were made, and more might be hoped for when success was attained. Some men were made prefects and procurators, and a number, somewhat unconstitutionally, were granted senatorial rank. It accords with this that, deficient as our records are, we know of at least four orientals who entered the Senate in Vespasian's reign, and the trend was accentuated in the following century. But lavish bribery of the troops was avoided, though the emperor-to-be held out the prospect of a modest sum, payment being conditional upon services.[54]

It remained to cater for the defence of the eastern frontier. A mission was sent to Parthia and Armenia, and steps taken to safeguard the Euphrates frontier during the confrontation with Vitellius. Vologaeses I of Parthia wrote in friendly strain to Vespasian, calling himself 'Arsaces, King of Kings' and correctly addressing the Roman leader merely as 'Flavius Vespasianus'. Later, when it became clearer even in Parthia that the Flavian cause was succeeding, Vologaeses was more forthcoming. But it was reasonably clear already that neither Parthia nor Armenia had any interest in either rebuffing a future Roman emperor or, if Vespasian failed, stealing an advantage which they could not hope to retain. The prosecution of the siege of Jerusalem would be resumed in the spring and Vespasian decided that while he himself went to Alexandria, and if need be moved further along the coast to occupy the Roman province of Africa, the honour of delivering the coup de grâce in Judaea should go to Titus, assisted, as his relative youth and inexperience made advisable, by Tiberius Julius Alexander.

The latter was therefore relieved of the governorship of Egypt, and replaced, after a stop-gap, by L. Peducaeus Titus and his chief-of-staff
began their preparations forthwith, though the opening of the main
campaign would be in April.[55]

A document was also circulated to all the various armies and commanders throughout the empire which, among other things, urged the
stepping-up of the recruitment of ex-Othonian Praetorians, the bait
being of course re-admission to the Guard from which they had been
ejected by Vitellius. Indeed all competent soldiers and enthusiastic
supporters would be welcome. When the message reached Liguria, one
officer at least responded with alacrity: he was Gnaeus Julius Agricola
of Fréjus.

Early in August, Mucianus moved out of Antioch with the Sixth
Legion and the 13,000 assorted legionaries. His way lay through Cappadocia and Galatia to the Bosporus, and thereafter to the Adriatic. The
Anatolian portion of this long march, even by the shortest route via
Adana and Kayseri, amounts to 765 miles, at least fifty-one days' steady
foot-slogging. Excessive haste was unnecessary, since what was envisaged was a spring campaign, and Mucianus knew enough about
orientals to suppose that as the dust rose over the open plains of the
Anatolian plateau, rumour might acceptably magnify his strength. By
early October, he was a hundred or so miles west of the Bosporus in
Thrace, moving along the Egnatian Way in the direction of Durrës and
the Achilles' heel of Italy.

8

The Second Battle of Cremona

The province of Pannonia was bounded on the north by the knee of the Danube from a point a little to the east of Vienna to the confluence of the River Sava and the Danube at Belgrade: here Moesia began. Its southern limit, towards Dalmatia, followed the Bosnian mountains along a line south of the Sava to Istria and the Julian Alps. It thus embraced much of the courses of this river and of the Drava, the lakes of Balaton and Neusiedl, the wooded hills of Slovenia and the more open and gently undulating plains of western Hungary. Economically and politically it could not at this date be called highly developed. This was frontier territory. In the oak forests lurked bears, boars and wild cats. The broad acres towards the Danube had hardly been exploited. But that its geographical position, contiguous to the Alps and linking, like them, the Rhine and Danube, gave it an importance for the Roman empire is proved by the presence in it of two legions in the autumn of 69: VII Galbiana lay at Petronell on the south bank of the Danube thirty miles east of Vienna; and the Thirteenth, on the south bank of the Drava, looked across the river to the citadel hill of Ptuj, a key point on the road from Ljubljana to Szombathely and Petronell.

Pannonia's importance for our story, however, arises from its possessing a legionary garrison nearer to Italy than any other. From Ptuj to the Julian Alps is a mere 150 miles by an easy road, and its fellow Petronell was only another 180 miles further off by an even flatter route: contrast the relative remoteness of Windisch, separated from Italy by some 300 miles and the Alps around the Great St Bernard. A circle whose centre is Rome and upon whose circumference stands Ptuj cuts the valley of the Dora Baltea well within Italy, between Ivrea and Aosta. Augustus himself had been much concerned to strengthen this weak point in Italy's defences against non-Roman invaders. At his death in A.D. 14 a further complication arose: a dangerous mutiny of the Pannonian legionaries themselves. The story of this movement as told by Tacitus in the first book of the *Annals* makes it clear that at that time it was the practice to hold late-summer manoeuvres of the united Pannonian legionary forces in the neighbourhood of Ljubljana, obviously an exercise designed to test the defences of the Birnbaumer

Wald (Hrušica) where the road to Italy meets in the Karst range its only considerable obstacle. It seems likely that a similar exercise in the late summer of 69 brought VII Galbiana and XIII together in circumstances where contact between the commanders was feasible and unobtrusive. In August came Vespasian's circular letter addressed to all commanders and announcing his recognition in the East. It was read to a mass parade of the troops and expressions of opinion were canvassed. Many officers thought it advisable to confine themselves to ambiguous generalities which could later be glossed to suit events. But there was one who provided a striking exception, one who showed his hand openly in favour of Vespasian and called for immediate action in words which clearly corresponded with the general feeling of the troops. This was the commander of VII Galbiana, Antonius Primus, destined to play the leading role in the remaining months of the year, his memorial the third book of Tacitus' *Histories*. Such heroes perform great deeds, seldom to their own ultimate advantage.

Antonius was born at Toulouse about A.D. 20, and all we know of his appearance—in default of the portrait prized years later by his young admirer Martial, who kept it poetically garlanded with violets and roses—is what we can deduce from his nickname 'Beaky' (*Beccus*) and from indications of commanding physique, stature and presence. His early career is a blank, but it was certainly senatorial, and his *nomen* Antonius suggests the enfranchisement, during Mark Antony's Gallic period in 43 B.C., of a Toulousain family supporting his faction. In A.D. 61, as his enemies tirelessly reminded their hearers and readers, he was ejected from the Senate by Nero on the ground (which by a law of Sulla inflicted *infamia*) that he had connived at witnessing a forged will designed to secure to conspirators the fortune of an elderly and childless capitalist. The action seems a little out of character, and the offence may have been a technical one. A new check upon forgery had been discovered in Nero's reign. Every testament now contained three waxed tablets. Of the six sides thus presented, the first and sixth contained the title of the document and the seals of witnesses, the second and third the names of witnesses and the fourth and fifth the text of the will. Its terms could then be kept invisible to the witnesses who guaranteed its authenticity, the identity of the witnesses was established by their full names, and the genuineness of the whole document attested by the passing of a thread three times through two matching holes pierced in each of the tablets, followed by the sealing. Furthermore, no one drafting a will for anybody else might insert in it a legacy for himself. An infringement or neglect of any of these elaborate new provisions would certainly catch some victims, and Antonius appears to have been among them. He was condemned to the relatively easy punishment of exile from the dominions of the Roman people, and Marseille—technically a free city—would have been a convenient and agreeable retreat for a Toulousain. In 68 he promptly joined Galba in the guise of a victim of Nero. The new emperor was in no position to make elaborate researches into the details of the Roman Newgate Calendar, but he could well do with enterprising officers. Antonius recovered his senatorial rank and was given command of the new legion; and whatever Galba's need for supporters this sudden promotion seems to show that the stickler for discipline was not unduly disturbed by Antonius' alleged offence. Antonius with his men accompanied Galba to Rome, but was almost immediately thereafter sent off with them to the Pannonian camp at Petronell, vacated by its previous occupants the Tenth, who were pleased enough to get back to the Spain they knew so well. Galba's exchange of formations seemed at the time to secure a double advantage of gratitude and self-defence: it was to prove fateful in a way he could not have imagined. We have seen that Otho's order to move came too late for Antonius to provide at Cremona the support he had already offered to Galba's successor, and he took no part in the spring fighting. From Este he and VII Galbiana were sent back to the Danube. For the moment he was foiled; but now, four months later, it seemed that his luck was about to turn.[56]

In the latter part of August and shortly after the reading of Vespasian's letter, the governor of Pannonia, his legionary legates, some centurions and representatives of the other ranks met in Ptuj at the headquarters of XIII to consider what action should be taken in the light of the legions' declared support for Vespasian. Knowledge of Vespasian's proposed strategy, if not of the tenor of the deliberations at Beirut, was available, but much must have been unclear. It seemed that the Pannonian legions were to block the Julian Alps, but not advance into Italy beyond Aquileia. On that line they would await, so Vespasian ordered, the arrival of Mucianus on the Adriatic, whether in Istria or further south opposite the heel of Italy. Further movements would be decided in the light of events. There was no reason why the blockade should not be effective, and in that case a physical invasion of Italy in the spring could hardly meet with serious resistance.

The plan was acceptable enough to Tampius Flavianus. It was less attractive to troops who had cast themselves for the profitable role of liberators. Moreover, on purely strategical considerations there were objections to several months' delay, and these were strongly put to the conference at Ptuj. It would be dangerous to fritter away the present enthusiasm and allow Vitellius a breathing space to get his troops into shape during the autumn. He had already called for auxiliary reinforcements from the Rhineland and their arrival must be prevented. A position upon the Julian Alps could be easily turned by a naval expedition from Ravenna or Ancona. Supplies might become difficult, especially if Mucianus' force were added to their own. Most serious of

all, it must be remembered, said Antonius, that if Caecina and Valens
had penetrated Italy in early spring, followed by Vitellius, then reinforcements from Germany, Gaul and Britain could and probably
would flow in before the winter to give Vitellius a very decided numerical superiority. At the most optimistic reckoning and at the cost of
stripping the frontier of legionary defences, the Flavian cause could only
muster the best part of nine legions (2 from Pannonia, 1 from Dalmatia,
3 from Moesia, 3 from the East). This army, when once assembled (and
how long would that take?), would certainly outnumber the present
garrison of Italy, about five legions. But with each passing week the
chances were growing that the balance of advantage would be tilted
against the Flavians. Before the winter began, the odds might well be in
Vitellius' favour. Antonius, who felt that Otho had thrown away the
moral certainty of a victory by procrastination and faintheartedness,
called for invasion forthwith, while northern Italy was only lightly held
by Vitellian auxiliaries. Possession of the plains of Piedmont, Lombardy
and Veneto would enable the Flavians to seal off all the Alpine passes
against the Vitellian provinces. 'All I ask for, gentlemen, is this,' exclaimed Antonius in his peroration: 'give me a few auxiliary cohorts
now and I guarantee to open up Italy and let in the legions without a
blow struck.'

This carefully-reasoned and impassioned argument aroused intense
enthusiasm. Even cautious and wary officers were swept off their feet by
Antonius' powerful personality and eloquence, to say nothing of the
logic of his strategy. He was hailed as the one real man and leader. It
was easy, in the light of what followed, to dismiss the hesitations of
Tampius Flavianus and others as mealy-mouthed and chicken-hearted.

Yet Tampius had every reason to walk warily. If his attitude was
ambiguous, it was not necessarily that of a poltroon; and many men in
authority must have found themselves in similar predicaments. Appointed governor of Pannonia by Galba (as we may justifiably assume),
he promptly recognized Otho. The adhesion of the governor, dependent
in the delicate circumstances upon the attitude of the troops, must have
taken place immediately, for though the mileages involved make it
likely that Otho could not have heard of the support of XIII before
7 February, or of VII Galbiana before 14 February, already on 26
February Tampius was rewarded by a notable honour accorded *in
absentia*: the minutes of the meeting of the Brethren of the Fields for that
day (the first occasion since 30 January) record that in the presence of
the fraternity, including the vice-president, Otho's brother Titianus,
and the brother of Vitellius, L. Tampius Flavianus was co-opted in the
room of Servius Sulpicius Galba. But however faithful an adherent of
Galba and Otho, Tampius was also a relative of Vitellius. It was because of this that he was to be unfairly blamed by the troops who failed

to make Cremona in time for the First Battle. In the summer, when the overbearing attitudes of Vitellius' representatives and the pressure from III Gallica in favour of Vespasian led to unrest among his troops, the unfortunate governor found himself in a predicament which he could not solve. He resigned his command and made for Italy. Then, yielding to the appeal of his energetic financial secretary, Cornelius Fuscus, who had pursued his retreating superior, he agreed to return to Pannonia and provide the Flavian movement there with the prestige associated with a consular governor. The arguments by which Fuscus achieved this conversion are not recorded, but they can be readily imagined.

The pro-Antonian element of the Flavian historical tradition presents us with an unflattering portrait of Tampius: he was old, rich, indecisive and cowardly. He is a convenient butt for the ironies of Tacitus, no lover of many of his senatorial colleagues and predecessors. But Fuscus' eagerness to enlist his support speaks otherwise. His career continued with distinction under Vespasian. In 70/1 or 72/3 he was governor of Africa, in 73/4 superintendent of the Rome aqueducts. Soon after he received a second consulship. A highly fragmentary inscription found at Fondi relating to him and to his services on the Danube frontier (almost certainly in the autumn of 69) mentions the award of the *ornamenta triumphalia*, the substitute under the principate for the triumph of the republican commander of distinction. Tampius, too, served his country well.[57]

Thus the decision to invade Italy immediately was not such a clear-cut choice between vigour and sloth as it appears in the highly dramatic account of Tacitus. Even Antonius was aware of the risks. Apart from the danger of robbing one part of the frontier to hold another, he was acting without the sanction of Vespasian and indeed in conflict with his instructions. On the other hand he could plead that he and his brother-officers on the spot were necessarily better qualified to decide on immediate action than a superior two thousand miles and many weeks away. That Antonius' main fear—the likelihood of further Vitellian reinforcements from Germany and the west—proved groundless does not necessarily condemn his decision to live dangerously in September 69.

The council of war at Ptuj approved the immediate invasion of Italy by Antonius Primus; he would command a modest auxiliary force and take Arrius Varus as his cavalry commander. If this strike were successful, the legions would follow.

The decision was fateful, no less than those of Vitellius on 3 January and of Otho a week later. It was to have momentous consequences unpredictable and undesired. From it flowed the course of events that led to a second bitter conflict at Cremona, the sack of that city, the bloody occupation of Rome, the death of Vitellius, of his brother and of the brother of Vespasian, and—most sinister prefiguration of doom in the eyes of distant observers—the destruction of the national shrine of Rome. Rome's unparalleled sufferings in 69 hardly confirmed divine benevolence. They indeed supplied proof, says the eloquent historian, that the gods, however indifferent to Rome's tranquillity, were eager enough to punish her sins. The curse of Romulus and Remus still pursued their descendants.

On a date which might be argued to be about 20 August, an appeal was sent in writing to Aponius Saturninus to bring up the army of Moesia at top speed. That governor, more decided or more reckless than Flavianus, needed no prompting. His rapid arrival at Verona (by 15 October) makes it probable, on a careful calculation of dates and distances, that he was, even in August, prepared to mobilize and march fast. Stimulated by the enthusiasm of the Third (Gallic) Legion for Vespasian, he may well already have edged the two lower legions, III and VIII, towards the west of his province. So, despite the extra distance, they arrived in northern Italy on the heels of the Pannonian formations.[58]

Antonius Primus and his colleagues realized that some precautions were after all necessary to ensure that a frontier where auxiliary forces would have to be brought in to man the legionary forts should remain unmolested. The lower Danube seemed quiet after the invasion of the spring. The corridor of flat ground between the Rivers Tisza and Danube (the Bácska of the Hungarians and the Bačka of the Yugoslavs) was then inhabited by Sarmatian horsemen from southern Russia called the Iazyges, who had arrived and settled in the open and fruitful plain some twenty or thirty years previously. Their chiefs, possessing absolute power in the community, were enrolled in the Flavian army, ostensibly as an honour, in reality to serve as hostages for the good behaviour of their tribe; but an offer from the Iazygan leaders to contribute a force of cavalry for the campaign was diplomatically refused as too dangerous. Further west up the Danube, north of the river and between the longitudes of Esztergom and Vienna, lay the client-kingdom of Vannius, a branch of the German Suebi, then ruled by Sido and Italicus. These potentates, like their predecessors, had long shown fidelity to Rome, and in this instance kings and people alike were taken into the Flavian army. Towards Germany, the front was constituted by the River Inn marking the border between the Vitellian Raetia (closely linked with the nearby legionary camp of Windisch) on the west, and, on the east, the friendly province of Noricum, roughly equivalent in extent to modern Austria less the Tirol and the Vorarlberg. Sextilius Felix, governor of Noricum, was instructed to occupy the bank of the Inn, whose importance had already been underlined by the action during February of Petronius Urbicus in breaking the bridges at Innsbruck–Wilten and Langenpfunzen near Rosenheim. No contact was made in this theatre with the opposing forces, for the Rhineland had its own problems nearer home. But, though the threat here never materialized, it would have been absurd, unless one possessed second sight, to attempt to occupy Veneto in September without securing one's rear in the Alpine area. In this respect the Flavians at Ptuj acted with marked prudence. The same, however, cannot be said of the promptness with which Saturninus, obeying or anticipating the call from Ptuj, stripped the lower Danube of its legionary forces.

As soon as the conference broke up, Antonius Primus moved out his auxiliary strike force of infantry and cavalry south-westwards. Topographically there were only two possible obstacles: on the road to Italy the hills between Celje and Ljubljana, and the Karst range west of the latter town. Neither—and they were both within the province of Pannonia—caused delay or suggested danger. The small force moved rapidly, crossed the Italian frontier on the Birnbaumer Wald, whose road summit is only one half the height of the Great St Bernard Pass mastered by Caecina in winter, and within a week had without incident occupied Aquileia, the prosperous harbour at the head of the Adriatic. Beyond the vast stony bed of the Tagliamento the road westward divided at Concordia south of Portogruaro, the right arm of the fork, the Postumian Way, making for Vicenza and Verona, the left for Altino (near Mestre) and Padova. These routes, if pursued southwestwards, would take one across the Po at Cremona and Ostiglia respectively, and provided some of the lowest crossings of the river by bridge. On the Postumian, Oderzo a little short of the Piave was taken, but the main spearhead turned towards Ostiglia. Everywhere the invaders were warmly welcomed. It was desirable to have an emblem for the new cause which could be publicly exhibited. Antonius had no stock of likenesses of Vespasian, had he even been recognizable to the local populace, but with ready ingenuity he gave orders that the busts of Galba, hurriedly put in store in January and carefully preserved, should be dusted down and replaced in the piazzas. The Flavians, it seemed, came as the avengers of the martyr-emperor, the bringers of sober and stable government.

A garrison was left at Altino owing to its accessibility from Ravenna, whose fleet, though thought to be lukewarm towards Vitellius, might still offer a threat or require a leader, and soon after a cavalry regiment under Memmius Rufinus was pushed forward as far as Adria on the Lower Tartaro only fifty miles from Ravenna. Padova and Este quickly opened their gates. At the latter spot it was learnt that three Vitellian cohorts and a cavalry regiment (the Sebosian) were encamped by a bridge which they had built over the Adige, probably at Legnago, possibly a little lower down at Castagnaro. These simple-minded troops seemed to be unaware of the approaching hurricane. There was a good chance of winning the crossing by surprise. At first light the Flavians fell upon the enemy while their victims were still largely unarmed. Instructions had been given that only a few should be killed and the rest frightened into charging sides. In fact some surrendered immediately, though more succeeded in halting the Flavian advance by cutting the pontoon bridge. And there were still the wide marshes of the ill-defined Tartaro to negotiate before reaching the Po. Quickly abandoning this thrust, Antonius decided to exploit the slightly longer route towards Cremona.[59]

The occupation of Padova on 3 September and the general welcome extended to Antonius had by now been reported to Ptuj, whence the legions were set in motion according to the agreed plan. On 23 September or thereabouts the Seventh (Galbian)—Antonius' own legion—and Thirteenth (Twin) arrived at Padova after a brisk march, and spent a few days here, resting after the hard slog. In consultation with Vedius Aquila commanding the Thirteenth, Antonius decided that Padova, large and prosperous though it was, seemed too exposed to possible naval attack and too far off the now chosen Cremona route to serve as a base. Verona, no less a city, offered superior advantages, lying directly on the Postumian fifty miles to the west. On three sides the town is surrounded by a loop of the Adige, while across the river to the north the ground rises immediately to form the tip of a finger of mountain stretching down from the Alps. Only to the south is there unimpeded access, and this the Flavians now had troops enough to bar. It was a large town, well able to feed, at any rate for a time, a considerable force. Above all, it commanded the descent into the plain from the Brenner and the Reschen–Scheidegg Passes; a dozen points in the north-south valley of the Adige above it could offer strong positions of defence against the dreaded incursion from Germany. Admittedly, Antonius' fears in this respect proved to be groundless, for reasons which he could hardly have known. But Verona was still an excellent choice. From it radiated the Postumian Way (backwards towards Pannonia, forwards to Cremona) and a main road to Ostiglia in the south-east. During the move from Padova to Verona, the Flavians passed through little Vicenza, birthplace of Caecina. The omens seemed good.

Meanwhile, what of that general and his colleague Valens? On 1 September the two entered office as colleagues in a suffect consulship due to last two months. There was no reason for them to expect immediate danger. The emperor's birthday celebrations on 7 September, attended and directed by his two consuls and lieutenants, proved the last glint of the Vitellian sun. A day or so later came news that Antonius had entered Italy. The gathering clouds would soon obscure in darkness and death the good days, the pleasant memories, the junketings, the profitable deals. Already as the strains intensify, a rift is developing between the pliable Caecina and the determined Valens. In reconstructing events, some historians writing a little after the Long Year believed that Caecina's loyalty was first undermined by remarks dropped by the Urban prefect Flavius Sabinus, the brother of Vespasian. It would certainly have been consistent with Sabinus' pacific character to attempt to avoid a collision between Roman armies; and Caecina's acceptability to Vespasian after 69 seems to attest gratitude for services rendered. It was easy enough to exploit the man's jealous spitefulness towards Valens, who he thought stood higher in Vitellius' esteem than he himself.

On or about 17 September (at a time when Antonius was already at Este), Caecina at last got the army moving northwards out of Rome. He was given an effusive and gratifying send-off by Vitellius. Once out of the capital, Caecina sent on part of his cavalry in advance to secure the familiar and friendly city of Cremona. The remainder formed his own vanguard. Then came the drafts from the First, Fourth, Fifteenth and Sixteenth Legions, and after these the Fifth and Twenty-Second. The rearguard consisted of the Twenty-First (Hurricane) and First (Italian), accompanied by elements of the three British legions and by selected auxiliaries.

Valens, however, had been immobilized by illness. Once Caecina had gone, he had misgivings. He sent orders to the army which had been under his command (that is, the First (Italian), the main body of the Fifth, and the drafts from the army of Lower Germany, those of the First, Fifteenth and Sixteenth Legions) to wait for him on the Flaminian Way: this, he said (no doubt truthfully), was what had been agreed between Caecina and himself. But Caecina had other views. He was on the spot and held the trump cards. He pretended that the plan had indeed been made, but had been altered subsequently so as to permit of their deploying their full forces against the enemy penetration. Such a strategy was obviously plausible, and Caecina was obeyed. So some of the legions were hurried on to Cremona, and others told to make for the nearer Ostiglia. All travelled together as far as Bologna, and before that moment Caecina had left his legions and turned off to Ravenna, ostensibly to address the men of the fleet. In fact, his intention was to discuss the whole political and military situation with its commander Sextus Lucilius Bassus, of whose misgivings about a resumption of the fighting he may already have had some inkling through Flavius Sabinus. It is more than probable that Vespasian's brother should have been kept aware of any written approach by Vespasian to the fleet and army commanders. Feelers put out to Bassus had not been rejected; and Caecina could now take the matter further; indeed, if he contemplated a change of allegiance, the support and agreement of the fleet based in his rear would be essential. As for Bassus, he had his own reasons for disliking Vitellius. Previously commander of a cavalry regiment, he had suffered illusions of grandeur on joining Vitellius: hoping for the post of Praetorian prefect, he took umbrage when given a lesser though considerable appointment, the command of both Italian fleets, one at Ravenna, one at Miseno. Moreover many of the Ravenna sailors came from Dalmatia and Pannonia, provinces which had declared for Vespasian and in which they had relatives who were now in a sense hostages.

During the conversations between these two would-be turncoats, datable as they are to the period between 2 and 10 October, it must have become known that Flavian legions were already at Padova or Verona. A second civil war was unwelcome for better reasons than seem to have prompted this vain and ambitous couple; and it was hard for anybody in his senses to imagine that Vitellius would prove a better leader than Vespasian. Patriotism and selfishness worked in harness. The bargain was struck. Bassus would bring over the fleet to Vespasian soon after Caecina had left, and on receipt of the news Caecina would attempt the rather more difficult task of swinging the legions at Ostiglia to the Flavian side. One slight difficulty arose from a doubt about Antonius Primus: how far was this impetuous—and successful—condottiere apprised of, and acting under, Vespasian's instructions? Some delicate negotiation would be required of Caecina. Once this was done and the plot successfully executed, both he and Bassus could claim credit for promoting an inevitable victory. Their calculations proved largely correct. Caecina and Bassus were to profit under the new master, and were described by the Flavian historians as 'patriots', inspired by a 'concern for peace'. The humbug attracts a bitter comment from Tacitus, placed strategically at a point in his narrative where it would linger in the mind of the reader—the end of the second book of the *Histories*.

On 12 October Caecina caught up with his legions at Ostiglia and made them encamp a little to the north of the town in a position where they commanded the approaches to the Po bridge, yet were themselves protected by the wide belt of marshy land through which wandered the lazy Tartaro. The enemy, if he decided to attempt the crossing here, could only approach along the banks of the Po from east or west, or by a single highway piercing the marches and coming from Verona, partly along the upper Tartaro. Caecina's chosen site was strong, almost impregnable, and provided that Cremona was held by the other portion of his army, promised to be as good a base as that of the Flavians at Verona thirty miles away. If Antonius proved uncooperative or demanded impossibly high terms, Caecina could still make things difficult for him. He would be bargaining from a position of strength.

But Antonius' hand had also been strengthened by the arrival of

Aponius Saturninus with one of his legions, VII Claudia, temporarily commanded—in the regrettable absence of Tettius Julianus—by one of its staff officers, the honest, competent and educated Vipstanus Messalla, to whose memoirs, in part transmitted by Tacitus' sombre lens, we owe a more than usually accurate picture of these days.

It is not surprising that the negotiations between Caecina and Antonius, though they ran smoothly enough, lasted several days. They were initiated by Caecina when, on 13 October, he received news that Bassus had successfully brought off his coup.

At Ravenna a meeting of the plotters had been held in the headquarters building of the Portus Augusti, which lay a little to the southeast of the town, on the right bank of the modern Fiumi Uniti and not far from the future site of the sixth-century church of S. Apollinare in Classe Fuori. Bassus himself was not present, but awaited the upshot in the commander's residence. Agreement reached, the captains removed the portraits of Vitellius to be found in the base and quickly overcame the slight resistance offered. Bassus then appeared and attempted to put himself at the head of the mutineers. But though the men readily accepted Vespasian as emperor, they were less happy with Bassus as his representative. It was decided to offer the command to an officer of the invading Flavian army. Cornelius Fuscus, the procurator of Dalmatia and Pannonia, apparently awaiting such a summons at Altino, speedily hurried forward to take over. This smooth transition argues a good deal of preparation, and an early approach to the Ravenna fleet by Vespasian himself, whose personal envoy, the imperial freedman and civil servant Hormus, now makes his appearance as a man of authority. As for Bassus, he was taken in a fast ship under open arrest as far as Adria which lay on a canal communicating with the Po, near its mouth, where he was at first closely confined by the local Flavian commander (obviously not in the diplomatic picture), but later released by the intervention of Hormus. Bassus, like the other discarded leaders, in due course received his modest reward, the restored command of both the Ravenna and Miseno fleets.

Caecina could now negotiate with Antonius with greater security to himself, but with some weakening of his bargaining position. However, Antonius was sensible of the advantage to be gained by the prospect of an unopposed crossing of the Po by the Ostiglia bridge and by the very considerable accession of strength which Caecina's defection would bring to the cause. Caecina for his part avoided any hostile move, and his proposals were couched in accommodating language, stressing the folly of civil war, hinting at the danger of further influxes from Germany, and carefully omitting all reference to Vitellius and Vespasian. In reply Antonius pointed out the strong position of the Flavians, already the object of a warm welcome in many Italian towns, and soon to be massively reinforced. But Caecina and his army must openly acknowledge Vespasian as emperor and take an oath of loyalty to him. No promises could be made concerning Vitellius, whose fate would be decided by Vespasian. However, promotions made recently and concessions accorded to the troops would be honoured by the new régime. It was also to be understood that Bassus accepted these terms.

This correspondence, publicly read to the Flavian troops at Verona, boosted their high morale. Negotiations were already in train when the two remaining Moesian legions appeared: III led by Dillius Aponianus and VIII by Numisius Lupus. Additional numbers made it both necessary and practicable to construct or extend a large camp on the undefended southern side of the city, which in the period since Augustus had spread far beyond the Augustan city walls, whose position is indicated by the still existing Porta dei Borsari. An earthen rampart was constructed along the line of the nineteenth-century Adigetto canal, almost a mile long, linking the southern ends of the two parallel reaches of the river. But the presence of two governors and four other legionary commanders put in question the authority of Antonius. It was answered by the undisguised preference of the troops for a unified command under Antonius, and by a sharp reaction against the claims of the consulars to assert themselves. Both Tampius Flavianus and Aponius Saturninus were in peril of their lives. One evening, owing to a silly misunderstanding, ill will against Flavianus came violently to the surface, and a mob assailed him. The unfortunate man behaved badly, grovelling on the ground, his clothes torn, his chest heaving and his lips quivering with inarticulate cries for mercy. In an attempt to save the governor from physical assault, Antonius ordered his arrest and got him away the same night. Soon after leaving Verona, Flavianus encountered a message from Vespasian which consoled and protected him: the emperor had summoned, or at least complimented, the governor of Pannonia. Indeed he survived the disgraceful episode at Verona (long a good story in military messes) to render notable service to the new master and to win a second consulship. On the following morning, another disorderly scene led to the expulsion of Saturninus when the men surrounded the mansion on the outskirts in which he was staying. Their intended victim escaped, less thanks to the efforts of Antonius and the commanders of III and VII Claudia than to his going to ground in a highly undignified lair. Creeping on all fours into the furnace house of an unoccupied villa nearby, he lay motionless on the cold ash between the pillars of the dark place until the pursuit died down. Later he made his escape to Padova, and thence, we may assume, to Egypt. It is possible, though not certain, that he too retained the favour of Vespasian despite the strange allegations in the Tettius Julianus affair, and the endangering of the Danube frontier.[60]

The disappearance of the two consulars, the backing of his brother officers and the enthusiastic support of the men now gave Antonius the undisputed leadership and secured for the Flavian cause in Italy the overwhelming advantage of a determined and unified strategy put into effect by forces numerically and morally superior. There were of course a few backbiters; and later controversy claimed that Antonius had fomented both disorders for his own advantage.

At Ostiglia, the coup which Caecina, satisfied with Antonius' terms, now attempted to pull off was risky, for he was dealing with the fanatical and interested devotion to Vitellius of an army the larger part of which looked to Valens rather than to himself as leader. On the morning of 18 October, when the troops were scattered on their various training and maintenance duties, Caecina summoned the senior centurions and a few representatives of the rank and file to his headquarters. There he put his cards on the table, speaking highly of Vespasian's qualifications and of the strength he enjoyed. The Ravenna fleet had changed sides, the supply situation would soon be subject to the blockade, Gaul and Spain were thoroughly disaffected, and Vitellius had made a poor showing as emperor. Those who were already in the plot took the lead in swearing allegiance to Vespasian, and before the rest could recover from their surprise, Caecina made them do so too. Vitellius' portraits were removed from the standards and his name from public view. Word was sent to Antonius that all was well.

When the main body of the legionaries returned for the evening meal, however, the situation rapidly changed. The removal of Vitellius' name and of the medallions representing him was immediately noticed, and rumour quickly retailed the events of the morning. A crowd gathered round the headquarters, and after a moment of profound and sinister silence, exploded in protest. Led by the Fifth Legion—that which had taken the lead at Vetera on 1 January in favour of Vitellius—the men replaced the portraits, put Caecina under close arrest, and elected as their leaders Fabius Fabullus, the commander of the Fifth, and the camp commandant, Cassius Longus. The unlucky crews of three Ravenna galleys, who happened to be at Ostiglia on detachment, were murdered out of hand. The legions of Germany were in no mood to throw away the fruits of the spring campaign, in no mood to deal gently with those who wished to rat. Perhaps only the fact that Caecina was known to enjoy the favour of Vitellius and was not only general but consul saved him from sudden death.

That evening the heavens themselves betokened their anger with Caecina—or with his troops. The moon itself was turned to blood. Its eclipse, which entered its maximum phase of near totality at 9.50 p.m., four hours after dusk, give it a sinister copper-coloured appearance as the light of the sun, drained of its blue component, was refracted round

the earth by the latter's atmosphere, and fell dimly upon the almost full
orb of the moon. This must surely be a portent of disaster and death:
but whose?

Alarming to the ignorant, the heavenly phenomenon was much less
terrifying to Fabullus and Longus than the very down-to-earth responsibility thrust upon them. They must decide immediately upon the best
way to adapt the fighting spirit of the troops to the facts of the strategical situation. The textbook remedy was to withdraw by night, leaving
campfires lit to mislead the enemy. For one had to assume the possibility, indeed the probability, that the Ravenna fleet, in concert with
Antonius, would send ships up the Po and Tartaro to cut communications between Ostiglia and the outside world, particularly Cremona;
and the encirclement by the fleet would probably coincide with an
offensive mounted from Verona with troops now decidedly outnumbering their own. Clearly, Ostiglia was no longer tenable. Fabullus and
Longus quickly concluded that with maximum speed and secrecy they
must move their forces to join those at Cremona. One day, 19 April,
had to suffice for deliberation and preparation.

During the night the army marched out as quietly as possible to
Ostiglia. At first light on the next day, the river was crossed, and the
pontoon bridge cut and rendered unusable, at any rate temporarily.
Within the next five days (20–24 October), the legions completed the
100-mile march at speed, covering about eighteen miles on each of the
first four days, and more on the fifth. This urgency was prompted by the
perfectly sound calculation that even though Antonius might not learn
of their departure until the evening of 20 October and could not move
instantly, he would be certain to try to defeat the small Cremona force
of 10,000 legionaries before those from Ostiglia reinforced it. In other
words, an attack on Cremona must be imminent. The distance between
Verona and Cremona was sixty-two miles. If one day were allowed
Antonius for preparation and three days for the march at top speed,
Antonius would be outside Cremona on the evening of 24 October.
This then was the time by which, at latest, the Vitellian rendezvous
must take place. Fabullus' route lay along the Aemilian Way, via
Reggio and Parma. The night of 23 April found him at Fidenza.
Twenty-four hours later, after a final day's march of thirty miles, his
forces crossed the Po and entered the city. Cremona was still just in
Vitellian hands. Piecemeal destruction had been avoided.

Antonius meanwhile had reacted much as Fabullus had supposed he
would. The news of the evacuation of Ostiglia, which reached him on
the evening of 20 April, was highly disturbing. The campaign was not
to be a picnic after all. A head-on collision between the total legionary
forces on either side might be inevitable: the plains of Cremona were
perhaps to recall the plains of Pharsalia, Modena, Philippi and other

fearful names of civil strife. It might be now too late to attempt to lure the Cremona garrison out in conditions favourable to the Flavians. But Antonius had information that Valens, about whose military capacity he was not in doubt and who was no Caecina, had recovered from his illness and left Rome on 25 September. Though he had so far been delayed en route, he would certainly hurry forward on hearing of Caecina's betrayal, and could be expected in the Po area in late October or early November. This further blow at least could be fore-stalled by fighting forthwith. There was still the Brenner to be feared, though there was no sign of immediate danger in that quarter. A few hours' debate was sufficient to secure agreement on the necessity of an immediate move of the whole army towards Cremona, and an attempt to destroy the Vitellians, piecemeal or en masse, before their morale recovered from the defection of Caecina and before Valens could arrive.

On 22–23 October the whole Flavian army moved along the Postumian Way to Bedriacum, a little to the west of the bridge over the Oglio, at a distance of forty miles from Verona and twenty-two from Cremona. A camp was made outside the village of Tornata, or that of April rebuilt. There were many to whom the spot seemed fateful. But Antonius was not the man to repeat the mistakes of April. It would be an error (even granted the very different numerical odds) to offer battle, as Otho had done, at a distance from one's own base and in proximity to the enemy's. Some quick and strong inducement must be found to lure the Vitellians out eastwards into the open country at once.

Something has already been said of this flat chequered land of corn and vine, whose nature conditioned the course of the Second, as of the First, Battle of Cremona. As the Flavian army marched south-west-wards from Verona, they traversed, between the rivers Mincio and Oglio, a corner of the territory of Mantua—the area which, one hundred and ten years previously, had been confiscated by Octavian to provide plots for his demobilized troops in a cruel redistribution of land that had cost Virgil's father, like many others, his farm. It was along this very road that the carrier's van had carried the child to his school in Cremona. The process of centuriation—the systematic survey, divi-sion and distribution of farming land in neatly rectangular plots whose limits and sub-divisions are preserved today by tracks, roads, field boundaries and watercourses—is a phenomenon well known from literary sources and still strikingly visible (especially from the air) in certain areas of Italy and other Mediterranean lands governed by Rome. Relics of the Mantuan grid (on a NW–SE and SW–NE alignment slightly different from that of the Postumian Way as it traverses it) can be traced westwards as far as the Oglio. But once the Flavians had crossed the bridge near Mósio, they soon found themselves in the area of Bedriacum and within another grid, that of the Cremonese centuriation first detectable today, if you come from the east, on the south side of Calvatone. Tornata itself stands upon a north-south *limes* (*cardo*) of this grid, and over many miles to the west the Postumian Way coincides with a main *decumanus* (east-west *limes*) of the same. The rectangles of the Cremonese grid (contemporary with that of Mantua and datable equally to 40 B.C.) measured, according to Frontinus and Hyginus, 210 *iugera*, that is, an area of 709 by 740 metres (21 by 20 *actus*, each measuring 35·48 metres). This grid (on an ESE–WNW and SSW–NNE alignment) extends to the northern outskirts of Cremona, whose streets, however, reflect an earlier orientation, that of its foundation in 218 B.C., and are tilted in yet another direction. The substantial accuracy of our literary information and the care of the Roman surveyors are proved by a detailed study of the Cremona–Bedriacum area. Then, as now, this land was rich; tidily parcelled out to the soldiers whose heirs or successors now tilled the plain, it constituted a large part of the wealth of Cremona. It was now to be a means to lure the enemy from behind the walls of city and camp.

Antonius sent his auxiliary cohorts into the countryside on either side of the highroad with orders to burn and plunder the farms as obtrusively as possible: the rising columns of smoke would instantaneously convey the message to Cremona. He himself moved forward with 4,000 cavalry to a point eight miles from the Bedriacum camp and fourteen from Cremona: here the Postumian Way changes direction to follow the main *decumanus* towards Cremona. His position, immediately south of Casa d'Andrea, can be fixed. Immediately behind him to the east a fork permitted rapid communication on two or more routes with Bedriacum. Some reconnaissance parties were sent on to probe the Postumian Way westwards.

The reaction he had expected was quick to come. During the morning of 24 October the signs of destruction had already prompted an urgent demand by the Cremonese that I Italica and XXI Hurricane, the two full legions sent on by Caecina to hold the town, should move out to prevent further losses to the farmers, inflicted, as it seemed, by a merely auxiliary force. At approximately 11 a.m. a scout galloped up to Antonius with the news that the Vitellian army was approaching, headed by a small advance party of cavalry. But the movement of a large force could be heard over a wide area. Antonius held a quick consultation with his staff. The plan was going according to expectations. A message was sent to the legions at Bedriacum telling them to arm and advance. By noon, no later, they were on the move, clear proof that there was no surprise. As for the auxiliary infantry spread about the countryside, a trumpet call was sounded, and repeated by each unit in turn to its neighbour, to indicate that they should drop every-thing and close in on the Postumian Way at the nearest point.

While Antonius was issuing these orders, Arrius Varus, without per-mission, it seems, dashed out with a spearhead of cavalry to confront the Vitellian advance guard. After initial success, exploited recklessly, he was thrown back, and though Antonius correctly left a gap in his main force to allow the fugitives to pass through into safety, the pursuing Vitellians were so close behind that the breach could not be closed in time, and the whole body of Flavian cavalry was thrown off its balance. Wounded or unscathed, they all fled, jockeying for position on the narrow Postumian Way and the other *decumani*, especially that upon which the village of Recórfano now stands. In this moment of chaos and demoralization Antonius did whatever a commander possessing pre-sence of mind and courage could. Finally he put a spear through a retreating ensign, seized the flag and turned with it to face the enemy. Some troopers—not more than 100—were shamed by the incident into standing their ground. The spot helped. The road narrowed at this point, and the bridge over the Delmona near Voltido, perhaps de-molished in the spring, was still down. The banks of the stream were steep and fell some eight feet below the level of the surrounding country, while the bed, lacking a clean masonry bottom, was of slippery mud. Here the pursuers were held. Antonius, ever resilient, was quick to press an advantage which soon developed into the wholesale rout of the Vitellians. The foragers joined in the harrying. The pursuit took the Flavians ten miles, as far as a point rather more than four miles from Cremona. Here—it was now afternoon—they caught sight of a glint of light through the trees as the westering sun picked out the silver standard-tips of the enemy. The Italian and Hurricane Legions had marched out as far as this during the hour or so occupied by the initial success of their cavalry. But their commanders (identity unknown) were not as good as Antonius. They failed to part and close ranks to admit the refugees and hold off the pursuit. Their front line wavered. The Flavian cavalry charged, closely followed by Messalla leading some Moesian auxiliaries, their rapid pace matched by many of the legionaries, presumably mounted on this occasion. Thus a mixed force of cavalry and infantry broke the Vitellians, who made for the shelter (all too near for desperate courage) of their camp and city. Antonius broke off the pursuit.

At about 5 p.m., as the light of the October afternoon was fading, the Flavian infantry arrived in full strength. Since noon they had covered almost eighteen miles along the endless ribbon of the Postumian. Despite the inevitable weariness, morale was high. The cavalry en-counter had gone well, and it was now the legions' turn. There was a strong demand for an immediate assault, which Antonius had the ut-

PLATE 7　A Roman
secondary road in the
Vosges

PLATE 8　The Postumian
Way in northern Italy

PLATE 9 Auxiliary
infantrymen in
conversation

PLATE 10 Part of the bronze
facing of a military chest
belonging to a unit of the
Fourth (Macedonian) Legion,
lost at Cremona on
25 October 69

most difficulty in preventing. Indeed his appeal to considerations of
common prudence seemed likely to fall on deaf ears, had not news
arrived that changed the whole course of the encounter. While riding
right up to the walls of Cremona, and therefore into the outer suburbs
of the town, some Flavian cavalrymen had captured a few townsfolk. On
interrogation these pro-Vitellian simpletons gleefully boasted that some
23,000 legionaries from Ostiglia had arrived: these, the 8,000 from
Britain, the full Fifth and the 10,000 drafted from the other legions in
Germany, had come in over the Po from the south and east, having
covered thirty miles that very day, and on hearing of the defeat of their
comrades were at that moment arming for battle and would soon be at
the Flavians' throats. The information secured Antonius instant
obedience.

He caused the advanced elements to move back some two miles along
the Postumian Way, through the very area in which the spring battle
had been chaotically fought. The men of the Thirteenth and some of
the ex-Othonian Praetorians knew these roads and fields only too well.
Vedius Aquila, too, the commander of the former, was there to impress
upon his colleague, had such a lesson been required, the need, this
time, for orderly deployment. Despite the darkness this was in large
measure achieved. Antonius allotted the Thirteenth itself a key position
astride the Postumian Way—only about eighteen feet wide, with
ditches on either side—at a point immediately south of the present-day
Casa de' Marozzi. In contact on its left, the Seventh (Galbian) occupied
open ground looking at the lie of the main road as it stretched athwart
their field of vision, receding from right to left towards the west—part
of the shallow dog-leg which harmonized the early course of the second-
century highway with the later centuriation grid. To the legions of
Pannonia Antonius had assigned the places of honour—and of danger.
Further to the south, the Moesian VII Claudia was protected by one of
the drainage ditches characteristic of the Po plain. This, the Dugale
Gambalone, here flows in from the west and follows for 700 metres the
line of the Casa de' Marozzi *cardo* towards the south and the great river.
Insignificant as it was and still is, a blue streak in the brown and green,
it provided with its deeply sunken banks and autumnal prickles a
formidable obstacle to close infantry fighting. Once down in that deep
and narrow ditch, a man would be helpless. South of this well-protected
formation lay auxiliary infantry. But on the north side of the Postumian
Way, the same *cardo* was held by the Eighth Legion without benefit of
cover, though now the massive walls of Marozzi cast a welcome shadow
on a hot day. After that came its Moesian fellow, the Third, split up in
a plantation of trees serving as vine props, and at the end some ex-
Othonian Praetorians and the remainder of the auxiliary infantry. The
cavalry were assigned the task of protecting the flanks and rear, and the

F

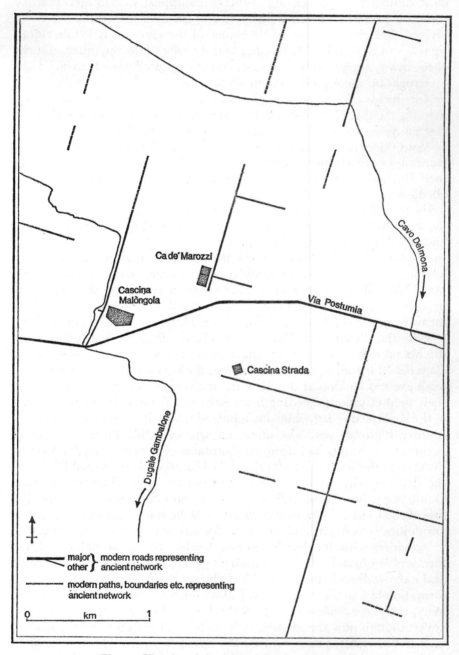

Fig. 4 The site of the Second Battle of Cremona

best of the Suebic horsemen moved up and down in advance of the line.

The Vitellians would have been well advised not to risk a night battle, for the Ostiglia legions were tired, and the Cremona garrison had already received hard knocks. But Roman endurance, the desperation of civil war, the encouragement of Cremona and conceivably the calculation that the enemy also had marched and suffered seemed to restore the balance of fatigue and failure. The Vitellian base was close, that of the Flavians far away; and numerically the former were at an advantage, having some 35,000 legionaries against the enemy's 25,000—though these proportions were not necessarily reflected in the auxiliary presence. And if the Ostiglia force had not even paused to take an evening meal, this was made good by the services of Cremonese women as vivandières, some losing their lives in the front line.

At about 8.30 p.m., by which time the Flavians were ready and in position, the Vitellians hurled themselves violently on their foe. Their centre, apparently assigned the task of splitting the Flavian army into two, was a powerful force of 15,000 legionaries: the men drafted from Britain, the Fifth Legion from Vetera and the detachment of XV from the same camp. The weak right consisted of 2,000 men of IIII Macedonica only, the left of XXII with the draft of 4,000 from the First and 2,000 from the Sixteenth (both from Lower Germany). Elements of the battered Italian and Hurricane Legions filled in the gaps, and the auxiliaries and cavalry had their usual role at the extremities.

Throughout the night the fighting was varied, indecisive and bitter, inflicting destruction on either side. The confusion normal in battle was at first increased by the darkness. For a time things went well for the Vitellians. In the vital central area their 15,000 legionaries faced the two formations: XIII on and around the road, VII Galbiana on the open ground immediately to its south. The more experienced and vindictive formation stood firm, but the Seventh was raw, despite Antonius' training, and had seen no battle experience, let alone Roman in action against Roman; and Antonius himself may have been elsewhere, his command now general. VII Galbiana suffered heavily. Six centurions of the leading companies were killed and a few manipular standards lost. Even the eagle was only saved by the desperate stand of the senior centurion Atilius Verus and at the cost, finally, of his own life. Antonius therefore stiffened the wavering line by transferring the Praetorians from their relatively quiet spot at the north end to the threatened area. After relieving the Seventh, they succeeded in driving the Vitellian centre back for the moment.

At 9.43 p.m. the moon rose and as it cleared the trees shed a deceptive glimmer upon the scene. Although approaching its last quarter, it was autumn-bright, and the sky was mostly cloudless. The eastern light exaggerated the shadows of the Flavians, confusing the aim of the Vitellians so that their shots fell short. Meanwhile the latter were brightly lit by the rays falling full on their faces, and presented an easy target for the small arrow- and stone-throwing ballistae of the Flavian legions. True, as the night wore on, clouds appeared and passed momentarily across the face of the moon, producing uncertain alternations of light and shadow, and rendering more confounded the confusion of the night encounter. The fighting became intermittent. Frequent challenges revealed the watchwords upon which depended recognition of men so similarly armed and equipped. Even flags were inextricably confused as they were captured by this group or that and carried hither and thither. One incident, recorded by Vipstanus Messalla, symbolized both the confusion and the impiety of the night's work. A young soldier, recruited into VII Galbiana in Spain, inflicted terrible injuries upon an older man of the Twenty-First. As he examined more closely the prostrate and semi-conscious figure, he recognized his own father, who had left home years before to serve at Windisch. Embracing the dying man, the son, choking with sobs, sought forgiveness for the unintended parricide, and gave his father such burial as was possible. The story ran through the ranks; men cursed the fighting—and fought on.

South of the road, the ex-Othonian Praetorians had their own difficulties. After initial success they too were driven back. Fabius Fabullus had not abandoned his plan of pressure on the Flavian centre. The Vitellian legionary artillery had at first been scattered among the several formations, and its fire in some cases, for example where the Third Legion confronted it, had been neutralized by the presence of vine props, solid tree stumps. Almost opposite the Third stood the Sixteenth, the legion of that enthusiastic artilleryman, Gaius Vedennius Moderatus, whose heirs placed upon his stone, years later, one of our best representations of a ballista. These pieces, fifty-four of which were allotted to a legion, must have been available to the Vitellians (if their vexillations were equipped in proportion) to the number of some 300. They were now concentrated between Cascina Malóngola and Casa de' Marozzi on that part of the road which made an angle of forty-five degrees with the parallel fronts through which it ran. Facing half-right, the ballistae could concentrate a very heavy fire on the exposed Praetorians, at any rate up to 400 yards, the maximum effective range. But the deceptive moonlight, coming now from south-east and south, made accuracy difficult. However, one particularly large piece hurled enormous stones and did considerable damage. Two Flavian soldiers, probably Praetorians, secretly picked up shields of fallen Vitellians, and taking advantage of this simple disguise (a difference of pattern, possibly a unit sign) and of the passage of clouds across the moon, mingled with the enemy, moved up to the monster ballista and suddenly hacked with their swords at its most vulnerable parts: the two skeins of sinew or hair whose torsion imparted thrust to the slider, and which, however large the engine, would be accessible at the lower end. The two men were of course instantly detected as enemies and killed, but not before they had done damage that could not quickly be put right. Their names are lost, for their bodies lay among the many dead around Malóngola, unknown warriors whom the record of history could not repay.[61]

The night wore on without bringing any clear decision. Towards dawn, when the moon shone high from the south, Antonius could be seen by his men as he turned to address each formation, calling for a final effort, praising or taunting as the case required. Everywhere there were cries of enthusiasm from the troops, weary as they were. As the sun rose into a clear sky, the Third greeted it with a cheer: such was the custom of Syria, their long-held station.

This led to a spreading rumour—not contradicted by Antonius or his officers—that Mucianus had arrived, and that the hurrahs were greetings exchanged between the two Flavian armies. Under the impression that they had been reinforced, and spurred on by Antonius' words, the troops moved forward to find the Vitellian positions only thinly held. So, despite the earlier successes, the generalship of Fabius Fabullus had been unable to hold his men, who had begun to drift back to their camp. Antonius reacted by massing his troops for a hard push along and alongside the Postumian Way. The loosely knit Vitellian front collapsed. Vehicles and guns in retreat blocked the road, hampering coordinated resistance. Down the straight road to Cremona the withdrawal developed into a disorderly flight, harried at every point by the Flavians.

But a new and formidable task confronted the victors on the northeastern outskirts of the town. Between 18 and 23 October the legions Caecina had sent to occupy Cremona—I Italica and XXI—had had time to recondition and strengthen the defences of the camp constructed in the spring. Here the remnants of the Vitellians held out. The Flavian command was reluctant to begin an assault with an army tired by a long day and a long night of marching and fighting. But the men, incredibly, could not be held back. Indeed the alternative for the Flavians—building their own camp in the immediate neighbourhood of the enemy's and of Cremona—would itself be dangerous. Antonius therefore agreed to an immediate attack. At first the Flavians suffered heavily from the plunging fire from the ramparts. But their commander distributed his legions around three sides of the camp (the fourth, towards Cremona, was wisely left as an escape route or because attackers would have their backs turned to the city). The south wall, nearest the Postumian Way, was allotted to the Third and Seventh (Galbian) and the east to VII Claudia and VIII, while the Thirteenth made for the north side, from which a track led to the highway to Brescia. Axes, scythes, ladders and other implements were hastily collected from the nearest farms, for the rapidly marshalled Flavian legionaries had naturally come without their full equipment except in so far as this had arrived during the course of the night. Then, interlocking shields above their heads, they moved in under the 'tortoise'. This walking carapace, a uniquely Roman contrivance, repelled the average missile: it could even sustain the weight of another party of armed men, poised aloft. But of course the Vitellians knew its weak points. They dropped heavy boulders, and when the 'tortoise' staggered, prised apart the individual shields with lances and poles. If the structure fell to pieces, they could flatten their maimed and bleeding opponents.

The hardest fighting was at the south gate, where Antonius reinforced the eager Third and much-tried Seventh with a strong force of auxiliary infantry, who provided covering fire for the attack. In the end the defenders resorted to desperate measures: a great gun (either that which had figured in the battle, now recovered and in position, or one of similar type) was tipped over upon the enemy beneath. For the moment this made a gap as it crushed those on whom it fell; but it also involved in its fall the merlons and upper part of the vallum; and simultaneously an adjacent gate-tower succumbed to a hail of stones hurled by Flavian pieces. While the Seventh kept up the pressure on the wall, the Third managed to hack its way through the gate with axes and swords. The first man to penetrate the camp, and therefore awarded the crown that bears the representation of a palisade, was a private of the Third, Gaius Volusius. He climbed the rampart from within, hurled down any still attempting resistance, and then, waving and yelling to attract the attention of his fellows, cried out, 'The camp is ours!' All the Vitellians now abandoned the ramparts and streamed out towards the walls of Cremona a few hundred yards away, or scattered into the surrounding countryside. Heavy losses were inflicted on the defeated enemy throughout the open space between the camp and the walls of Cremona. In the stampede a company chest belonging to the Vitellian Fourth Legion, hastily caught up by the *signifer* responsible for it, was dropped. Fragments of its bronze facing—remnant of pillage or jetsam—were found in the nineteenth century. The find-spot, fifty yards outside the Porta Venezia, explains and corroborates nearly two thousand years later the brief narrative of Tacitus.[62]

9

Antonius Moves South

The Flavians had now a camp in which to pass the night and begin to recover from more than twenty-four hours of continuous marching and fighting. The third day imposed a possibly more exacting enterprise: the capture of Cremona itself. The city walls were lofty, at any rate by comparison with the earthen rampart and wooden palisade of the camp, and they were manned in apparent strength; the gate-towers were not of timber, but of stone; and the gates themselves boasted the refinement of the portcullis. On the other hand, the remnants of the beaten army did not find their task of defence facilitated by the presence of numerous Italian visitors who were attending the Cremona autumn fair and found themselves caught up in the sudden return of a civil war which they had believed would pass them by. Antonius adopted a standard method of weakening the inhabitants' will to resist: he ordered the most attractive suburban houses to be fired. Such buildings as stood close to the walls and equalled or surpassed them in height were manned by picked Flavian troops with instructions to dislodge the Vitellians on the parapet by the use of joists, tiles and firebrands. When it became apparent that the attackers intended an immediate assault with artillery and tortoise tactics, Fabullus and his brother officers, already without hope of sustaining a siege for more than a very few days, felt that all further resistance was pointless. The camp commandant Cassius Longus had the portraits of Vitellius and the indications of his name removed from military equipment and public places. Caecina, still in confinement, was released and asked to act as an intermediary between the Vitellians and Antonius. In view of their earlier contacts he was the obvious choice. After satisfying his injured pride by a brief show of reluctance, he agreed. The white flag was prominently displayed from the walls, and Antonius thereupon ordered a ceasefire. Terms of capitulation were duly arranged by Caecina, in accordance with which the Vitellian garrison marched out, disarmed but in their units and formations, and encamped close to the city.

Caecina now had the spirit, or the conceit, to reappear ostentatiously garbed not as a soldier but as a consul, wearing the ceremonial bordered toga and preceded by the regulation twelve lictors. This ill-timed gesture caused a violent reaction among the Flavians (and equally, one may conjecture, among the Vitellians). They taunted the man with charges of insolence and treachery, but Antonius managed to get him away under escort to Vespasian, from whom he received the same benevolent welcome accorded also to Tampius Flavianus and Aponius Saturninus. For several years Caecina was to enjoy Vespasian's favour until, in mysterious circumstances, he was put to death by Titus as a conspirator. He was consequently portrayed by those historians who wrote before his fall as a patriot inspired by a love of peace, and by those who wrote later as a hypocrite and renegade, who had betrayed Nero, Galba, Vitellius and Vespasian in succession. Tacitus deals with him contemptuously and perhaps unfairly, sparing little of the gossip, even that which retailed the sartorial extravagancies of his wife. But whatever his weaknesses of character, he had shown undeniable re- source and ingenuity in the spring campaign, and his decision to forget his oath to Vitellius when Vespasian appeared as a pretender was one shared by many Romans capable of rational choice, whether interested or disinterested. Had not Tacitus' own father-in-law held office under Galba and Otho at Rome and after being called away to Liguria by his mother's death quickly transformed himself into a Flavian? In civil war, where allegiance is puzzling, oaths of fidelity are feeble bonds.

In October 69 Caecina was not the only object of Flavian hostility. The populace of Cremona, twice selected as a Vitellian stronghold, had supported that cause too vigorously to escape retribution now. The amphitheatre built by the Thirteenth, the floral tributes along the Postumian Way and the cantinières' help must now be paid for. Antonius tried to quieten scuffles that developed in the suburbs by assembling the men, congratulating them on their victory and directing words of clemency to the vanquished without any explicit reference to Cremona. He seems to have decided to let things take their course, hoping for, rather than expecting, restraint. With an abnegation of authority which might be harshly criticized by historians or pro- pagandists, never themselves faced by a situation rendered unmanage- able by the bitterness of civil war, Antonius vanished to a suburban villa in order to wash away the stains of battle. There a chance witti- cism of his was remembered and afterwards construed as an admission of guilt. The temperature of the baths (not surprisingly in the circum- stances) was insufficient, and Antonius, apparently already informed of acts of arson in the town itself, remarked, 'Lukewarm! We'll soon be in hot water, though.'

Cremona was already burning. Some 40,000 men, a large part of the Flavian army, and their camp followers had made their way into the city, intent on loot, and indeed there are some signs that public order had already broken down during the preparations for capitulation. Demoralized Vitellians who had failed to march out were already at this work, facilitated as it was by the fact that many Cremonese of substance had fled. Whatever the exact course of events—and a detailed investigation is not at all likely to have been held—arrests, thefts and vandalism were followed by fire-raising as the looters threw torches into rifled houses and temples. Cremona burned for four days. All its buildings, sacred and profane, collapsed in the flames with the sole exception of the Temple of Mefitis, goddess of infernal and pestilent exhalations, defended by its position outside the walls or by the power of a divinity glutted with the fumes of death and conflagration.

The ferocity of the disaster was unparalleled, and it became the talk of Italy and of the Roman world. Antonius issued a proclamation to the effect that no one should keep prisoner a citizen of Cremona. When foreign cities had been sacked, it had long been customary that both property and persons were shared at the general's discretion between officers and men; in Homer prisoners of war are sold into bondage as the victor's perquisite. But this was an Italian city whose citizens were also citizens of Rome, it was not some stronghold of barbarism on the fringe of the world. The troops had already found that there was no market in which a Roman citizen could legally be sold into slavery. When the probably grossly exaggerated rumour spread that the unfortunates were being murdered by their captors, they were stealthily ransomed by their relatives. In due course the surviving inhabitants returned to Cremona. The temples and fora were restored by public subscription, under the patronage (this he could afford) of Vespasian.

After the holocaust Antonius moved his troops out of the Vitellian camp and built another three miles away. The Vitellian formations were held intact, the stragglers and deserters rounded up; and in a short time the beaten formations moved out of Italy to strengthen the dangerously undermanned Danube line: I Italica and V Alaudae certainly, and probably the remnants of the drafts from Germany (I, IV Macedonica, XV Primigenia and XVI). The Twenty-First, however, seems to have gone back to Windisch, empty of legionary troops since its departure thence in February. The Flavian VII Claudia returned to Kostolać. XXII Primigenia, with its eagle, went temporarily to Pannonia, probably to Petronell in place of VII Galbiana. Finally, the British contingents were packed off to their distant isle, carrying with them—especially those from the Twentieth—little love for Vespasian. Official news of the Flavian victory was sent to Britain, Spain, Gaul and Germany, and of course to the East. At the same time the Alpine passes by which Vitellian forces might still conceivably attempt to penetrate north-eastern Italy (the Brenner and Reschen-Scheidegg) were sealed off by troops sent thither or placed at Trento, the focus of roads north of Verona.

We must now trace the fortunes of Valens, whom illness had prevented from leaving Rome in the company of Caecina and the army.
Soon after his colleague's departure on 17 September, well-grounded
distrust caused him to send a special order to those units which had
composed his own expeditionary force (I Italica, and the vexillations
from Vetera, Neuss and Bonn). They were to halt and wait for him,
Valens, on the Flaminian Way in accordance with a plan agreed with
Caecina. We have seen that Caecina overrode the order and hurried
northwards to expedite his change of front. Valens set out from Rome
about 25 September without troops, but soon halted in uncertainty,
perhaps in the Faliscan area. No word had come from Caecina, still
less word that his troops were waiting for him on the Flaminian Way.
Valens may even have toyed with the idea of returning to Rome, where
at any rate there were some troops to command; but his suspicions became moral certainties when on 14 October fast messengers arrived
with the information that the Ravenna fleet had changed sides. It is
perhaps just possible that if Valens had hurried forward alone, he might
have reached Ostiglia in three days, in time to prevent the defection of
18 October; and without question he could have reached Cremona
before the fatal battle. Even so, it is doubtful whether he could have
done much better than Fabullus. But such a scheme was now im-
practicable without troops, since the proximity of Ravenna to the
Aemilian Way—only some sixteen miles separate them at the nearest
approach—meant that the main road would be barred. Some of
Valens' advisers suggested that he should circumvent the danger area
by crossing the Apennines by the Florence–Bologna road fifty miles
west of Ravenna or by minor tracks via Pistoia: again a possibility, but
time-consuming, and, if things developed too fast, stultifying. Valens
wrote to Vitellius to ask for help, no doubt expecting Praetorians. A
force was indeed immediately sent, but it consisted merely of three
auxiliary cohorts and a cavalry regiment from Britain—too few men to
cut a way through the presumed barrier near Ravenna, too many to
permit undetected movement. One can understand the reluctance of
Vitellius to deplete his Praetorian forces in a venture of questionable
practicability. But however trusty, 2,000 auxiliaries could hardly deal
with 5,000 naval men or many thousands of legionaries; and their
trustworthiness was in question. Valens decided to jettison this encum-
brance, and move fast and alone. The cohorts he sent on to occupy
Rimini, telling the cavalry to hold the Flaminian Way further south,
probably at Bevagna, west of Foligno and the Apennines. With only a
small party, he himself made his way north by the Via Amerina,
entered Umbria below Orte, proceeded to Todi and beyond, recrossed
the Tiber north-westwards into Tuscany, and made his way via Perugia
and Arezzo to the northern part of that region. Here, about 28 October,

he heard of the battle fought and lost three days before on the other side of the mountains. The game in Italy was up. But Valens had spirit. He quickly formulated another plan which, if successful, might have had dreadful consequences. This was to get hold of some shipping, land on the coast of Gaul, and incite the Gallic provinces and the depleted garrison of Germany to renew the war. He communicated this intention to Vitellius and sailed from Pisa Port north of Livorno, but was soon compelled by unseasonably contrary winds to put in to the sheltering harbour of Monaco. Ten miles away was Cimiez, behind Nice, the capital of the small district of the Maritime Alps and the headquarters of its governor, Marius Maturus, who despite wavering neighbours remained notably faithful to Vitellius' cause. Marius warned Valens against entering Southern Gaul, where the imperial procurator Valerius Paulinus (we know nothing of the identity or activity of the governor; but the recent passage of Valens had not endeared the populace to Vitellius) had made the local communities swear allegiance to Vespasian, and having recruited the ex-Othonian Praetorians according to the new ruler's instructions, was now holding the town and naval base of Fréjus in strength. This last blow of fortune Valens could hardly parry. Accompanied by only four bodyguards, three civilian advisers and three centurions, he returned to Monaco, and sailed past the dangerous Fréjus, uncertain what to do next. In the event, recurrent bad weather solved his problem: he was forced to land on one of the Iles d'Hyères, and there a flotilla of four galleys sent by Paulinus effected his arrest. It was now late November. The valuable hostage was immediately dispatched to await the pleasure of Antonius, now thought to be heading for Rome.[63]

It was indeed so. By the end of the first week in November, the Flavian commander was ready to resume the advance. The caution of his colleagues and his own pride dictated that once again only his light forces should lead the way. The beaten Vitellian legions, though set in motion towards Britain and Illyricum as soon as practicable after the battle, were still quite near, and the main Flavian legionary force must be kept at Verona for the time being, in order to prevent any attempted about-turn. It was not in fact moved until a month after the battle, though the offensive went on.

The first acquisition came quite soon, at the end of October. The faint-hearted Vitellian auxiliaries had barely occupied the town of Rimini which it was their duty to hold, when Cornelius Fuscus rapidly surrounded it by land and sea with his Ravenna force. After two or three days' siege, the defenders were only too pleased to open the gates. Fuscus then quickly overran the eastern seaboard of Italy as far as Ancona and beyond it, perhaps even, if we may press Tacitus' language, up to the River Pescara. He met no resistance.

Informed of this satisfactory situation, Antonius started off from Verona on 9 November, marching quickly through the lowlands of the Po, now waterlogged by the rains of autumn. At Verona he had left the headquarters and main bodies of the legions, the wounded and the unfit, confident that his own force, some auxiliary cohorts and cavalry with a stiffening of legionaries, would be adequate for his task. The war, it was felt, was virtually over. Besides, soon after leaving Verona, Antonius was at last overtaken by the Eleventh Legion from Dalmatia, remarkable now, as in March, for its slowness. At first the painfully indecisive governor of the province, Pompeius Silvanus, had hesitated to obey the summons issued from Ptuj, and then, when Antonius prospered, became uneasy at his failure to cooperate. Luckily he was supported by one of those admirable and largely unsung heroes of Rome, the professional servants of the state. Annius Bassus, the legionary commander, knew how to show his superior proper deference; he knew also how to manage him, and whenever there was work to be done he was on the spot, ready to act with quiet efficiency. The legion was accompanied by 6,000 Dalmatians recently recruited for auxiliary or naval service, presumably at the orders of Vitellius, when uncertain of the loyalty of Ravenna under Bassus. Together with the Dalmatians there came the pick of the naval force—perhaps those who had done well at Rimini—who were anxious to sell their support at the price of transfer into the better-paid legionary service. They were accepted to make good past casualties, and were replaced in the navy by the Dalmatians.

At Fano, Antonius halted for a week or more (20–28 November). The main reasons were the receipt of information that the Vitellian Praetorians (certainly a force superior to Antonius' immediate companions) had left Rome on 13 November, and a calculation that by this time, seven days later, they could be approaching the Apennines. There might well be a race between the two sides to occupy the Furlo gorge, the narrow valley between Cagli and Cantiano, or the Scheggia Pass. It was not inconceivable that some very strong strategic point was already occupied by the Vitellians. It seemed sensible to send out reconnaissance parties to see what possibilities were offered by other passes, notably those between Ancona and Nocera (or Foligno), and between Ascoli Piceno and Rieti. But Antonius' fears proved groundless, and the lengthy reconnaissances unnecessary. Comparable doubts about the enemy's position and intentions had already slowed the Vitellians, who for their part at no time advanced beyond Bevagna, only eighty-seven miles from Rome, and fifty miles short of the Burano gorge. This, however, Antonius could not immediately know, and he was right to await his scouts' reports, particularly as the wet autumn promised difficult going, with snow on the mountains. Moreover, as he

could now safely call the legions forward from Verona, it was desirable
not to outdistance them too far. Sending the order to Verona and waiting for confirmation of its execution called for some five days, less than
the time required by reconnaissance. During this period, also, arrangements were made for concentrating at Fano the supplies necessary
before the mountains were tackled, and the Ravenna fleet was used to
convey corn down the Po and along the Adriatic coast.

It is now that we hear of lively exchanges by letter between Mucianus
and Antonius. A note of acrimony resounds. The former had already
from time to time sent reports of his progress to Antonius, together with
mysterious hints about the necessity for caution and the need for speed.
It was obvious that this language could be interpreted to suit events,
and sprang from the mortification of seeing the Flavian thunder stolen.
But the letters which now arrived at Fano had something more particular to relate.

Mucianus' long march from Syria to Rome must be reconstructed, if
at all, from fragmentary allusions and hints in our main source. The
weeks since early August had been largely spent by Mucianus and his
18,000 legionaries in toiling across the interminable plateau of central
Anatolia. By early October, as we have seen, he was on the Egnatian
Way in Thrace, perhaps a hundred miles west of the Bosporus. The
general's plan of campaign was still unclear, even to himself; but his
concentration of the forty vessels of the Black Sea fleet at Istanbul
suggests that he was preparing himself for the obvious contingency of an
opposed or unopposed crossing of the Ionian Sea to the heel of Italy,
whatever harbour, Taranto, Brindisi, Bari or another, seemed best for
achieving surprise. However, about the middle of the month, his
ruminations had been rudely cut short. Alarming news from Moesia in
the north reported that the Transdanubian barbarians had taken
advantage of the weakness of the frontier and their knowledge that an
Italian death-struggle was imminent to stage one of their customary
raids into the Roman province along the lower Danube.

A change of plan was inescapable. However, by the end of the first
week in November, Mucianus had managed to stabilize the situation
and by chasing the Dacians back across the Danube to lessen the threat
of a possible pincers attack by them and the Germans acting in concert.
This threat evaporated completely when news arrived of the Second
Battle of Cremona. There was now the prospect of a further reinforcement of the threatened frontier by the return of its legions or equivalent
troops. But at the same time the good news rendered more urgent
Mucianus' need to catch up with a rival now more than ever likely to
beat him to Rome. On 7 November, Mucianus resumed his march
westwards, not before despatching some cold congratulations and
complaints to Antonius.

This, then, was the background of the wait at Fano. Antonius for his part bitterly resented Mucianus' criticism, the product, he remarked, of jealousy and pique. He retorted by writing to Vespasian in a tone which some found to be unnecessarily arrogant and which contained veiled attacks on the emperor's supporter, whose services, he hastened to point out, were vastly inferior to his own. The retort, however understandable, did not help Antonius. It should have been obvious to him (as it was to some of his more cautious officers) that in the end Mucianus was bound to exert tremendous influence over an emperor whose elevation he had greatly assisted. A quarrel between the two champions, whatever the rights and wrongs of the case, could only harm Antonius, however grateful and tolerant Vespasian might be. Already Cremona was a talking point in which it was difficult to rebut the comments of political enemies. In the controversy between the two, Antonius said what he thought quite frankly, while Mucianus, said his enemies, concealed and fed his grudge with patient and implacable cunning.

But it was time for action, not words. It had become clear that the Vitellians showed no obvious signs of an intention to challenge the invaders in the mountains, so that the Flaminian Way could be used if no time were lost. On 28 November the Flavian van marched out from Fano towards the gorge of the Furlo, soon to be tunnelled by Vespasian, but presenting in 69 a stiff and tedious climb. Then came the narrow valley of the Burano and finally the passage of the Sierra Maggio before Scheggia. But by 6 December the army had passed the worst in difficult weather and reached Bevagna. The Vitellians had evacuated it just four days previously, retiring thirty-four miles to a strong position at Narni and Terni. This was a clear sign that the enemy were unable or unwilling to face an encounter in the plain of the Clitunno in which Bevagna stands: they had run for the shelter of the hills to the south. The news that Bevagna had changed hands without a blow induced a clear swing of public opinion in favour of the Flavians in central-southern Italy. Antonius wasted no time. Without pausing he moved on to Carsulae, two or three days' journey nearer the enemy, where he was within sight of their positions. It seemed that the retreating Vitellians had really decided to stand and fight here, at Narni. It would be necessary to halt for five days to allow the legions to catch up.

Carsulae makes a good base. Placed high on a shoulder of mountain on the eastern side of the main Umbrian valley, it commands wide and distant prospects on three sides. To north and west it dominates the low ground in which the modern main road runs. To the east it is protected by the steep slopes rising to Monte Torre Maggiore. On the south it looks down over the low triangular plain of Terni to the line of hills in which a V-shaped notch marks the course of the Nera as it flows south to the Tiber, Narni on the height beside it. Easily defensible, capable of holding several thousand troops on its ridge, Carsulae could rely for supplies upon prosperous towns in its rear like Spoleto, Todi and Foligno, and indeed central Umbria at large. Today the town reveals a monumental centre, a theatre, and a solitary arch upon the Flaminian Way.[64]

According to some historians—clearly those who wrote to vindicate Antonius—it would have been quite possible for Flavius Sabinus and Domitian to have left the capital for the Flavian army. Antonius claimed to have got messages from Carsulae to Rome promising a rendezvous outside the capital where an escort would pick them up and bring them northwards. The anti-Antonian historians retorted that the reason why this offer was not accepted was that Sabinus was a sick man and not fit enough for the exhausting plan of secret flight and a ride by night along rough trails. In fact, a more probable reason is that Sabinus was at that very moment in the early stages of negotiations with Vitellius which he hoped would lead to a peaceful solution, and to disappear at this stage would have been entirely irresponsible. Domitian, for his part, used to say that he had been quite willing to escape, but Vitellius had put him under open arrest and though the guards (as it became clear later, in perfect sincerity) promised to join him in the venture, he had feared that this was a trap. In fact, Vitellius himself avoided any ill treatment of Domitian (as of Sabinus) in the endeavour to secure a guarantee which would, if the worst came to the worst, save his own family.

But Antonius did receive one welcome visitor: a man in peasant's dress who came down a mountain track from the north-east. It was that reckless but spirited commander, Quintus Petilius Cerialis Caesius Rufus, close relative (perhaps even son-in-law) of Vespasian. He had arrived from Rieti, and possibly from Rome, circumventing the Vitellian lines in disguise and using his knowledge of the country routes. After all, this must have been familiar ground for the connection of Vespasian. He was welcomed and co-opted as a leader. In less than a year he was to improve a somewhat chequered military reputation by the recovery of the rebellious Rhineland in a lightning campaign.[65]

But more important even than Petilius was another arrival. The captured Valens in the custody of his jailors had retraced the weary journey from Gaul to Pisa, Arezzo and Perugia. When it was realized that the Flavian vanguard had just passed through Bevagna, the news was sent on to Antonius. The reply came back immediately. At Collemancio, a hamlet west of Bevagna, where he was being kept in custody, Fabius Valens was put to death, the one loyal and determined commander of the Vitellian faction. From December at Bonn to December in Umbria, the last year of his life had been long indeed. He should have served a better master, and a better cause.

Since Valens left Rome, Vitellius had done little. The climate of Rome is oppressively hot in August and September, and if you are rich enough and have a site, you will build yourself a villa where elevation brings relief from the dusty and oppressive atmosphere. Such a villa, splendidly situated on Monte Mario, on which the Rome observatory now stands, is described by Martial as belonging to a wealthy and genial patron. When the mist hid the curved valleys, the gently-rounded summit of the hill enjoyed a purer light; at night the graceful villa's roofs were silhouetted against more brilliant stars. From it you could enjoy a bird's-eye view of all Rome. To the north-east were visible old Fidenae beyond the Tiber, and this side of it the hamlet of Rubrae at the end of the pink cliffs. To the south-east, just outside the city, the meadow and grove of Anna Perenna, where the poor caroused in shacks at the annual festival, were visible between the Flaminian Way and the river. The vehicles on the Flaminian and Salarian Ways could be seen to move, but no sound was heard. The cries of the bargees on the Tiber immediately beneath were imperceptible. But if you looked from the Monte Mario over the heart of the misty city, the south-eastern horizon was occupied by the Monte Cavo, the sacred mount of the early Latins, and the Colli Albani around, holding in their craters the still lakes of Alba and Nemi. Cicero had his favourite villa at Tusculum, near Frascati, Pompey a grand place at Albano, and at Ariccia Lucius Vitellius, father of the emperor, three times consul, the faithful friend of Claudius, had stocked a great park with the by-products of his governorship of Syria: such exotics as Syrian and Carian fig trees (in Caria the natives fed their flocks on figs, if you can believe Philostratus), not to mention the pistachio, whose tasty nuts Joseph's brethren took as a present to Egypt. To this agreeable and familiar retreat his son, once Caecina and Valens had left for the front, retired with relief, as if duty were done. He was not a man made to endure the heat and dust of battle or even administration. Nero's Golden House with its lake was itself too cramped. The woodlands of Ariccia offered shade, the lakes of Alba and Nemi freshness. For fully a month, from 25 September to 26 October, when duty or mere prudence might have counselled training, recruiting and activities to catch the public eye, we hear nothing of him. Caustic critics, then or later, complained that he had consigned past, present and future to universal oblivion, like a rabbit in a hutch, content to lie, eat and doze so long as it was fed. A more charitable explanation—the exact sequence of events is in fact in doubt—is that illness, followed by convalescence in the Servilian Gardens on the southern outskirts of Rome, was concluded by the stay at Ariccia. However that may be, it was here that news of Bassus' treachery and of the defection of the fleet jolted him into life. Soon after, reports arrived of Caecina, good mixed with bad, telling of his desertion and arrest.

Vitellius rode back to the capital and addressed a crowded meeting, lavishly praising the devotion of the troops. Publilius Sabinus, the Praetorian prefect, was put under arrest as a friend of Caecina, Alfenus Varus, Valens' competent camp commandant, taking his place. On 30 October the Senate met. To a carefully prepared speech delivered by the emperor members responded with studied flattery, avoiding never-theless any precise reference to Antonius or Vespasian: it was necessary to keep one's options open. But Caecina could safely be attacked as no true friend to either side. His term as suffect consul, almost at an end, was declared null and void. A senator obsequiously petitioned, and was allowed, to occupy the one-day vacancy created. On 31 October, Rosius Regulus, a man otherwise unknown to history, entered, and resigned, office. Such brief power, contemptible both in the giver and in the recipient, was not entirely without precedent; but constitutional pedantry, paradoxical in this year of revolution but typical of Roman ritualism, observed that never before had a suffect consul been ap-pointed in these circumstances without the passing of a formal act of abrogation.

But this was play-acting. Harsh reality broke in upon it with the devastating knowledge, on 1 or 2 November, of the Second Battle of Cremona fought a week before. At first Vitellius attempted to hush up the news, of course without success. By pretending that all was well, he aggravated the difficulty. In the emperor's presence there was an un-canny conspiracy of silence, while throughout Italy rumour multiplied sensational versions of the disaster to spite the censorship. Antonius was astute enough to take Vitellian spies on conducted tours of the battle-field and of the Flavian forces, and then send them back to their in-credulous master. A remarkable—and perhaps true—story is told of the Praetorian centurion Julius Agrestis, stationed at Rome. Having failed to induce Vitellius to accept the truth and act accordingly, he asked to be sent to Cremona to find out precisely what had happened. On arriving, he made no attempt to hide the purpose of his mission from Antonius, who for his part readily enough provided officers to take him round the field of battle and allowed him to speak to the legions which had capitulated. When the emperor still refused to believe and accused Agrestis of having been bribed, the centurion replied, 'Well, since you need irrefutable proof and have no further use for my services, alive or dead, I will give you evidence which you *must* believe.' With this he left Vitellius and committed suicide.

Finally, but only towards the middle of November, Vitellius drew the consequences. He sent his Praetorian prefects, Julius Priscus and Alfenus Varus, to hold the Apennines with fourteen Praetorian cohorts and all the available cavalry regiments; and this force was backed up by a legion recruited from the sailors at Miseno. The remaining cohorts (two

Praetorian and nearly thirty auxiliary) were allotted to the emperor's brother Lucius for the protection of the capital. The expeditionary force reached Bevagna in Umbria on 19 November, and its commanders rightly decided that no good purpose would be served by pushing into the mountains now that the weather had broken: let the enemy suffer the hardships of snow and cold if they were so foolish. However sensible strategically, this policy was less good for morale, and there was a demand that the supreme commander should show himself in the camp. Towards the end of the month, Vitellius yielded, and spent a few days with his men. At first, isolated by his staff and as puzzled as they about the whereabouts and intentions of the enemy, he found himself helpless. But as reconnaissance parties returned from the north, it became apparent that the enemy were at Fano, preparing to cross the Apennines. The last thing the Vitellians wanted was another Cremona fought in the Clitunno valley against an enemy superior in numbers and morale. They must gain time and give Valens a chance to open another front. Since Bevagna was not a good defensive position, it would be better to retire thirty miles to the Narni gap.

This sound decision was reinforced by the alarming news that the Miseno fleet had defected. Vitellius moved back, leaving at Narni eight Praetorian cohorts and some cavalry, and taking the remaining six Praetorian cohorts and 500 horse to the capital. Pending his arrival, a scratch force was ordered to Campania. Back at Rome, and all too late in the day, Vitellius set about recruiting the urban populace, whose enthusiasm was encouraging though unmatched by any knowledge of fighting. Helped by the freedmen of the imperial civil service, he caused the people to be mustered by wards and had volunteers sworn in. The response was so overwhelming that the two new consuls suffect, Gaius Quintius Atticus and Gnaeus Caecilius Simplex, were asked to supervise the levy. Senators, knights and freedmen offered contributions in money and slaves, plus a certain unreasoning enthusiasm which soon faded. Vitellius even assumed the title 'Caesar', which he had been unwilling to accept before. Now even straws must be grasped at. In this way something was done to counter the bad impression caused by the navy revolt south of Rome, to which we must now turn.

In late November, Claudius Faventinus, a centurion of the Miseno fleet who had been cashiered by Galba, induced the rebellion by producing a letter—forged or genuine, who could say?—purporting to come from Vespasian and offering the same sort of inducement, legionary service and pay, as appears to have led to the movement at Ravenna more than a month before. Indeed, the interval suggests that Faventinus was an agent of Cornelius Fuscus or of Hormus. An ex-praetor, Apinius Tiro, who happened to be conveniently near at Minturno, forty miles up the coast, put himself at the head of the move-

ment. Vitellius' stop-gap force under Claudius Julianus (one Urban
Cohort and some gladiators) promptly sided with the rebels, who now
made themselves masters of the seaport of Terracina at the lower end
of the Pontine marshes.

News of the occupation of this town, only sixty-five miles from Rome,
induced Vitellius to detail his brother to crush the naval rebels with the
aid of six of the nine Praetorian cohorts then available in Rome. These
were determined and reliable troops, and Lucius was not the man to
stand any nonsense. There should be no difficulty in mopping up a
disorderly rabble. He left Rome on 9 December and two days later was
encamped a little short of Terracina, at the spring and grove of Feronia.
At this point, the Punta di Leano, a projection of the Volscian hills,
impinged momentarily upon the Appian Way, terminating the canal
which accompanied the road for the nineteen miles from Tor Tre Ponti.
Here the canalized river turned away right towards the sea, so that
peacetime travellers who, like Horace, used the slow overnight barge
through a land of frogs and malarial mosquitoes, must disembark;
then, having washed in Feronia's water, they would crawl the remaining three miles on foot or vehicle. This well-watered spot, known to
every traveller, was an obvious base now for Lucius Vitellius, as he
studied the problem of taking Terracina. The rebellious sailors and
gladiators showed no inclination to venture beyond the city walls, at any
rate in the direction of Feronia. On the other side, towards the sea,
their ships gave them assurance. And was it not the season of the
Saturnalia, when even soldiers and sailors have holidays? The beach
rang with shouts of revelry re-echoing from the bastion of Monte Sant'
Angelo on the north. Fighting, says Tacitus, was merely a topic for
discussion at the dinner table. One omission of the rebels was indeed
serious: the garrisoning of the great hill, 225 metres high, which
dominates town and bay and still displays the impressive substructures
of the great Temple of Jupiter, visible afar. This eyrie was the more
important because it blocked the passage of the Appian Way, its seaside
course not yet opened up by Trajan's passion for excavation; in 69,
having entered the town from the Rome direction, the road was compelled to turn sharply left and make a steep climb to the rear of the
citadel on its way to Fondi.

Vergilius Capito, governor of Egypt in 47–52, seems to have had
property in Terracina, though he came from Capua. One of his slaves,
misusing the freedom of the Saturnalia and perhaps anxious to secure the
household from damage, appeared in Vitellius' camp and offered to
guide a party to the undefended height. Under his instructions some of
the cohorts proceeded in battle order around the half-moon of plain
between Liano and the town, following, perhaps at the 200-metre
contour, the line of the aqueduct that brought Feronia's water to

Terracina. The march of several miles was accomplished noiselessly in the darkness. Without attracting attention, they reached the saddle towards Monte Sant' Angelo and the Appian Way after its climb north-eastwards, and before first light on 18 December charged down the road south-westwards upon the sleeping town. It was a massacre, not a battle. The defenders were struck down while still fumbling in the dark for their clothes and weapons. A few gladiators offered serious resistance and inflicted some damage before they fell; the rest made a rush for the ships, which, since the old circular harbour was by now silted up, had merely anchored in the bay or been beached. Here the scene was one of panic and chaos, in which civilians were mixed up with soldiers and suffered a similar fate at the hands of the Vitellians. Six galleys got away. The rest were captured on the beach, or else capsized under the press of fugitives and sank. Claudius Julianus was taken before Lucius Vitellius, flogged and strangled before the victor's eyes. Lucius knew how to avenge a stab in the back. He lost no time in sending a laurelled dispatch to his brother, announcing the victory and enquiring whether he wanted him to return immediately or complete the disciplining of Campania. The delay involved was providential for the Flavians and the city of Rome. The Vitellians at Terracina were flushed with an easy victory; if they had made for the capital at full speed, they could have arrived on the evening of 19 December, prolonged a dying agony, given Vitellius a chance of escape and perhaps brought nearer the necessity of Vespasian's policy of attrition. From this at least Good Luck, a goddess frequently favourable to Vespasian, saved his compatriots.[66]

None of this could be foreseen on 9 December. When Lucius left Rome, his brother's empire had shrunk to the small part of Italy that lay between Narni and Feronia, and that narrow dominion was soon to be further reduced. Antonius and the Flavian advance force had been resting for some days at Carsulae when, on 13 December, the Verona legions finally caught up. As news of the concentration of a vast army spread, the Vitellians at Narni began to waver. Their officers competed in desertion, better informed than the men. One or two actually brought over a company or a squadron with them to ensure a welcome. From these the Flavians learnt that Terni, five miles from Narni in the eastern apex of the plain, was garrisoned by only 400 cavalry. Varus was instantly dispatched with a battle group. He killed a few who resisted, and the majority, completely demoralized, threw down their arms and asked for quarter. A few escaped to carry the sorry tale to Narni, exaggerating the strength of the foe to exculpate themselves. The answer of the two prefects was to vanish to Rome, thus freeing everybody from the need to be ashamed of giving up. The situation was indeed hopeless. Even those who still fancied that another army might get through from Germany were brutally disillusioned. One day, a group of Flavians approached close under the hill of Narni, holding an object stuck on a pole. It was the head of Valens.

Terms were arranged, and the change of allegiance was effected with some shreds of dignity. On 15 December the Vitellians marched out over the bridge of Augustus down to the plain on the north, with banners flying and standards borne aloft. The Cremona procedure was repeated. The Flavian forces, ready and armed for all eventualities, formed up in close ranks on either side of the Flaminian Way. The Vitellians were shepherded into a square and addressed by Antonius in a conciliatory tone. Some were told to stand fast at Narni, others at Terni; others, again, were to accompany the march. One or two Flavian legions were left behind to keep an eye on those who remained, but they gave no trouble. On the following day the Flavian army marched through the gorge in which the milky sulphureous waters of the Nera flow, and halted that evening at Otricoli by the Tiber. They could look forward to Happy Saturnalia, a few days' relaxation followed by a ceremonial entry into Rome.

In the palace the atmosphere was gloomy. Vitellius' brother had gone south, and good news could hardly be expected from the north. Aulus sank even more visibly into pessimism and despair. Adversity showed the man in his true colours, pallid and yellow. Both Antonius and Mucianus (the latter was already in Italy) sent him a stream of messages offering him his life, a pension, and a place of retirement in Campania if he would lay down his arms and throw himself and his children on the mercy of Vespasian. Often Vitellius was weakly tempted to take the invitation seriously: he would talk of the number of servants he would need and the best seaside resort to choose. The emperor himself had no stomach for heroics or for honour, and not much even for his own survival. But he was overwhelmed with pity for his family and by the thought that, if he resisted to the bitter end as honour and his Praetorians demanded, he might leave his widow, son and daughter to face the harsher vengeance of a resentful victor. Then there was his elderly mother, the excellent Sextilia, a lady of breeding with recollections of a happier past. She was in poor health now. By a happy dispensation she died a few days before the doom of her family, having gained nothing from the circumstance that her son was emperor except grief and the sympathy of the public.

During the week following the departure of Lucius Vitellius, the emperor on his own initiative held a number of private meetings with Flavius Sabinus, his city prefect, and clearly also the representative, official or unofficial, of the new power. Both men were under pressure from extremists and both resisted it. The commanders of the Praetorian cohorts left in Rome and those politicians most closely associated

with Vitellius pointed out to him the folly of believing that any compromise was possible: neither Vespasian nor his followers could in the
long run countenance the survival of Vitellius or his son. Moreover, he
was popular in Rome and should fight it out; even if they failed in the
end, at least let their end be glorious. Sabinus' advisers urged him to
declare himself military governor of Rome in reliance on the Urban
Cohorts, whom he controlled *ex officio*, and the Watch, if only in order
that all credit for the recovery of the capital should not go to Antonius:
Vitellius was in an impossible situation, without will to cling to power
further. But Sabinus had no desire to provoke a challenge which would
inevitably lead to bloodshed in the streets of Rome. The negotiations
would continue.

The two men were soon near agreement, and on 16 December the
news of the Narni capitulation decided Vitellius to take the final step.
On the following day, which was the first day of the winter festival of
the Saturnalia, a meeting was held in the Temple of Apollo, attended
by Vitellius and Sabinus, and, as witnesses to the instrument, Cluvius
Rufus and Vitellius' friend Silius Italicus, the orator and poet. Observers outside the temple remarked on the demeanour of the principals:
Vitellius, bowed in gloom; Sabinus, his usual mild and sympathetic
self. A melancholy interest attaches to a compact immediately and
fatally overturned. Its exact terms were difficult to ascertain thirty
years later when Tacitus wrote, for by then both witnesses, as well as
both principals, were dead. But it may be inferred that at the very least
a timetable for the act of abdication was fixed. On the following morning this was to be performed publicly at a ceremony in the Forum
Romanum, at which the consul Caecilius Simplex would preside. After
this, Vitellius would retire to his own private house on the Aventine
until such time as a more remote place of residence were determined.
The lives of himself and his family would be spared and he would
receive a suitable financial allowance. On the same morning, Flavius
Sabinus, accompanied by the other consul, Quintius Atticus, would
assume control of all military forces and address the people in the
Forum after Vitellius had gone. He would then proceed to the palace,
and hold the Palatine Hill in the name of Vespasian. Antonius Primus
would be informed, and his troops would occupy Rome and the
Praetorian barracks in an orderly takeover.

On the afternoon of the same day Vitellius paraded the Praetorian
cohorts in the square before the palace. Standing at the head of the
flight of steps, he informed them that he was retiring from a position
which had been forced upon him against his will. There were cries of
protest, and Vitellius dismissed the parade, merely saying that he would
bear their views in mind. At the same time, Sabinus issued orders in
writing to all military commanders telling them to confine their men to

barracks until further notice. Only the cohort of Praetorians on duty in the palace was excepted from this, as it would accompany the emperor from the palace to the Forum. The news of these momentous arrangements spread immediately throughout the city. These would indeed be Saturnalia to remember.

Rhine and Nile

Soon after entering Batavian territory at Schenkenschanz, following a course slightly different from today's, the Rhine divided, as it still does at roughly the same point, into two arms. The northerly one reached the North Sea by Leiden and Katwijk and marked the boundary of the Roman dominion. The southerly arm, the Waal, wider and slower, was the main highway for waterborne traffic, moving silently and majestically through the flat, green lands at the end of Europe. In antiquity it entered the sea by a huge estuary called Helinium, into which a little further south, the Maas (Meuse) also emptied itself. Of the Lek we hear nothing, and it seems not to have been important. The two main arms embraced the so-called Island of the Batavians, almost 100 miles long. Behind the dunes of the coastal strip, the western portion of the Island was inhabited by the Cannenefates, numerically inferior to the Batavians to whom they were akin, but, like them, tall, sturdy, pugnacious and lacking nothing in tribal patriotism. Their capital lay at Voorburg behind the Hague. In A.D. 69 they had an ambitious chief called Brinno, son of a leader who, thirty years before, when the emperor Gaius had been staging important manoeuvres in the Low Countries, had rejected with impunity an order to participate. The son had a reputation to live up to. In the spring of this year, 69, amid a surge of anti-Roman feeling caused by the activities of the Vitellian recruiting centurions, he was placed upon a shield in German fashion and raised shoulder high by his cheering followers to symbolize his election as leader in a war against the suzerain. The action, unexplained by Tacitus, was also perhaps stimulated by the knowledge that a furious and deadly clash between Otho and Vitellius was imminent. Brinno immediately called upon the Frisians in Noord-Holland, just beyond the narrow water frontier, to join him in a two-pronged attack upon the oppressors. The lower Rhine was protected by a series of small auxiliary forts whose sites are known: Katwijk, Valkenburg and Roomburg around Leiden; Alfen and Zwammerdamm; de Meern and Vechten around Utrecht, and Utrecht itself. The western forts were obvious targets. Assaulted simultaneously without warning by the Cannenefates from the land and the Frisians from the sea, the cohort garrisons were unable to hold out, and two of the furthest forts were captured and sacked. It was then an easy matter to fall upon unsuspecting supply contractors and merchants scattered over the countryside or travelling by barge along the Fossa Corbulonis, the canal (now the Vliet and the Schie) constructed in A.D. 47 by the then governor of Lower Germany, to protect from the perils of the unpredictable North Sea the river traffic of the Waal moving up to the western end of the frontier. The next Rhine forts were about to suffer similar attacks, when they were set on fire by the cohort prefects as being indefensible; and the garrisons fell back to the upper end of the Island. It was now the beginning of May.

At this point we must turn to a more considerable character than Brinno, and to Brinno's neighbours. The Batavians, a German tribe, once formed part of the Chatti on the upper Weser, but, driven out by domestic feuds more than a century previously, they had occupied—perhaps with Roman approval—the larger part of the Island, the Betuwe, together with the territory between the Waal and the Maas and a strip of land south of the Maas, between Ravestein and Crèvecoeur. Their tribal capital, Batavodorum or oppidum Batavorum, occupied the site of the present-day Hunerpark, opposite the big bridge at Nijmegen. Like the Cannenefates, they paid no tribute in money, but lay under the obligation of furnishing an exceptionally large contingent of auxiliary troops. Nine cohorts of these appear in the history of the first century, as well as a strong cavalry militia specially trained for amphibious operations in order to defend their homeland and the empire. These men were capable of swimming rivers while keeping hold of their arms and mounts, and maintaining perfect formation; and similar feats were performed by the equestrian element in the infantry cohorts, as we have seen from the story of the First Battle of Cremona. Batavian cohorts had fought with distinction both in Germany (under Drusus, Tiberius and Germanicus, between 12 B.C. and A.D. 16) and in Britain (during the invasion of A.D. 43 and again in helping to crush the uprising of Boudicca, seventeen years later). They were commanded, according to long-standing custom, by their own chiefs, who enjoyed Roman citizenship and bore Roman names.

In A.D. 68 the most prominent Batavians were two brothers (or cousins), Julius Civilis and Claudius Paulus, of royal descent. Paulus seems to have been suspected (perhaps rightly) of complicity in the uprising of Vindex, and was put to death in May or June by the then governor of Lower Germany, Fonteius Capito. Civilis, himself suspect, was sent in irons to Nero and after suffering a few months' confinement was liberated by Vindex' friend Galba when he reached Rome late in the year; and he was then sent back to command a cohort serving locally. The Rhineland legionaries, however, some of whom had helped

to crush Vindex at Besançon, continued to regard him with a suspicion
and dislike that were mutual. In January, the proclamation of Vitellius
as emperor brought him once more into danger, though Vitellius had
too much sense to punish a chief whose people might be useful friends
and dangerous enemies.

These checkered experiences had not sweetened Civilis' temper or
lessened his tribal following. He had served in the Roman auxiliary
army for five-and-twenty years. He had made the acquaintance, perhaps won the friendship, of the legionary commander Vespasian,
presumably during the invasion of Britain in A.D. 43. But the death of
Paulus rankled. Julius knew both the strengths and the weaknesses of
Rome. When Vespasian's name began to be whispered in July and
proclaimed in August, he conceived a grand design. Would it not be
possible at one stroke to take vengeance on the Vitellians, ingratiate
himself with the Flavians and achieve the liberation of his people under
his own leadership, by organizing what purported to be support for the
new emperor but would, in fact, be a tribal uprising? After all, there
was no reason why Vespasian's gratitude (or caution) should not ac-
quiesce in a redrawn frontier which at least followed not the lower
Rhine but the Waal or the Maas. Why should not he, Julius Civilis,
who at the moment was only one Batavian leader, however influential,
among many, aspire to the dignity accorded to the feeble potentates of
Armenia? By August 69 Civilis believed that his hour of destiny had
come, the hour when he might become another Arminius, unquestion-
ably the liberator of his country. Vespasian, his friend, had rebelled
against the wretched Vitellius. He had (perhaps) written to Civilis. A
prolonged and evenly-balanced war was in prospect, the winner of
which would be in no position to take umbrage. Antonius Primus,
anticipating Ptuj, had put out feelers for support; the eight Batavian
regular cohorts, dismissed from Pavia and ordered to Britain by
Vitellius in June, must be at no great distance from the homeland,
disillusioned and discontented by a series of marches and counter-
marches at the order of one or other emperor. The Roman garrisons in
the Island were in confusion, those of the Rhineland depleted. And
finally, within his own people there was resentment at the hasty and
extraordinary levies ordered by Vitellius, levies that bore particularly
hard upon a people already heavily recruited.

Civilis played his hand cleverly. He encouraged the Batavians to
refuse service, alleging corruption and violence on the part of recruiting
officers. When feeling was running high, he invited the nobles and some
prominent burghers to a banquet, carefully stage-managed in a sacred
grove such as must have been common enough in the thickly-wooded
land. There, by the altars of their gods, under the branches to which the
bear and dragon standards were fixed, a table was spread in a Rem-

brandtesque setting of light and dark. As the August dusk fell, and their host observed that wine and food had inflamed their imaginations and reinforced their courage, he launched into an inflammatory speech. It was listened to with approval. Civilis exacted from his hearers an oath of loyalty according to barbarous rituals made potent by ancestral curses upon the perjuror. Strong in this authority, he came to an understanding with Brinno, whose forces now acted in concert with the Batavians. He further sent emissaries to explain the position to the eight Batavian cohorts and to invite their cooperation. As for the Romans, Civilis wrote to Hordeonius Flaccus criticizing the prefects for abandoning their forts in the spring and insincerely offering to deal with the Cannenefates by himself, with the help of the cohort under his command: the prefects should return each to his station; there was no real danger.[67]

But this ingenious stratagem was soon detected. The Batavians talked too much. Hints gradually leaked out, and the trick was revealed: the scattering of the cohorts was calculated to make it easier to pick them off one by one; the real enemy was not Brinno, but Civilis. In this conviction, the dislodged Roman garrisons remained concentrated at the upper end of the Island. In September a front was formed at no great distance from the Rhine, perhaps in north-east Betuwe between Driel and Huissen, opposite modern Arnhem. It was supported by a naval force which had made its base here after the destruction of the forts further downstream. But the attempted front soon disintegrated into chaos. Fighting had hardly begun when an auxiliary cohort from Tongeren went over to Civilis; and the naval force proved equally disloyal. Some of the rowers were Batavians, and these men intentionally got in the way of the sailors and marines as they attempted to carry out their duties. Then they resisted forcibly, steered the ships downstream towards enemy-held territory, and finally murdered those helmsmen and centurions who refused to throw in their lot with them. In the end, all the ships were either abandoned or captured. On land, a number of standards and prisoners were taken, though the Roman historian's principles forbid his being arithmetically precise. The losses in killed and wounded must have been heavy, and the sequel was the complete evacuation of the Island.[68]

News of the defeat spread rapidly among the Gauls and Germans. The latter immediately sent Civilis offers of support. As for the Gauls, the victor returned to their homes such of the captured cohort prefects as were of Gallic origin, and gave the men the choice between discharge and soldiering on as a Batavian force. Those who stayed were offered the same terms of service as before, and those who were sent home were incriminated by the offer and acceptance of Roman spoils. Before they disappeared, they were subjected to anti-Roman indoctrination. In fact, Civilis harboured no illusions about the practicability and utility of a Gallic revolt, but as much unrest as possible would serve his purpose.

The disastrous effects of civil war were nowhere more severely felt than on the Rhine. The unhappy Hordeonius was in a most difficult position, with insufficient forces, an adversary whose intentions were far from clear, an army suspicious of its officers, and a total bewilderment as to how loyalty to Vespasian could be reconciled with lip-service to Vitellius. He and most of his officers were secretly pro-Flavian, their men suspicious, sullen and openly pro-Vitellian. By the end of September he had received the circular letter issued by Vespasian after Beirut, to say nothing of a possible earlier missive announcing the proclamation of July. Antonius Primus had pointed out to him the desirability of conniving at an apparent offensive, or threat of offensive, from the Island, which would preclude the sending of further Vitellian reinforcements to the south. Impressed by this, Hordeonius actually summoned Civilis and explained the position in a confidential interview: a less than vigorous prosecution of the war against the Cannenefates, the encouragement of a feeling of insecurity in the Rhineland regions—this, but nothing more, might be acceptable to Vespasian. Indeed, it cannot be supposed that the cautious Vespasian, or the worried Hordeonius claiming to speak on his behalf, would have sanctioned actual warfare against Roman troops. Civilis kept his own council, convinced that he was master of the situation.

The exact degree to which the Flavians—Vespasian, Antonius Primus, Hordeonius Flaccus—may be regarded as accessories to the revolt of Civilis is as doubtful to us as it was to contemporaries. The documents that might have settled the issue were too incriminating to survive long. By whom, when, and on what matters letters were written and received cannot be deduced beyond doubt from the vague allusions of Tacitus, himself probably baffled and ignorant. But the tendency of the Flavian historians must inevitably have been to absolve Vespasian of all responsibility, and to blacken Hordeonius and Antonius. The latter, in particular, was still alive when the earlier Flavian historians were writing, and Mucianus, if no one else, would see to it that an impression was given that his rival had fostered the rebellion that led to the loss of the Rhineland as irresponsibly as he had endangered the frontier of the Danube. Hordeonius was dead, and could be maligned, poor man, without fear of contradiction. And for Vespasian in September 69, far away in Judaea, every consideration makes it obvious to us that no apologia was really needed; all his hesitations and actions show that he believed that the blockade and Mucianus' appearance on the frontiers of Italy were sufficient weapons to use against Vitellius.

The news of the catastrophic defeat on the Island at least made it clear that Civilis was an enemy of Rome, not merely of Vitellius. The legate therefore ordered Numisius Lupus, commanding the remnants of the Fifth and Fifteenth Legions at Vetera (of the former some 1,000, of the latter some 3,000 men still remained in the vast camp), to move out against the enemy. From these legions was selected a body of perhaps 2,000 men, with some auxiliary (Ubian) infantry and Treviran cavalry who were stationed in the vicinity. This poor force was hurriedly shipped across the Waal below its confluence with the Rhine, together with a Batavian cavalry regiment, in whose loyalty it was remarkable that anyone should have placed confidence at this late date. The second battle, fought in the Huissen–Elst area at no great distance from the site of the first, proved equally disastrous. Civilis had massed around himself the captured Roman standards, and in the fashion typical of the Germans caused his mother and sisters (his wife and son were away at Cologne), as well as the wives and young children of all his men, to take up a position behind the front to offer a spur to victory and taunts to the routed. Then the Batavian warriors raised the threatening strain of the war chant, at first a low whisper, but swelling to a roar like that of ocean breakers. It was accompanied by the shrieks and wails of the women. As the din rang out over the plain, it evoked in response only a feeble cheer. The Roman left was soon exposed by the defection of the Batavian cavalry, who immediately performed a volte-face and attacked their former comrades. The auxiliaries were scattered to the winds in wild flight. The few legionaries stood firm, and as, luckily, the Batavians pursued the easier plunder, eventually they managed to withdraw and make their way back to Vetera. It is curious and instructive to hear that the prefect of the defecting Batavian cavalry regiment, Claudius Labeo, was soon involved in a petty squabble with Civilis. As his murder (however convenient) might be unpopular and his continued presence embarrassing, Civilis kidnapped him and had him kept in exile among the allied Frisians. Such a welcome soon turned this weathercock Romeward once more. For the moment, however, the second defeat of the Romans led to serious demoralization and recrimination among the officers and men at Vetera and the other Rhineland forts.

Civilis now sent a second message to the eight cohorts of Batavians and Cannenefates in Upper Germany, asking them now to march northward to join the cause of the liberators. Only a few days before, they had received an order from Vitellius, issued in mid-September, to return to Italy in view of the Flavian invasion, and they were already beginning the march south. The request from Civilis at this moment presented their leaders, who were all Batavian nobles, with a dilemma. It was true that they had already been approached confidentially; but their first and traditional loyalty was to the Roman Caesar. Recent months, however, had strained their patience. The latest contact with Vitellius' army in northern Italy had been far from harmonious. To fight for a ruler so uncongenial and perhaps so little likely to survive might seem inadvisable. And if, indeed, their countrymen were to become completely independent of a weakened empire, it may have seemed desirable to some of the Batavian officers that they should not owe that independence entirely to Civilis. The more sober and far-sighted may well have calculated that Roman discipline and tenacity, qualities strikingly exemplified by Vespasian, would in the end over-come the difficulties of the present. One must therefore insure oneself against either contingency: a Roman or a Batavian success. The cohorts halted and their officers demanded of Hordeonius Flaccus at Mainz patently unacceptable terms for compliance with Vitellius' order—a bounty, double pay and an increase in the effectives of the higher-paid cavalry element in the predominantly infantry cohorts. It was alleged that these increases had been promised by Vitellius. But Hordeonius was not willing, authorized or able to make any such concessions, and he refused. The Batavians then marched north to join their countrymen, hoping to avoid as far as possible any contact with the legionary garri-sons.

Where this literal and metaphorical about-turn took place we do not know, but there is some probability that it was south of Mainz. If so, it would have been easy to by-pass that fortress by taking the short cut across the arc of the Rhine to Bingen via Alzey. Hordeonius knew that it would be impossible, or at any rate imprudent, to use his own reduced and diluted force to block the progress of 4,000 determined troops at Bingen, the obvious bottleneck. But it might be practicable to catch the Batavians between the united forces of Mainz and Bonn. He wrote to Herennius Gallus, commanding the First Legion at Bonn, 100 miles downstream, telling him to bar the passage of the Batavians and promising to follow closely on their heels with his own men. On a cal-culation of numbers, the rebels might well have succumbed to a well-timed pincer movement. But suddenly Flaccus countermanded the order to Gallus, telling him to allow the departing cohorts to pass through the town of Bonn without molestation. The reason for this surprising change of heart can only be conjectured. Certainly, Tacitus did not know it. It can only have sprung from the receipt of fresh in-formation or fresh orders. To reconstruct the correspondence between Vespasian, Vitellius, Antonius and Hordeonius Flaccus in this complex situation is, as we have seen, a desperate matter. But it could be argued that it was at this moment in late September that Flaccus received from Antonius an urgent request to head off any Rhineland reinforcements from Italy: Civilis, he added, had been asked by him to mount a feint attack on the Rhineland, and this was part of that plan. If this is some-thing like the truth, it is unnecessary to despair of Flaccus' sanity. He may have felt himself obliged, as a secret sympathizer with the Flavian cause, to refrain from annihilating the Batavian cohorts and thus neutralizing the threat of Civilis. Perhaps it would all work out for the best. But it would be as well to keep Antonius' letter, in order to safeguard himself in the event of any later enquiry after a Flavian victory. By an unfortunate mischance, the compromising document was kept and its existence revealed: at Neuss Hordeonius was to be compelled to read it to the troops, with disastrous effects upon discipline. But already in September and early October, these rapid changes of plan had bred suspicion and uneasiness: something not known to the ordinary soldier seemed to be going on behind the scenes. Worse still, Antonius' letter arrived at an awkward moment: there was insufficient time to enable the countermanding order to reach Herennius Gallus before the Batavians, some five days after passing Mainz, were approaching Bonn. On nearing the fortress, which could be less easily circumvented than Mainz, they sent a representative to explain their attitude. There was no question, they said diplomatically, of waging war against the Romans, for whom they had long fought. The fact was, they were wearied by the hard stint of twenty-five years, and longed for home and demobilization. If no resistance were offered, they would march on through Bonn without doing damage; but if any attempt were made to prevent their passage by force, they would cut their way through. Against his better judgment, pressed by his troops, and ignorant of the change of plan, Herennius Gallus allowed his 3,000 legionaries, some raw Belgian cohorts and a mob of camp followers to make sorties at several points in the hope of surrounding the numerically inferior Batavians. What the latter lacked in numbers, they more than made up for in experience and cohesion. They formed into squares, broke through the tenuous Roman line and drove Herennius Gallus' men back helter-skelter to the camp with heavy losses, particularly as they converged on the gates. The victors resumed their march, and gave Cologne, a walled city without a Roman garrison, a wide berth by marching well to the west on the flat plain surrounding the capital. Without further incident at either Neuss or Vetera, they reached Nijmegen. It was now mid-October.

Civilis was well placed. He disposed of nine trained cohorts of Batavians, some cavalry and a number of units who had deserted from the Romans on the Island—a force of some 15,000 in all. But from free Germany, eager would-be heroes were flowing in daily. He must proceed against Vetera. But even at this late stage, cunning or caution impelled him, tongue in cheek, to make his men swear allegiance to Vespasian, and to send an invitation to the garrison of Vetera to accept the same oath. He had miscalculated Roman pride. The impudent suggestion backfired, and the pro-Vitellian legions replied loftily that they were not in the habit of taking advice from a traitor or an enemy.

They already had an emperor in Vitellius, and in his defence they would maintain their loyalty and arms to their dying breath. As for Civilis, he would get his deserts, the punishment of a felon.

The site of Vetera has long been known and, in this century, carefully, though so far only partially, investigated. Between Xanten and Birten, by the main road that accompanies the Rhine on its west bank from Nijmegen to Neuss, is the slight eminence of the Fürstenberg (69 metres). On the ground sloping southward from it, and alongside an arm of the river, lies the site of the two-legion fort of Vetera. Its walls, defended by a single ditch six metres broad, and a double row of *cippi*, described a rectangle roughly 900 by 620 metres, within which 10,000 men, their stores and services could be easily, indeed spaciously, accommodated. Beneath today's ploughland, the layout of barracks, headquarters building, the houses of the two legionary commanders and the tribunes, and a hospital survives in foundations and footings, excavated, recorded and decently reinterred. The site was chosen in Augustan times and the fort of A.D. 16 was preceded by others of smaller size and quite different, if unintelligible, plan. The gentle slope guaranteed good drainage, and the proximity of the Rhine arm easy accessibility. During the first century, the fort underwent a number of improvements by the addition of timber and stone to reinforce the earthen walls and ditches. There seemed no real possibility that the place would ever have to stand siege, but the garrison had to be kept employed in the long years of peace, and the technique of fortification was not static.[69]

In the centre of the vast area of the camp of A.D. 69, the *principia* or headquarters complex, its outer wall measuring 120 by 95 metres, consisted of the usual unroofed and cloistered court, surrounded by a double range of storerooms and offices on three sides, the fourth being occupied by a covered parade hall like that reconstructed at the Saalburg. Adjacent lay a tribunal for allocutions, flanked by chapels guarding the standards and eagles—those of the Fifth on the left, of the Fifteenth on the right—and rooms which may have constituted the double armoury. To left and right of the headquarters, and separated from it by an eight-metres-wide road, stood the houses of the legionary commanders, their doorways opposite entrances to the central building. The ground plan of the house of the commander of the Fifth is particularly clear. The visitor, entering by a pillared vestibule behind the arcade of the street, found himself in a passage leading to the central hall or *atrium*, on to which opened a series of rooms, including the study of the master of the house, a second peristyle court and even a stadium-shaped, enclosed garden (83 by 18·8 metres) that recalls the great circus-like promenade of the Palatine, built soon after our date by Domitian, twice as long and more than twice as broad as the Vetera examples. In Rome, the modern visitor readily appreciates the seclusion

PLATE 11 Leonardo da Vinci's bird's-eye view of the country around Terracina

FOEDVSVECVMQVIBVS VOLET FACERE LICEAT ITA VTI LICVIT DIVO AVG
TI IVLIO CAESARI AVG TIBERIOQVE CLAVDIO CAESARI AVG GERMANICO
VTIQVE EI SENATVM HABERE RELATIONEM FACERE REMITTERE SENATVS
CONSVLTA PER RELATIONEM DISCESSIONEMQVE FACERE LICEAT
ITA VTI LICVIT DIVO AVG TI IVLIO CAESARI AVG TI CLAVDIO CAESARI
AVGVSTO GERMANICO
VTIQVE CVM EX VOLVNTATE AVCTORITATIVE IVSSV MANDATVVE EIVS
PRAESENTEVE EO SENATVS HABEBITVR OMNIVM RERVM IVS PERINDE
HABEATVR SERVETVR AC SI E LEGE SENATVS EDICTVS ESSET HABERETVRQVE
VTIQVE QVOS MAGISTRATVM POTESTATEM IMPERIVM CVRATIONEMVE
CVIVS REI PETENTES SENATVI POPVLOQVE ROMANO COMMENDAVERIT
QVIBVSVE SVFFRAGATIONEM SVAM DEDERIT PROMISERIT EORVM
COMITIS QVIBVSQVE EXTRA ORDINEM RATIO HABEATVR
VTIQVE EI FINES POMERII PROFERRE PROMOVERE CVM EX RE PVBLICA
CENSEBIT ESSE LICEAT ITA VTI LICVIT TI CLAVDIO CAESARI AVG
GERMANICO
VTIQVE QVAECVNQVE EX VSV REI PVBLICAE MAIESTATE DIVINARVM
HVMARVM PVBLICARVM PRIVATARVMQVE RERVM ESSE
CENSEBIT EI AGERE FACERE IVS POTESTASQVE SIT ITA VTI DIVO AVG
TIBERIOQVE IVLIO CAESARI AVG TIBERIOQVE CLAVDIO CAESARI
AVG GERMANICO FVIT
VTIQVE QVIBVS LEGIBVS PLEBEIVE SCITIS SCRIPTVM FVIT NE DIVVS AVG
TIBERIVSVE IVLIVS CAESAR AVG TIBERIVSQVE CLAVDIVS CAESAR AVG
GERMANICVS TENERENTVR IIS LEGIBVS PLEBISQVE SCITIS IMP CAESAR
VESPASIANVS SOLVTVS SIT QVAEQVE EX QVAQVE LEGE ROGATIONE
DIVVM AVG TIBERVMVE IVLIVM CAESAREM AVG TIBERIVMVE
CLAVDIVM CAESAREM AVG GERMANICVM FACERE OPORTVIT
EA OMNIA IMP CAESARI VESPASIANO AVG FACERE LICEAT
VTIQVE QVAE ANTE HANC LEGEM ROGATAM ACTA GESTA
DECRETA IMPERATA AB IMPERATORE CAESARE VESPASIANO AVG
IVSSV MANDATVVE EIVS A QVOQVE SVNT EA PERINDE IVSTA RATAQ
SINT AC SI POPVLI PLEBISVE IVSSV ACTA ESSENT

SANCTIO

SI QVIS HVIVSCE LEGIS ERGOA DVERSVS LEGES ROGATIONES PLEBISVE SCITA
SENATVSVE CONSVLTA FECIT FECERIT SIVE QVOD EVM EX LEGE ROGATIONE
PLEBISVE SCITO S VE FACERE OPORTEBIT NON FECERIT HVIVS LEGIS
ERGO ID EI NE FRAVDI ESTO NEVE QVIT OB EAM REM POPVLO DARE DEBETO
NEVE CVI DE EA RE ACTIONEVE IVDICATIO ESTO NEVE QVIS DE EA RE APVD
... SE NITO

PLATE 12   Part of the text of the Instrument conveying the imperial prerogatives
to Vespasian: the *Lex de Imperio Vespasiani*

of this private *rus in urbe*: and Vetera was a little Rome. A similar, but not identical, plan marked the corresponding house of the other commander. A more modest area (41 by 39 metres) with a single central hall was allotted to each of the tribunes. Of particular interest is the camp hospital, comparable with that of Windisch, its main building 83 metres square, having sixty small wards (each capable of holding three beds), a bath, foyer and operating room, all grouped around the central exercise area. Medical facilities were hardly available on this scale to any Roman civilian. Outside the fort, in what is now the village of Birten, there was a lively civilian settlement of camp followers, traders and retired soldiers, with their families: their little amphitheatre still serves the purposes of public entertainment today.

But these refinements brought small comfort to Munius as he strolled in his walled garden within the fort of Vetera, or to Numisius as he surveyed the defences of his own camp at Neuss. For them, the future was precarious. Vetera was clearly the enemy's next target. What imperilled it in the last months of 69 was not any shortcoming in preparedness—there had been a last-minute check of rampart, palisade and gate-towers—but the smallness of its garrison. Scarcely 5,000 men were available to maintain the day- and night-guard of a periphery of more than three kilometres.

The initial attack by Civilis came in October. It was lively, but quite unsuccessful. The Batavians and the German volunteers from east of the Rhine were formed up in separate armies, in order to encourage healthy rivalry. They first challenged the defence with long-distance volleys. But most of their missiles embedded themselves uselessly in the solid wall and palisade, while the attackers were exposed to plunging showers of stones. So, with a wild yell, they rushed forward, placing scaling-ladders against the timbered vallum or clambering over tortoises formed by their comrades. Any who managed to get up to the palisade were sent hurtling down, buried under stakes and javelins. Natives were always full of fire at the start of an engagement; and now the prospect of rich booty made Civilis' men willing to take considerable punishment. Moreover, Roman deserters and prisoners of war had shown them how to build a long timber shed like the superstructure of a bridge, put it on wheels and move it forward, some champions doing battle aloft and others, concealed beneath, undermining the wall. But they were amateurs at this game, and an artillery discharge of heavy stones soon flattened the crazy contraption. Finally, the Roman ballistae propelled ignited spears to set fire to the enemy equipment. This was too much. Civilis called off the attack and resorted to a siege that seemed to offer better prospects in a relatively short time, in view of the lack of Roman supplies.

Before the siege began, Flaccus had sent out recruiting officers to

G

enrol auxiliaries in Gaul. He mounted a relief expedition from Mainz, apparently in the last week of October, putting Dillius Vocula, commander of the Twenty-Second Legion, in charge of a contingent drawn from all the available legionaries, with orders to move at a good pace along the main road that followed the Rhine. Too lame to march himself, he travelled in one of the naval ships that accompanied the infantry. The troops distrusted Hordeonius, and discovering somehow or other that he had previously received a letter from Vespasian, compelled the unfortunate governor to read it at a parade: it announced the acclamation in Egypt, Judaea and Syria, and asked for support. The message was badly received, and Hordeonius thought it expedient to send the bearers of the letter to Vitellius in custody. But arrival at Bonn meant more recriminations. Herennius Gallus tried to excuse his defeat at the hands of the Batavians by accusing Hordeonius of failing to appear in support or take effective action to gather reinforcements in time. His superior could hardly explain publicly the real reason for his change of plan, and sought to rebut the frivolous and untrue charge of failure to recruit by reading out copies of his instructions on this matter. His version of events seems to be confirmed by the appearance at Cologne of the first Gallic levies, who came in readily enough, at least for a time. But there were seditious elements in the legionary army, which seems to have lost its pride and self-confidence. Yet by merely arresting one of the ringleaders and ordering his summary execution, which was carried out, Dillius Vocula was able to restore some kind of discipline. This induced Hordeonius, who was in a totally false position, to resign to him the total command of the expeditionary force, though he himself travelled on as far as Neuss.

The expedition was dogged by all sorts of bad luck. The autumnal rains of northern Italy had made the Po valley uncomfortably damp; the autumnal drought of the Rhineland had serious consequences on the flow of services along the river. The climatic and meteorological conditions in the basins of the two rivers are quite different. November is frequently a time of low water in the Rhine, and the early spring and hot summer seemed to have lowered the water-level disastrously. At certain notorious shallows, such as those at Bingen, supply ships were held up, and the same weather factors may have affected the Mosel as well, even supposing that all was well in the state of the Treveri. A second effect of the drought was that it lessened the defensive value of the river and made it easier for the Transrhenane Germans to creep across in their canoes, hollowed from single tree trunks and capable of carrying thirty men apiece. Under cover of darkness it was not difficult to stage fleeting raids, despite an increased watch along the many miles of river bank by static guards or mobile patrols of the Roman fleet. Thus, late in the year and in the rear of the relief expedition, a mixed force of Chatti, Usipi and Mattiaci managed to get across in some strength, obviously in the Taunus–Bingen area. Their attempt upon Mainz itself was a failure, but the marauders collected a fair amount of booty in the area, though the Treveri vigorously defended their own frontier along the Hunsrück, and some of the Germans were caught by a Roman force from Neuss. The whole defensive system along the Rhine frontier seemed to be crumbling.

At Bonn the relief expedition had received some addition of strength from the First, and at Neuss from the Sixteenth, Legions. Since the situation further north was obscure, advance headquarters were set up at Gellep and garrisoned with a small striking force by which reconnaissance and raids could be mounted against the territory of the Cugerni around Vetera, who, willingly or perforce, had joined Civilis. The physical labour of digging and building, together with a programme of training, did something to improve morale, and soon Vocula was able to explore the area towards Vetera. But beyond Neuss the Germans of the right bank controlled movements on the river, which was therefore no more available for bringing up supplies to Vetera than it had been for the same purpose further south during the November drought. Meanwhile, the Ubii around Cologne and the Treveri on the Mosel were being distracted by attacks from their neighbours. A quite separate Batavian enterprise was the dispatch of a force against the Menapii and Morini, south of Helinium, an exercise designed to soften up Gallic opinion and encourage the whole of Northern Gaul to join the independence movement. Civilis' ambitions were ramifying with success.

In December, he pressed the siege of Vetera harder, drawing a tight cordon round the place to prevent any news of the approach of the Gellep relief force from getting through to the besieged. But it was now clear to the Batavian commander that it was useless to expect his enthusiastic but unsophisticated German allies to handle anything but the weapons to which they were accustomed. They were used as cannon-fodder in head-on attacks upon the rampart and when repulsed sent in again and again. So unskilled were these warriors that, on one occasion, they lit a huge bonfire and held a night carousal within range of the fortress. As the wine went to their heads, they surged forward with a reckless folly that failed to achieve anything. Their own shots went astray, and the Romans were presented with targets silhouetted against the flames. Finally, Civilis made the Germans put the fire out, and there was a confused mêlée of darkness and battle in which discordant howling and uncoordinated attacks merely created a senseless pandemonium. The Romans on their rampart, reserving their missiles and blows until they could see the enemy, and throwing the latter down from the ladders as they scaled the wall, had little to fear from attackers as ill-organized as these.

The Batavians, however, had served in the Roman army, and used their knowledge or observation of Roman engineering, though hardly with great success. They built a siege-tower with two superimposed platforms, thirty feet high and theoretically capable of dominating the palisade and perhaps the gate-towers of the fort. This they moved up on wheels to the main gate near Birten, where the ground was flatter. But the defenders knew the appropriate reply. The tower was allowed to approach the walls. When it was in contact, sturdy metal-shod poles were used to spear the enemy attackers, and heavy beams swung out to batter the wooden structure, whose collapse caused many casualties. Then a sudden sortie by men waiting behind the gate completed the rout. Indeed, good fighters as the Batavians obviously were, it seems that such mechanical skills as the Roman army possessed were carefully husbanded within the legionary component. One of the more interesting pieces of equipment—not new in absolute terms, but evidently novel to its victims—was the *tolleno*, a grab or sweep, consisting of a long pole pivoted at a universal joint upon a solid support, and capable of lifting weights thanks to a counterbalance adjusted at the near end of the arm. The long pole, suitably equipped with a forked end, would be suddenly let down, and one or more unsuspecting enemy soldiers whisked up into the air before the eyes of their comrades, swung round, and deposited inside the fort.[70]

The second direct assault upon Vetera thus failed, and Civilis turned against Gellep. A raiding party, led by two officers (of whom one was his nephew), rode south from Vetera, sacked in passing the head-quarters of a cavalry regiment at Asberg (opposite Duisburg), and arrived so suddenly at Gellep that Vocula, whose reconnaissance must have been poor, was caught unawares. In an untidy battle (this time, Nervian auxiliary cohorts ran) things might have gone hard for him but for the opportune arrival of some Basque cohorts recruited by Galba, stationed in Spain or Gaul, already summoned by Hordeonius Flaccus, and now directed by him to Gellep. As these newcomers neared the fort, they heard the shouts of men fighting. While the Batavians' attention was elsewhere, they charged from the rear and caused tremendous havoc, their victims imagining that this was the main army from Neuss or Mainz. In this curious encounter of skill, inefficiency and luck, Roman casualties were numerically higher, but those of the Batavians, men picked for a special operation, more serious. Vocula was afterwards criticized for not exploiting the victory by moving direct to Vetera while the enemy were still in disarray; but he himself needed a few days to reorganize, bring up fresh men from Neuss and Bonn, and plan the advance over the remaining stretch of twenty miles.

Before he arrived, Civilis tried psychological warfare in hopes of a quick kill. He had captured some auxiliary and legionary standards and cavalry flags in the initial stages of the attack on Gellep. These emblems were now paraded round the walls of Vetera to create the impression that the relief attempt had been foiled and that surrender alone was left for the garrison. Even prisoners of war were put on show. One of these ventured an act of great courage. He shouted out what had really happened, and was instantly cut down by the guards. But this merely served to confirm his story; and indisputable evidence was provided by the smoke rising from the farms of the disloyal Cugerni, sacked by the advancing force from Gellep. When Vocula was within sight of the beleaguered fort, he halted and constructed a temporary marching-camp, the correct procedure before a battle, though it was criticized by some. From the walls the garrison of Vetera could see everything that happened. At the right moment, when Vocula had marshalled his men, they dashed out from the four gates of the camp. By a lucky mischance, Civilis' horse stumbled and threw him. Both armies believed a rumour that he was injured or dead, and the Batavians and German besiegers melted away. Vocula let them go, determined to husband his small force for what a realistic appreciation of the situation seemed to forebode.

Despite the success of the relief of Vetera, its lifeline was tenuous. No prospect yet existed of creating an army which could crush the Batavians in their homeland. It was obvious that Civilis would return, for his encounters with the Romans had been by no means unsuccessful, and the maintenance of his own position among the Batavian chiefs demanded a posture of attack. Beyond Neuss, the Romans had a very insecure hold upon the Rhineland, and as far south as Mainz marauders had been able to cross the river. For the defence of Vetera, necessary as a northern outpost to stem or reduce the pressure from the Low Countries, two things were immediately necessary. The number of non-combatants inside the fort must be reduced to the minimum, and the supply of food and stores greatly increased. Additional men could hardly be spared, but the existing small garrison had already shown that it had the capacity to resist, so long as provisions lasted. It was the lack of Roman supplies that was the dominant feature of the Rhineland campaign in the last months of 69.

From Vetera, the legionary transport, laden with evacuees, was sent to Neuss, returning northward with grain, which could no longer be moved by river. The first convoy got through unscathed on both outward and return journeys, since Civilis was still licking his wounds. The second was ambushed on its way south, the victim of excessive self-confidence and of Civilis' re-emergence with superior intelligence that told him when the transports were to set out again with their auxiliary guard. The train was proceeding on its way as if the enemy were miles away. Only a few men were at the command post, their arms were stowed away in the waggons, and everybody was wandering about with a complete lack of march discipline. But Civilis had sent parties ahead to hold the bridges where the road narrowed to cross the Mörs and other watercourses in the low-lying ground south-west of Rheinberg. Here, fighting suddenly flared up along the whole column, but it was surprisingly indecisive, despite the carelessness of the auxiliaries; and finally night forced a disengagement. The cohorts hurried the train on to Gellep and safety. This incident was, of course, reported to Vocula when the column returned to Vetera. It was obvious to him that a third attempt at the double run would involve serious risk. But as food was urgently needed, he took the risk and, this time, provided legionary protection: 1,000 men from the Fifth and Fifteenth. This guaranteed some sort of safety. Civilis was probably wise not to attempt a second ambush when the first had failed. But it was significant of the lowered morale at Vetera, which was clearly being provisioned to stand a resumption of the siege, that more than the appointed 1,000 men in fact joined the detail selected for convoy duty, and the garrison left at Vetera in its turn complained that it had been left in the lurch. On the march, the malcontents roundly declared that they had no intention of putting up any longer with short rations and disloyal commanders. They refused to return to Vetera, though Vocula himself had joined the third southward-bound convoy.

This refusal helped to seal the fate of Vetera. The reduction in the number of its defenders, the loss of the third convoy, the unexpectedly violent sedition at Neuss and the slowness of the eventual advance in the following year were factors which were destined in combination to frustrate Vocula's reasonable expectation that a resumed siege of Vetera could be successfully endured.

Shortly after his arrival at Neuss, Vocula won a victory over enemy cavalry who had followed him to the area. But success and failure seemed equally irritating to the legionary troublemakers. They demanded the donative which they understood Vitellius had sent. Hordeonius promptly handed it over, but in the name of Vespasian. This step, however understandable, was fatal. In a wild orgy of dissipation and sedition, their longstanding distrust of Hordeonius revived, inflamed by his blatant dereliction of Vitellius. None of the officers dared to resist a mob which darkness had stripped of the last vestige of restraint. The troops dragged Hordeonius Flaccus from his bed, and murdered him. Vocula almost suffered the same fate, but he disguised himself in the night riot by dressing as a soldier's servant, and thus got away to Bonn. The ringleaders of this riot, who belonged principally to the Fifth and Fifteenth, soon fled; but the portraits of Vitellius were replaced both at Neuss and in the nearer native communities, though Vitellius was by this time no more. However, at Bonn the men of the

First, Fourth and Twenty-Second Legions put themselves under Vocula's orders, and swore allegiance to Vespasian before mounting the emergency rescue operation which moved upstream towards Mainz.

But, by this time, Civilis had made contact with Julius Classicus, the commander of the Treviran cavalry regiment detached by Valens to Fréjus and now apparently back in the Rhineland. Classicus was one of the richest and most prominent leaders of his people, descended from a line of kings, when kings still ruled in Gaul, and given to declaring that he counted among his ancestors more foes than friends of Rome. The reference was clearly to Indutiomarus, Julius Caesar's enemy, and to the Florus who helped to lead a transient rebellion in A.D. 21. However exaggerated, the boast conjured up in some heated imaginations grand notions of liberty and personal aggrandizement. Two such men as Classicus and Civilis—especially if they could spread the revolt to embrace the people of Langres—might well set the whole of north-east Gaul on fire. A conference was proposed, to be held in secret at Cologne. The attempt to put history's clock back was soon to be proved folly. But the proof was to be costly for everyone. Thus, in the Rhineland the year closed in dishonour, gloom and uncertainty, the Roman army divided and mutinous or demoralized, the German and Gallic tribes unsettled, Civilis successful and Vetera facing a renewed and desperate siege. Even the saner elements of the army, the leaders of the Gauls and the citizens of Cologne, might be forgiven for thinking that, while the Batavian and German uprising would finally be crushed, things would certainly get worse before they got better. Both the optimism and the pessimism were to be fully justified by the event.

Scarcely anything of the involved situation in the Rhineland was known to Vespasian at the other end of the Roman world, and even the first attack on the Rhine forts in late April cannot have affected a decision to claim the principate which must be dated to late May. Since Nero's death, the Jewish War had been quiescent. Vespasian had had no intention of hastening the final collision without a clear mandate from Rome. It was as impossible to obtain such a statement of policy in the first six months of 69 as it had been in the last six months of 68; and at the end of these twelve months, Vespasian had decided upon a strategy of his own which prolonged the period of inaction. Luckily, the suicidal factions of the Jews rendered any real danger from that quarter inconsiderable. In the spring of 69, a young and vigorous brigand chief from Jerash, Simon ben Giora, had begun to terrorize southern Judaea. After a spell at the Dead Sea fortress of Machaerus, he had made for himself a stronghold in the area of the Frank Mountain, the 880-metre-high castle hill of Herod, the Herodium, and of the ancient town of Abraham, Hebron. Near Hebron was shown the great terebinth tree, one of those of Mamre, beneath which the patriarch had set up his tent;

and Herod the Great had created a sanctuary here, embracing the tree, a well and an altar, so that its occupation bestowed a certain prestige upon the occupier. But Simon was no prophet or Messiah. For some months he and a large following ravaged the hills and the plain of Idumaea like locusts, but in the early summer they transferred themselves to Jerusalem and contributed their part to the internal dissensions within the stricken city.

It was clear then that the Jews could be relied upon to be their own worst enemies. Nevertheless, as we have seen, when all arrangements had been made for the declaration on 1 July at Alexandria and immediately afterwards in Judaea and Syria, Vespasian had thought it advisable to show the flag in the brief June excursion. Thereafter, the Jewish question could certainly wait until the spring of 70, since only Herodium, Masada, Machaerus and Jerusalem now held out. Nevertheless, the late date at which Vespasian finally made his way to Rome in 70 was in part determined by the fact that there was unfinished business in Judaea.

After the conference of Beirut and the departure of Mucianus from Antioch, where Vespasian had taken leave of him, a period of some three months passed about which we are ill-informed. Vespasian and Titus, perhaps in Syria and Judaea respectively, continued the work decided on at Beirut. The flow of talent from Rome was now beginning to reach the East. Vespasian carefully surveyed his resources in men as well as material; and the promotions which he made brought into prominence some men of exceptional calibre, who were soon to rise to highest senatorial rank. A mission had been sent to Parthia, and King Vologaeses had replied.

Only one cloud appeared on the immediate horizon. As we observed, Mucianus had concentrated the Black Sea fleet at Istanbul, and the absence of any Roman policing of the Black Sea was soon noticed. Some five years previously, as part of a move by Nero to strengthen the eastern frontier, the kingdom of Pontus (around Sinop, Samsun and Trabzon) had been added to the Roman province of Bithynia immediately to its west, and the last king, Polemo II, had been compelled to abdicate. The royal fleet now became the *classis Pontica*, under a Roman officer. Its ex-commander, who bore the splendid name of Anicetus, 'The Unconquered', was no more happy to see his command pass under alien control than he was to observe the end of the kingdom. An opportunity for revenge now presented itself. In the name of Vitellius, he called to arms the wild mountaineers of north-eastern Anatolia. The lure of plunder has always been acceptable enough in this part of the world. At the head of a considerable force, he swooped down on Trabzon, and cut to pieces a unit which had once formed part of the royal army but now, in the guise of a Roman auxiliary cohort, had been dignified with the special privilege of Roman citizenship and equipped with Roman standards and uniform. But its fighting capacity remained mediocre. Anicetus then fanned the flames of insurrection by creating a rebel fleet of triremes, which sailed the Black Sea unhindered and at will. The barbarian tribes took a leaf out of Anicetus' book by hastily constructing small craft called *camarae*, arks narrow above the waterline and broad in the beam, held together with wooden pegging or cordage. These unusual clinker-built vessels, which would hold up to twenty-five or thirty people, were designed to cope with the sudden storms of an unfriendly sea. When the water became choppy, the mariners would increase the freeboard by adding planks successively as the need arose, until they were wholly enclosed by a sort of shell. Identical in shape fore and aft, these craft could be rowed in either direction, stern or bow first, and when the boatmen returned to land, they put the *camarae* on their shoulders, as the Aran islanders their curraghs, and carried them into the thickets where they lived, tilling a poor soil.[71]

On hearing of Anicetus' activities, Vespasian formed a legionary force and sent it north under Virdius Geminus. This experienced officer soon dealt with the looters on land, and quickly constructing galleys with the timber of Pontus or Bithynia, caught up with Anicetus at the mouth of the Khobi under the Caucasus. The rebellious admiral had bribed the king of the local tribe of the Sedochezi to give him asylum. At first the potentate tried to bluster, in an attempt to save his protégé from extradition. But when he was confronted with the plain choice between war and a bribe, his loyalty to Anicetus melted away. Hoping to secure himself against both Romans and rebels, he struck a bargain providing for the execution of Anicetus and surrendered the refugee. That was the end of the episode.

In early November, reassured by this good news, Vespasian moved towards Egypt, leaving Titus in Caesarea. On the heels of one happy message came another. In mid-November, after crossing into Egypt at El-Arish, he heard the news of the Second Battle of Cremona. Whatever dissatisfaction he felt at the anticipation of his own plans, the unfortunate effect upon public opinion of the sack of an Italian city and the fear of possible jealousy between his two champions Mucianus and Antonius must have been far outweighed by relief at the prospect of a rapid end to the war. It was certain that Vitellius would capitulate, and it might well be that the need for an invasion of Cyrenaica and Africa to complete the blockade was now past. Nevertheless, this could not be assumed as a certainty, and Vespasian decided to carry on the preparations for the march westwards. Greatly encouraged, he hurried on to Alexandria, where the city which had greeted his proclamation so ecstatically five months before accorded him obsequious and optimistic attention.[72]

Alexandria, the second city in the empire for size and wealth, was to be Vespasian's place of residence for some four months. Until such time as the winds of March reopened the sea to the fleets that would accompany him, he held court. There was much to do and see. The capital of the Ptolemies, whose successor was the Roman emperor, had been founded by Alexander and still preserved his tomb. In the area of the Palaces lay the Sema, the Tomb, a sacred enclosure containing the crypt in which lay the remains of the greatest leader of antiquity. Within the enclosure, one descended some steps to an open, sunken forecourt, beyond which lay an inner room containing the couch supporting the body, which was enclosed in a glass coffin. Julius and Octavian had come here to pay their respects to the one Greek whom the Romans considered their equal, or superior, in the art of war and imperial dominion, in exploration and the founding of city-states in barbarous lands, and as the bringer of civilization. It was fitting that the founder of the second dynasty of Roman emperors should, in paying this visit, follow the founder of the first.[73]

Alexandria was eager to play the host. Flattery and superstition combined to render to the blunt old gentleman from Rieti honours which he found it difficult to take seriously. But he soon learned to humour the natives and indulge their perhaps not entirely baseless belief in his destiny. Perhaps it was true, as the Stoics claimed, that a Divine Providence existed, manifesting itself in many ways, and that a rational man should cooperate with its mysterious workings.

Among the lower classes of the Egyptian capital, there was a blind man whom everybody knew. One day this fellow threw himself at Vespasian's feet, imploring him with groans to heal his blindness. He had been told to make this request by the god Sarapis. Would it please His Majesty to anoint his cheeks and eyeballs with the imperial spittle? A second petitioner, suffering from a withered hand, pleaded his case, too, also on the advice of Sarapis: would Caesar not tread upon him with his imperial foot? At first, Vespasian laughed, and refused. When the two insisted, he hesitated. The situation was becoming embarrassing. A refusal would look churlish; if he agreed and nothing happened, his own reputation might suffer in the eyes of a credulous mob. Before committing himself, Vespasian asked the doctors for an opinion. These gentlemen discoursed at length on the various possibilities. The man's vision was not irretrievably damaged, and correct treatment could perhaps put right the dislocated hand. Perhaps this was the will of the god. Perhaps the emperor, the Pharoah, had been chosen to perform a miracle. Anyhow, if a cure were effected, the credit would go to him; if not, the poor wretches would have to bear the ridicule. Vespasian capitulated. With a deprecatory smile, he did what was asked in the presence of an expectant crowd. Instantly, the cripple recovered the use of his hand, and the light of heaven dawned upon his blind companion. Thirty years later, in Trajan's reign, these incidents were still vouched for by eyewitnesses, though there was now nothing to be gained by lying.

II

The Battle of Rome

At first light on 18 December a procession gathered at the palace to perform the public act of abdication. Vitellius walked down the slope to the Forum dressed in funereal grey, surrounded by his dejected household servants; and behind him his six-year-old son, the poor stutterer so proudly presented to the troops at Lyon a few months ago, was carried luxuriously but ominously in a litter, his last taste of the greatness his father had so often promised him. The cheers of the public were loud and ill-timed, but the Praetorian escort preserved a sullen silence. No man, however dull of heart, could have failed to feel some emotion at the scene. An emperor of Rome, so recently the acknowledged master of the civilized world, was leaving the imperial palace that had been his and was moving through the crowded streets of Rome on the road to abdication and exile. Assassination, suicide, poison and natural death were known as marking the ends of emperors. But there was something new in the obsequies of a reign celebrated in a glare of publicity by the ruler himself. Vitellius walked towards the rostrum, mounted it and came forward so that every eye rested on him. He made a short speech similar to that delivered to the Praetorians on the previous evening, this time, however, reading from a prepared script. In the interests of peace and of his country, he said, he was abdicating a position he had from the beginning been reluctant to assume. He asked his hearers not to think ill of him, and to deal mercifully with his brother Lucius, his wife Galeria and his innocent children. As he spoke, he held up the small lad so that he could be seen, appealing both to the crowd as a whole and to individuals in it. In the end he broke down, and silently drew from his belt the ten-inch dagger (such was normally worn by the Roman infantryman), which in Vitellius served as the symbol of the commander-in-chief's power of life and death, offering it to the consul Caecilius Simplex who was standing beside him. The magistrate refused it, and there were indignant cries of 'No, no' from the populace. Vitellius then retreated from the rostrum with the intention of laying down his insignia in a public building immediately behind the platform, associated with acts of state and by its very name symbolic: the Temple of Concord at the foot of the Register House. From here he

would take refuge in Lucius' residence close by. At this the shouts of
protest redoubled. The crowd surged around, preventing his mounting
the flight of steps to the broad pronaos of the temple and blocking all
egress from the Forum. 'You are Concord enough—go back to the
palace!' roared the crowd. Nonplussed, Vitellius retraced his steps
through the Forum but at the far end was again compelled by the press
of bodies to abandon his intention, which was now to make for the
Aventine and his own private residence. So he went reluctantly up the
sloping road that led to the forecourt of the palace. Even abdication, it
seemed, was beyond his reach. For Vitellius there was to be no way of
releasing the ears of the wolf without suffering its jaws.[74]

How he spent the following hours can only be inferred. He sent
Galeria and the children away from the palace by a secret exit, but for
some reason did not follow them himself. This decision to remain may
have been the result of the arrival of Lucius' message from Terracina,
accompanied by the slave who had betrayed the town to Lucius. In a
sudden upsurge of hope and confidence, Aulus rewarded Icelus with a
knight's rings. In Vitellius' eyes the success at Terracina, coming after
so many failures, shed a new light on the situation. Even if the abdication had failed, he might now exact better terms by capitulating from a
position of strength. The return of the six Praetorian cohorts from
Terracina to Rome could be effected by the evening of 21 December,
and their presence might make Antonius readier to avoid the use of
force in occupying the city. It was essential to play for time. He sent an
order to Lucius to return at full speed, told the superintendent of the
armoury in the Praetorian camp to issue arms to the People, who had
clamoured for them, and fixed a meeting of the Senate for the following
day, 19 December, to negotiate further with the Flavians.

But already, on the same morning, things had taken a surprising turn
in Rome without any initiative from Vitellius. At the moment when he
was making his abdication attempt in the Forum, nearly a mile away
to the north-east and at a spot south of the modern Manica Lunga of
the Quirinal Palace, a crowd of notables had gathered at the house of
Flavius Sabinus, prefect of the city, to whom supreme responsibility
had, it seemed, now passed. Among them were the other consul Quintius Atticus, some leading members of the Senate, a number of knights,
and representatives of the units of the Urban Cohorts and the Cohorts
of the Watch, both of which Sabinus commanded by virtue of his office.
It was a levée with a difference. Quite apart from the desirability of
paying homage to the elder brother of the new emperor, there were
practical matters to be settled. The oath must be administered to all
military personnel; the policing of Rome must be assured; the transfer
of some senior civil functions would be necessary; and arrangements
must be made for the removal of Vitellius and his family from Rome.

Quintius produced some pretentiously-worded consular edicts informing the civil population of the position, and arranged for these to be
published throughout the city. Suddenly the conference was interrupted. Word came that the abdication had not been carried through,
that the crowds in the Forum had strongly supported the retention of
Vitellius as emperor, and that the Praetorians were determined to
defend a leader whose disappearance would entail their own destruction. Vitellius had accomplished nothing and returned to the palace.
Among the Flavians there was consternation. But Sabinus and the rest
had gone too far to retreat, and the bitter reflection that it was Vitellius
who had failed to carry out his part of a bargain freely negotiated
helped little. The Flavians were now confronted with the very real
danger that, if they separated on their several errands, they might be
hunted down individually and dealt with as traitors. The prefect was
a moderate man, anxious at all costs to avoid bloodshed; but he was
not lacking in courage. He decided to proceed to the Forum to explain
the full facts of the situation to the crowds still gathered there in perplexity after Vitellius himself had retreated into the palace; and if
necessary meet Vitellius once more. With him went a number of
military and civilian dignitaries, though some of the less heroic Flavians
quietly disappeared.

The party had reached the Basin of Fundanus, a well-known land-
mark on the slope leading down to the centre of the city, when it was
confronted by a group of Vitellian activists, including some Praetorians,
who were obviously bent on barring the way to the Forum and the
palace. This encounter was unexpected. A scuffle developed, in which
the Vitellians came off the better. In the circumstances Sabinus thought
it wise not to attempt to push on towards the Forum, but to turn off to
the right and occupy the strong point of the Capitoline Hill. So the
motley force of soldiers and civilians, including some women (one is
mentioned by name, the courageous Verulana Gratilla), turned off to
the west and in due course reached and moved up the slope represented
by the modern Cordinata, passed the walled-in site of the Grove of
Refuge, where Romulus had accommodated the outlaws that flocked
to early Rome, and entered by a postern the sanctuary of the Temple
of Jupiter Best and Greatest on the southern summit of the two-peaked
hill. The Vitellian troops threw a loose cordon round the foot of the
eminence, but by about 10 p.m., when the pickets were growing careless, Sabinus was able to profit by the presence of an unwatched sector
to get his son Sabinus and his nephew Domitian to join him on the
Capitol; he also managed to send news to the Flavian army, pointing
out that the situation of the besieged, who had neither food nor proper
arms, would soon become desperate unless help were forthcoming. It
was later alleged, in defence of Antonius, that the night was so quiet

that Sabinus himself could have got away without danger, for Vitellius' men, though full of dash on the battlefield, were pretty slack when
it came to humdrum fatigues and guard duties. In addition, the sudden
onset of winter rain made seeing and hearing difficult.

Sabinus made no such attempt, and indeed any plan to escape from
the Capitol to the advancing Flavian army would have been extremely
hazardous. Even Sabinus' messages sent before the siege informing
Antonius of the abdication and related measures had had to pass a
strict control, and for this reason had been got out of Rome in such
ingenious containers as baskets of fruit, reeds used by fowlers to carry
bird lime and coffins (with their corpses).

At or before first light on 19 December the city prefect sent a senior
centurion, Cornelius Martialis, to the Palatine to protest to Vitellius
about the breach in their agreement. Vitellius received the envoy and
expressed his concern at the situation, apologizing for the exuberance
of troops over whom, he said, he no longer exercised any real control.
He was himself no less a prisoner than Sabinus. With this cold comfort,
which had an appearance of plausibility, Martialis was dismissed; and
Vitellius pointedly warned the officer to leave by a remote corner of the
hill in order to avoid being murdered by the soldiers as the intermediary
of an understanding that they abominated. He himself, he added, was
in no position either to command or to prohibit; emperor no longer,
he was merely the cause of fighting.

Still, there was no reason so far why some accommodation should not
be worked out if Vitellius had had the capacity and time to reassert
himself and assure the troops that Sabinus had acted in good faith in
accordance with a prior arrangement. But at this point Fortune, who
had so often favoured the Flavians, turned against them. After the
surrender at Narni and before moving on to Otricoli, Antonius had
ordered Petilius Cerialis to take 1,000 cavalrymen, including some of
those who had changed sides at Terni, and move up by a different
route towards Rome in order to reconnoitre what possibilities of entry
there might be if, after all, Vitellius' overtures came to nothing. This
force had started off early on 16 December, and in the course of that
day and the two following advanced via Rieti and the quiet Salarian
Way as far as Fidenae, an old town much decayed, on the left bank of
the Tiber five miles above Rome, represented now by the mound of
Castel Giubileo. The ride of some seventy miles was performed without
haste. It was the holiday season, and there seemed to be no urgency.
But on the evening of 18 December, Cerialis at Fidenae must surely
have got wind of the alarming developments in Rome. If so, he must
have felt that he should do something to relieve the pressure upon the
unfortunates gathered around Sabinus, whose character and ability to
withstand prolonged strain he was too close a relative to misjudge. In

any event, early on the following morning he ordered an attack on the north-eastern suburbs of the city, somewhat rashly expecting to encounter only a token resistance. He was much mistaken. This was precisely the neighbourhood in which lay the Praetorian barracks, and the Vitellian cohorts, even if easy-going in their watch upon the Capitol where there was no real danger, were sufficiently alive to the approach of Antonius to place pickets on the roads leading north. Cerialis ran into a mixed force of enemy infantry and cavalry amid the suburban villas, kitchen gardens and winding lanes of the Porta Salaria area, familiar enough to the garrison of Rome, but puzzling to cavalry from the Danube. Nor did the Flavian force work well together, for those elements who had, until four days before, considered themselves to be fighting for Vitellius now held back to see whether they should not revert to their previous allegiance. Julius Flavianus, the commander of one of the cavalry regiments, was captured, and the rest of the force was pushed ignominiously back, though the victors gave up the pursuit at Fidenae. Cerialis' motives may have been laudable; but the action had been typically reckless and was to have grave consequences.

The reaction of the Vitellians to this attack was understandably violent. It was obvious, they said to themselves, that the arrival of Cerialis had been a clumsy attempt to sneak into Rome while they themselves were preoccupied in containing Sabinus and Domitian. Indeed the whole comedy of the abortive abdication had been a deep-laid plot by the scheming old politician hoping to mislead Vitellius and stultify the loyalty of the Praetorians. So without waiting for heavy equipment and without their officers (who may have judged the situation more coolly and with longer views) most of the three Praetorian cohorts made off in a fury along the main road that led into the city. It must have been about midday when, descending by the Via di Marforio, they debouched on the northern corner of the Forum Romanum, rushed past between the Temples of Concord and Saturn, and charged straight along the Capitoline slope as far as the outer main gateway of the sacred enclosure. Their appearance could hardly have been expected by Sabinus, for its motive—revenge for the seemingly collusive synchronism of Cerialis' approach—was unknown to him. But there were soldiers among the party who could think and act quickly. In A.D. 69 a long portico lined the right-hand side of the rise as you ascended. The Flavian soldiers, coming from higher ground, rapidly posted themselves on the roof of this colonnade and from it assailed the Vitellians with stones and tiles as they tried to pass beneath them. The attackers for their part were armed only with swords. Beaten back at the first attempt, they decided that they would not wait for artillery to be brought up from the barracks two miles away. They set light to the portico at its lowest point and as the flames spread uphill, driving back the Flavians, they followed them up, and would have battered down the charred gates, had not Sabinus uprooted a number of the statues which thickly adorned the area and with them formed an improvised barricade.

Foiled at the main entrance, the Vitellians soon found three other ways of access. Redescending the Clivus Capitolinus, they divided at its foot. Some made for the Via dell' Arco di Settimio Severo, the Hundred Steps between the Register House and the prison, determined on an assault from the southern part of the Piazza del Campidoglio. Others rode round to the north face of the Capitol and mounted the ramp used by Sabinus and his followers on the previous day. Yet a third group entered the ground floors of the high tenements that hugged the Capitoline rock on the north and north-east sides, climbing up under cover from storey to storey and emerging at the tops of the buildings. In a time of peace which had encouraged a comparable situation at Verona and Cremona, these flatted houses had been allowed to mount level with the surface of the sacred area. This was much the most serious threat to the defenders. In an effort to snap off this attack, Quintius Atticus, it seems, employed the weapon already used by the enemy and ordered the houses to be set on fire. They blazed up with the notorious combustibility of the Roman flat complex, and from there the fire leapt to the portico that fringed the Capitoline area. In close proximity lay the rear of the great temple. Its old wooden rafters, despite the recent rain as dry as cinder under the well-tended tiles, caught fire, and fed a holocaust. As the whole building flared, forcing both attackers and defenders back the triple Temple of Jupiter, Juno and Minerva was burnt to the ground undefended and un-attacked. Three thousand bronze tablets containing the text of sena-torial decrees and laws going back almost to the earliest days of Rome perished in the fire. It had been a wonderful archive, whose loss was not easily made good.

The great pillar of fire and smoke announced not the help but the anger of the gods, working through the folly of men. To the Roman and non-Roman world the destruction of the national shrine, before which, almost a year ago, Galba had prayed for the welfare of Rome and him-self, seemed a portent of retribution. The Temple of Jupiter Optimus Maximus was coeval with the founding of the republic. It had been vowed by the good king Tarquin the Elder and dedicated by the heroic consul Horatius. Its first structure, whose foundations may still be seen beneath the Conservatori Museum, had lasted for 425 years, until on 6 July 83 B.C. a mysterious act of arson had destroyed it, in a disaster that heralded the tyranny of Sulla, the dictator whose example and succession had brought about the downfall of the republic. Now its replacement, dedicated in 69 B.C., had been destroyed 138 years later under the principate, in the madness of another civil war. Did the repeated doom foreshadow the accelerated approach of a final ruin?[75]

But there was little time for melancholy philosophy on that afternoon of calamity. The fire seems to have consumed Sabinus' will to resist and his ability to command. He gave conflicting orders, immediately supplanted by the instructions of others, none of them carried out. Soon the defenders threw down their arms and looked around for methods of escape or places of concealment: the cliffs or crypts or sacristies. As resistance died, the Vitellians forced their way in from the three sides. A few of the Flavian professional soldiers—tribunes or centurions like Cornelius Martialis, Aemilius Pacensis, Casperius Niger, Didius Scaeva—ventured to resist and were cut down. Sabinus was unarmed and made no attempt to run; together with Quintius Atticus he was surrounded and taken prisoner. Some of the defenders, disguising themselves as Vitellians and when challenged giving the Vitellian watchword which they had learned in the confusion, managed to get away through the smouldering tenements, and that these were fairly numerous is shown by the fact that many self-seeking characters who had had nothing to do with the fighting on the Capitol later claimed to have participated in it. As soon as the defences were breached, Domitian had disappeared.

Sabinus and Atticus, heavily manacled, were taken to the Palatine, where in the forecourt at the head of the staircase Vitellius received them with looks and words that showed little hostility. He was well aware of his own slender authority and of the innocence of the prefect and the consul, who had merely tried to carry out the agreement arrived at in the Temple of Apollo. But he was unable to save Sabinus. The prefect who had served his country so well was stabbed and hacked to death by the mob. His head was cut off and the decapitated body dragged to the point where the carcases of felons were exposed at the foot of the Gemonian Steps. Vitellius can hardly be blamed for a barbarity so obviously contrary to his own interest and so certain to be avenged; and he did succeed in saving the life of the consul. When asked about the origin of the fire, Atticus had admitted issuing the order to ignite the tenements, thus unintentionally causing the destruction of the temple. This admission, which relieved the Vitellians of the opprobrium of sacrilege, was no doubt honest, obscured though it later was by the efforts of the Flavian historians to shift the blame on to Vitellian shoulders. It was perhaps the consideration that such a valuable witness should be kept alive that enabled Vitellius to mollify the would-be executioners.

The death of Flavius Sabinus was a senseless act of lynch-law, a tragic end to a life of long service to the state. At the time of his death, Vespasian's brother was in his sixties, and his public career extended over thirty-five years. In 43 he fought in Britain with his brother. He governed Moesia for seven years (49–56) and was city prefect in 56–60 and 62–68 under Nero, and once again in the present year from Otho's accession onward. In 61 he seems to have held a special commission to conduct the census of the Gallic provinces, a particularly onerous post in a financially important part of the empire. Sabinus was a mild and honest man, lacking the ability to dominate events and yielding perhaps too readily to the pressures put upon him by circumstances and people. Thus in April, on hearing of Otho's death, Dolabella had left his place of banishment at Aquino and made his way to Rome as a possible candidate for the principate and rival to Vitellius. The threats of Triaria had forced Sabinus to report this potentially dangerous development to Vitellius, who demanded the man's death. It fell to Sabinus to arrange a discreet liquidation, accelerated by the impatience of the executioner, who murdered him at a wayside inn. It can neither be proved nor disproved that Sabinus discussed with Caecina the desirability of the latter's conversion to the Flavian cause; but from August onwards the news of his brother's salutation as emperor at Alexandria and in the East must have put him in an invidious position. It says something for his honesty—and for Vitellius' own regard for him—that he was maintained in the key position of prefect of the city until the end, that he was acceptable as a mediator to Vitellius, and that the latter had no complaint to make against him even on the occupation of the Capitol. There were few more innocent victims of the year of civil strife than he. In January 70, when Rome had fallen, something was done to make amends for his death. At the proposal of Domitian, the Senate voted him a state funeral, a medallion portrait, probably to be placed in the Senate House, and a statue in one of the two semicircular porticoes of the Forum of Augustus. Here, honoured in effigy and epitaph, he joined the company of the *triumphatores*.[76]

Meanwhile, forty miles to the north the army of Antonius Primus was celebrating the Saturnalia with a well-earned rest (the legions had scarcely paused at Carsulae) and the usual jollification. When such numbers of men were gathered in a small town, it may not have been possible to provide the plums, dates, figs and apples that traditionally accompanied such an occasion, but there were certainly no duties to speak of. The officers messed with the men without distinction of rank, and for once all could dice for nuts or money without breaking regulations. The necessity of leaving a number of troops, own and enemy, on the plain of Terni had made it advisable to march on immediately after the Vitellian capitulation at Narni to tap a fresh source of supply. The prosperous little town of Otricoli, already in the home stretch of the Tiber valley, was only twelve miles away, and an obvious choice. On 16 December, therefore, the main body of the Flavians had moved on, and

during the first two days of the Saturnalia, 17 and 18 December, they
rested, totally unaware that the president of the immortals, whose
colossal head may already have impressed the beholder at Otricoli, was
about to lose his temple at Rome and Sabinus his life. All seemed over
bar the ceremonial entry.

The unfortunate fact that the inactivity of Antonius synchronized
with the siege of the Capitol became a matter of heated discussion later,
when inquests on the events of December were held by gossips, pamphleteers and, in due course, historians. Wild allegations were made by
those who sought to please Mucianus by vilifying his rival: the general
had been bribed by Vitellius (correspondence was known to have been
exchanged between them) with the promise of a consulship, marriage
with his daughter and a rich dowry to go with her. In fact, there were
three perfectly credible and creditable reasons for the pause at Otricoli.
Military accounts of Domitianic date, preserved in a papyrus at
Geneva, mention among a number of stoppages deducted from pay a
saturnalicium k(astrense), or contribution to the cost of a camp Christmas
dinner (on the verso, incidentally, appears the name, in the rank of
camp commandant, of the forceful T. Suedius Clemens, who had been
the most effective among the leaders of Otho's naval expedition in
spring of the present year); so that even if Macrobius did not fill the
strange silence of Tacitus, we should still suspect that the Saturnalia
was a military as well as a civil holiday. Secondly, given time, there
were good prospects that Vitellius would abdicate, or that a compromise avoiding an attack on Rome would be achieved. Thirdly, it
was Antonius' duty, if not his pleasure, to await the arrival of Mucianus,
who by this time was traversing the Furlo only 160 miles, or eight rapid
marching days, behind. Vespasian's lieutenant had, if only in veiled
hints, made it abundantly clear to Antonius that he expected to be
present at the formal entry into liberated Rome. All these considerations—including that of exact chronology—were muddled in the
controversy, and only some appear in an ill-digested form in Tacitus.[77]

The holiday atmosphere was rudely interrupted in the small hours of
19 December when Sabinus' messenger announced the investment of
the Capitol and the precarious position of Sabinus himself, Domitian
and their company, who even if their lives were spared were likely to
make useful hostages. Antonius immediately struck camp and marched
hard southwards, covering in some twelve hours the thirty-five miles or
so to Grotta Rossa. When the weary troops reached the village well
after the winter nightfall, it was to find that their forced march had
gone for nothing. They were too late. The Capitol had been stormed
several hours before, Sabinus was dead and Domitian missing. Nor was
this the sum total of disaster. We must suppose, from the proximity of
Castel Giubileo to the Flaminian Way on the other bank of the river, that

Cerialis' ill-success of that morning was then reported to Antonius; and finally the apparent enthusiasm of the people of Rome for Vitellius, demonstrated by the rejection of the abdication and the demand for arms (answered by their distribution to slave and free), proved that the war was by no means over. Whether the intelligence also included, as it may well have done, the story of Terracina's capture by Lucius, is uncertain. But in any case it was one of unrelieved catastrophe, and Antonius can have enjoyed little sleep that night. Much later, when the Flavian general had lived for many years in retirement at Toulouse, Martial too glibly imagines his thoughts on reviewing his past life:

> No day recalled brings heaviness or pain,
> No day that's done makes memory aghast:
> A good man's span is long; for him the past
> Brings pleasure pure, and so he lives again.

To relive, and repeatedly, the events of 19 December in memory was no addition to life.[73]

In the morning morale had recovered somewhat. There was no note of uncertainty in the rejection of the enemy's request for a few days' armistice. At the meeting of the Senate on the afternoon of 19 December, Vitellius had recommended the sending of envoys both to Cerialis and to Antonius, to ask for peace or at least for a respite. The envoys received short shrift, and went in peril of their lives. At Castel Giubileo, the leader of the deputation, Arulenus Rusticus, was wounded in a scuffle, an incident thoroughly understandable in the circumstances, but stigmatized by Tacitus as particularly scandalous in view of Rusticus' high standing as a Stoic philosopher and political theorist, quite apart from the violation of the status of ambassador and praetor. Such nice considerations cannot have weighed with men smarting under defeat and incensed by the humbug of those who had hunted down the helpless Sabinus and then asked for concessions for themselves. Rusticus' fellow-negotiators, too, were roughly handled, and when his senior lictor tried to clear a way for the magistrate, he was killed. Eventually order was restored, and Petilius sent the mission back empty-handed under the protection of an escort. A calmer attitude marked the reception of the envoys sent to Antonius, though here, too, the Vitellians adopted a high-and-mighty tone ill-suited to their predicament. One of the party, another leading senator and Stoic, Musonius Rufus, evoked considerable ridicule by lecturing armed men on the blessings of peace. Many laughed in his face, more found him merely tedious, and a few of the rougher sort wanted to knock him down. Luckily Musonius held his tongue in time. The Flavians also received a deputation of Vestal Virgins carrying a personal appeal from

Vitellius to Antonius, in which he asked for one day's grace to facilitate a general agreement. But of course it was useless. The Vestals were sent away with the courtesy due to their sex and order, and Rome was brusquely informed that the murder of Sabinus and the firing of the Capitol meant that there could be no question of further negotiation.

However, Antonius was a reasonable man. He paraded the legions and tried to cool tempers, urging an encampment for the night three miles further on at the north end of the Milvian Bridge, before entering Rome on 21 December. This would have conceded the delay Vitellius had asked for, but Antonius' hearers were suspicious of any postponement; moreover the civilians whom Vitellius had armed had been told to station themselves on the Monti Parioli, immediately to the south-east of the bridge, and the glint of their banners in the morning sun gave the impression, false though it proved to be, that this was a part of a sizeable force bent on defending every inch of Rome. Antonius' army was set in motion, and Cerialis was informed.

The narrow Milvian Bridge was held by the Vitellians; but the position was soon turned by cavalry who forded the Tiber, its usual shallow self despite the very recent rain, and took the defenders in the rear. The armed militia on the Parioli Hills was soon swept away. By late morning the Flavian army was moving southward from the bridge on the last two miles of its journey from the Danube. At a point approximating to the Piazza del Popolo, the army divided into three. One column continued to follow the Via Flaminia, which beyond Agrippa's Portico became Broad Street. A second advanced along the Tiber bank, passing west of the Mausoleum of the Julio-Claudian emperors. A third turned to the left to move through the depression between the Pincian and the Quirinal in a south-easterly direction towards the Park of Sallust and the Praetorian barracks. There was a good deal of fighting outside the city boundaries: it mostly went in favour of the Flavians, helped as they were by better leadership and morale and a decided superiority in numbers. But the Vitellians fought back sturdily. When the streets closed in, the attackers were pelted with tiles from the rooftops, and severe losses were inflicted by small parties of determined men operating in confined passages, such as were typical of the less modern parts of Rome not swept away by the fire or Nero's town-planning. Despair sometimes drove the Vitellians forward wildly, and though routed, they re-formed repeatedly in the southern half of the Campus Martius within the city. However, the stiffest resistance was offered to the Flavians who had turned south-eastwards towards the Sallustian Park, where narrow and slippery tracks seamed an area not yet fully developed. The Vitellians standing on the park walls, which followed the escarpment of the Quirinal and formed in themselves a considerable obstacle, hurled back the attackers below them with stones and javelins until dusk. Finally Petilius' cavalry, set in motion a little later than desirable, forced the Colline Gate and enveloped the enemy position, avenging the disgrace incurred in the same area on the previous day.

By this time the position of the Vitellians in the centre had already become hopeless and organized resistance had ceased. It was now a matter of mopping up odd groups or individuals who had taken refuge in shops and palazzi. A macabre aspect of the fighting was that it was treated as a Christmas spectacle by civilians perched at the windows of tenement buildings: cheering and clapping, they would point out where enemy soldiers were lurking. The latter were then dragged out and killed at the instance of the mob, like gladiators judged unworthy to live in the amphitheatre. While the pursuit continued, the mob looted.

The heaviest encounters naturally occurred around the Praetorian barracks, which the most devoted Vitellians defended to the bitter end. Here it was a struggle between the ex-Praetorians of Galba and Otho, and those who had supplanted them under Vitellius. Every ounce of cunning, every form of tactical ingenuity was exerted by two sides between whose quality as fighting men there was little to choose. But the Vitellians had no battle cry of vengeance or hope to inspire them. Outnumbered and doomed, they fought on in professional pride, their only solace the assurance of being found worthy soldiers at the last. Men died hanging doubled-up from the crenellations and towers, and when the gates were torn from their sockets by the Flavians, the surviving Vitellian Praetorians formed themselves into a compact body and charged. They all fell with their wounds in front, facing the enemy, with honour.

Such consolation was not to be granted to the man for whom they fought. At about 2 p.m., when it was clear that the Flavian penetration was reaching the Campus Martius, Vitellius was taken in a chair through the back of the palace to his house on the Aventine, to which his wife and children had preceded him. His purpose at this time, provided he could lie low during the remaining hours of daylight, was to get away to the cohorts now presumed to be returning from Terracina with Lucius. Tacitus assumes that it was fickleness and panic that caused Vitellius to change his mind. A more probable motive may be discovered in his realization that the attack was developing more rapidly than he had expected and that the Flavian force advancing along the Tiber might well by-pass the centre and encircle it from the south before night fell, and long before Lucius could arrive. In that event the Aventine would soon be theirs, and it was easy to guess that the Flavian command would make a point of surrounding the Vitellian residence. His wife and family must be spared if possible. His own presence had become a menace to them. He told them to leave—time was short and the last hard parting must have been brief—and himself returned to the palace, either in the vague hope that resistance there could be prolonged until Lucius came to the rescue or more probably in the conviction—credible even in a character unfitted for heroics—that if the end must come, it should come while he was defending his palace with his personal servants. Whatever the motives of Vitellius, they played him false. Seeing their master depart, nearly all the palace staff had vanished. Vitellius wandered through the immense complex of buildings and found it forlorn and deserted. Many of the rooms had been locked by conscientious officials as they departed, and when a door did open, he shuddered to find emptiness. In a sudden panic, realizing that he was abandoned by everyone, he threw himself into the porter's lodge, disguised himself as a slave, took the watchdog from its kennel and tied it outside the door of the apartment, which he jammed from inside with a bedstead and palliasse.

By this time advanced elements of the Flavian central column had entered the palace and were ransacking it. Vitellius was soon discovered and dragged out, unrecognized by Danubian troops who had never seen the emperor except in unfaithful effigy. When they asked him who he was and where he supposed Vitellius to be, he lied to them. The subterfuge was futile and degrading. A cohort tribune, Julius Placidus, soon appeared and recognized the tall, ungainly, dishevelled figure. Vitellius then resorted to another fruitless stratagem: would they keep him in custody, even in prison, for the time being? He had information touching the life of Vespasian. This was obviously a hint that he and he alone knew the identity of assassins sent to murder his successor. The device was not unknown: it had already been attempted without success by himself and Otho, Vespasian was said to have feared it, and Mucianus was to employ it against Piso in Africa in the New Year. True or false, the statement was disregarded. Vitellius' hands were tied behind his back, a cord was placed round his neck and he was driven or hauled, like a reluctant ox dragged to the altar, through the jeering crowds filling the Forum. On the way a stray soldier from the German armies met the party. In the confusion the man had retained a sword. Either attempting rescue or trying to put Vitellius out of his misery, he aimed a blow which, partly parried, cut off the tribune's ear, and he was immediately run through. Amid a rain of missiles Vitellius was driven forward, his captors holding a sword under his chin and pulling his hair back to force him to look up and face the tormentors. He saw his statues as they fell, the spot where Galba, against whom he had rebelled, met his end, and then the rostra where stood—worst sight of all—the statue of his father with the proud inscription 'Unshakeably loyal to his emperor'. Finally they drove him to the Gemonian Steps where the body of Flavius Sabinus had lain two days before. His last words showed a not wholly degenerate spirit. When a tribune mocked him, he retorted: *ego tamen imperator tuus fui*—'Despite everything, I was your emperor.' Thereupon he fell lifeless beneath a rain of blows, and in his death the mob reviled him as viciously as it had flattered him while he lived. The body was later dragged by the hook to the Tiber, to be carried down, like a parricide's, to the sea that washes all things clean.

The historical tradition represents Aulus Vitellius as a gluttonous and drunken *bon viveur*, a frequenter of theatres and racecourses, and, typically and most frequently, the host or guest at a succession of Trimalchian banquets. It was inevitable that for the next fifteen years, the Flavian historians should deride the emperor against whom Vespasian had rebelled, while at the same time denouncing the revolt of Vitellius against Galba. The two rebellions were embarrassingly similar. It was not immediately obvious that Fabius Valens and Caecina Alienus were worse than Cornelius Laco and Titus Vinius, particularly as Caecina continued to enjoy Vespasian's favour, in common with a number of nobles who switched allegiance at the right time. The armies of the East and of the Danube were not palpably more altruistic than the garrison of the Rhine. The government of Vitellius had certainly not been revealed as insufferably bad by June, the month in which, at latest, Vespasian decided to rise against him. It was therefore necessary for these writers to stress the psychological unfitness of Vitellius to rule, even more than Vespasian's reluctance to move against him. The bias is transparent in Flavius Josephus, Suetonius and in Pliny the Elder (so far as his attitude can be reconstructed). Tacitus himself is too much of a sceptic and too great a devotee of antithesis and paradox to accept all that the Flavian doctrine taught, but even with him some of the mud sticks, and he not infrequently hedges and takes refuge in apophthegms and ambiguities painful to contemplate, however dazzling at first glance. A dispassionate study of Vitellius hardly confirms the usual caricature. Among those acts of state which (fairly numerous in a short reign) are attributable to decisions of the emperor himself, it is hard to find much amiss, apart from the first—the original decision to invite, and then to accept, nomination to the principate. For this post Vitellius was equipped neither by temperament nor by training. He was a comfortable, easy family man, ready enough to entertain his friends lavishly, taking a lively interest in the turf and the stage, a spendthrift pursued by creditors, perhaps just capable of running the great family estate at Ariccia; unluckily, he was also saddled with the damnable inheritance of a great name. It was a calamity for him that his father had been three times consul, the friend and colleague of Claudius. Galba should no more have chosen Vitellius to command in Lower Germany than Hordeonius Flaccus in Upper. Once he had become emperor, it was inevitable that some spoils should be handed out and some scores settled. The most expensive of them was the drafting of 20,000 legionaries into the Urban and Praetorian Cohorts and the consequent rise in their rates of pay, respectively 375 and 750 denarii annually in place of 225 denarii, plus bonuses in proportion. To make room for the new Praetorians, those of Otho were discharged, though honourably, so that they retained their lump sum or land in lieu as pension. The main political victims were Pompeius Propinquus, too loyal to Galba, and some centurions, too loyal to Otho. But Julius Burdo, Julius Civilis, Licinius Proculus, Marius Celsus, Galerius Trachalus and Quintius Atticus were spared, often despite the malevolence of the Vitellians; and if it cost Sabinus dear to be the brother of an emperor designate, his death was contrary to the wish of Vitellius, who had unhesitatingly retained him as prefect of the city even after the proclamation of 1 July was known. There were no reprisals against the Helvetii, or against the Othonian generals. It is true that Cornelius Dolabella was thought too dangerous to live, but he had invited his fate. Under Vitellius, his reign largely occupied by the actuality or threat of hostilities, the financial crisis naturally deepened, and his measures here—a wealth tax upon freedmen, and the rather dangerous expedient of reducing legionary strengths by ceasing to recruit—could hardly be expected to show any immediate result. It is to Vitellius' credit that he regularly attended the Senate, even when minor business was on the agenda, and his rearrangement of the consular list was tactfully managed. As between Caecina and Valens, he tried to hold the scales of favour level, and his frequent public appearances not only in the Senate, but also in the theatre and amphitheatre made him surprisingly, if superficially, popular in the city. In the purely military sphere he comes under heavy criticism from Tacitus, who never forgives failure. But here, too, he often made sensible decisions or accepted sensible advice. The invasion of Italy by three separate forces was well planned in Cologne, and in withdrawing troops from the Rhine frontier Vitellius showed more restraint and sense of responsibility than did Antonius Primus and Aponius Saturninus in respect of the Danube. For the defeat of his army at Cremona he cannot be blamed, except in so far as his absence facilitated the treachery of Bassus and Caecina. The decisions not to defend the Apennine crossings and to crush the mutineers at Terracina are not obviously wrong. Finally, at the family level he showed affection and even self-sacrifice. As a man, despite the odd impression created by above-average height combined with a flabby physique, he was amiable. The conversations which led to his decision to abdicate were initiated by Vitellius himself, and it was not his fault if the move failed. Only the failure of nerve in his last hours shows a character unable to take severe strain: here, his critic Tacitus is as merciless to Vitellius as he had been generous to Otho, spokesman of a society which demanded that, whenever and however the end came, it must be faced unflinchingly and with decorum. At the time of his death Vitellius was fifty-seven years old, and his reign lasted eight months.

On the day after the capture of Rome, Domitian appeared to claim the position of son and deputy of Vespasian Augustus. It was later alleged by flatterers that his role in the last days of Vitellius' reign had been heroic. The actual facts are less heady. As soon as the defences of the Capitol were breached on the afternoon of 19 December, Domitian, accompanied by the young Sabinus, had hidden in the house of the sacristan of the great temple, and perhaps later in the cellars of the burnt-out building. He spent the whole of the night in concealment. At or before dawn, he was smuggled down the slopes or descended through the tenement houses, and so reached the Velabrum and the house of Cornelius Primus, a dependant of his father. On the suggestion of this Cornelius, who had perhaps read of an incident in the proscriptions of 43 B.C., Domitian was dressed in the linen garment, ankle-long, of a priest of Isis. Even better, if available, would have been a papier-maché dog's-head mask. In this disguise he was thrust in among a band of real priests of Isis who, in view of the approach of the fighting, were hurriedly moving through the Velabrum, conveying some of the more precious objects of the great Temple of Isis near the Baths of Agrippa to a point beyond the Tiber. In the confusion the masquerade was not detected either by the priests or by Vitellian sympathizers, who at this eleventh hour had been told to secure Domitian as a hostage. Beyond the Tiber bridges, which might be expected to be heavily controlled, the young man managed to leave the procession, and once more baffled detection overnight, this time by hiding—again with one companion, presumably the same—in the house of the mother of a fellow-student in the Trastevere. By late evening of 20 December, Rome was completely in Flavian hands, but no prominent person in his senses would have dared to venture out. When daylight came on 21 December all seemed quiet. Domitian recrossed the Tiber and revealed himself to the Flavian leaders and troops camped in and around the palace. The men crowded round, hailed him as 'Caesar', and just as they were, without ceremony or smartness, still armed and stained with battle, escorted him to his father's house on the Quirinal.[79]

12

The Last Ten Days

At the Kazan Defile and the Iron Gates the Danube breaks through the only mountain barrier it encounters between the Wachau above Vienna and the Black Sea, if one disregards the slight eminence of the Dobrogea. The south-western prolongation of the Southern Carpathians, passing over from modern Romania to Yugoslavia, provides high ground through which the river, fed full by the Tisza and the Tisza's tributaries that flow westwards through Transylvania—Timiş, and Mureş and Someş—forces its way through a 100-mile-long gap, from Baziaş below Kostolać to Turnu Severin, where Trajan was soon to build his bridge. West and east of this barrier, the steppes of Asia die away in the Bácska and Wallachia, in A.D. 69 the homes of the Iazyges and the Rhoxolani respectively. Both were potential danger points for Rome. But danger lurked in the mountains also. Some ninety miles from the Danube, high up in the remoteness of the wooded mountain quadrilateral between Haţeg, Sebeş, Sibiu, the middle Olt, the Latru and the Strei, lies the walled city Sarmizegetusa, ringed by its satellite forts of Blidaru, Piatra Roşie and the rest. Only one valley, leading southwards from Orăştie, offers tolerable access to the redoubt, but it soon narrows and is guarded by the hill-top fort of Costeşti. This was the homeland of a sturdy race of shepherd-warriors, the trousered and bearded Dacians, whom the Romans were glad to acknowledge as worthy foes, and commemorate in literature and in the lively sculptures that encircle the Monument of Adamclisi and spiral up the Column of Trajan. Already in republican times, and still more when the province of Moesia brought a standing Roman presence to the lower Danube in Augustus' reign, the Dacians of the mountains, with their allies of the plain, were always ready to cross the river boundary on plundering raids or in aggressive self-defence. One of the topics upon which Horace's leech-like acquaintance wished to pump one whom he supposed to be in possession of court secrets—'Any news about the Dacians?'—betrays public anxiety on this score. History tended to repeat itself in 69. Just as the Rhoxolani had taken advantage of the news of Vitellius' move to strike in February, so now, in the autumn, the Dacians felt that an advantageous moment had recurred. The Danube was stripped of legions. In September, the barbarians studied the initial phases of Antonius' campaign, making no move at first. Then, when in the latter part of that month they realized that a savage civil war was about to be fought in Italy, they descended upon the Danube, stormed a number of auxiliary forts, now weakly held or quite abandoned by their infantry and cavalry garrisons, and proceeded to make themselves masters of both banks of the river. Like Civilis, they were ready to learn from their enemy, take prisoners and equipment and utilize both. The next step was to move in on the legionary forts at Kostolać, Gigen and perhaps also the lowest, Svištov.

News of the irruption reached Mucianus when he was already in Thrace, his eyes fixed on the Adriatic, to which the Egnatian Way led him. Suddenly, the plans had to be jettisoned. On the Danube was an immediate danger which suffered no delay. He turned north via Sofia and Niš, descended the Morava, and planted himself at Kostolać, reflecting bitterly that this danger and the diversion of his route were attributable to Antonius and Saturninus, who had irresponsibly denuded the forts in aid of an unnecessary race to Rome. Impatiently halting at Kostolać with his 13,000 legionaries, he sent the Sixth downstream to occupy Gigen and mop up the intruders. After a delay of more than a month, the worst was over, or seemed to be. Early in November, he received information of the Second Battle of Cremona which, while it lessened the danger of a simultaneous threat from the Danube and the Rhine, had at some cost in Italian lives and property awarded Antonius laurels to which he was not really entitled. Mucianus wrote immediately to Antonius demanding a rapid return of the Moesian legionary troops and pointing out that, while the success should, of course, be exploited, it had been no part of Vespasian's strategy: blockade would have sufficed without bloodshed. The same warning was expressed more forcibly to Plotius Grypus and Hormus, and they were instructed to slow up the advance if possible, and allow himself, Mucianus, to catch up with it. At the same time, leaving the Sixth Legion on the Danube and summoning the proconsul of Asia, Fonteius Agrippa, to coordinate defences, Mucianus moved on with the 13,000 legionaries and hurried towards Italy. But for the Capitol disaster, he would probably have caught up with Antonius outside Rome, at Otricoli. In the event, misfortune followed misfortune. He was still among the Apennines when, on 16 December, he heard of the capitulation at Narni on the day before, 100 miles to the south. It seemed that Rome was bound to fall at any moment. He immediately penned a dispatch addressed formally to the consuls, praetors, tribunes and Senate at large, which was read in the chamber on 21 December. It was less its language, urgent and peremptory, than the fact that the letter had been written at all, that caused antagonism among members who had hoped, as after the death of Nero, to make themselves important before the new emperor arrived. They remarked that Mucianus was, of course, a senator, and as such perfectly entitled to speak in person in the Senate, when present in the house. But as a governor of Syria, he had technically no right to communicate directly with the Senate by letter, still less to adopt an air of authority towards it. He could have said all he wanted to say a few days later, for much latitude was allowed in debate. Finally, it was quite intolerable that he should imply that he had conveyed the empire to Vespasian, as if it were in his own gift.[80]

These spinsterish objections throw a curious light upon the pedantry and petty-mindedness of the republican opposition. They were in a sense valid criticisms, were this the long-vanished age when the Senate was still undisputed master of Rome. Now, in the year of the four emperors, they reflected a legalism that came ill from a body that had played so miserable and undignified a role in recent months; and that they should be recorded so carefully and with such apparent approval by Tacitus shows that he, too, sometimes thought in this way and took pleasure in a posthumous revenge, at a time when the Flavian dynasty, and not merely Mucianus' ascendancy, was past history.

On the evening of 20 December, it had been quite impossible to summon the Senate. Its members were naturally in hiding, and had no intention of emerging from their places of refuge. On the following day, the Flavian army moved out south-eastwards to protect the capital from Lucius Vitellius, and it was now that the Senate met. After letters from Vespasian and Mucianus had been read, it voted to Vespasian, as to Otho in January and to Vitellius in April, all the titles and powers whose accumulation express what we understand by 'emperor': he was to be commander-in-chief, Augustus, Caesar, holder of the tribunician power. Valerius Asiaticus, as consul designate, prompted no doubt by Mucianus' instructions and anxious to efface the memory of the un-fortunate circumstance that he had been Vitellius' choice for son-in-law, proposed that Vespasian should be consul for the coming year, with Titus as his colleague, both, of course, *in absentia* for the time being. Mucianus received triumphal honours for his October campaign against the Dacians and Sarmatians, while Antonius Primus was given the insignia of a consul, and Cornelius Fuscus and Arrius Varus those of praetors. Valerius Asiaticus finally proposed something which ex-perts in senatorial procedure felt should have come first: the decision to restore the Temple of Jupiter Capitolinus. All these measures were readily voted. When asked, most of the senators rapidly signified assent by a glance or a gesture, though a few felt it incumbent or advantageous to offer some words of polished and insincere rhetoric. Helvidius alone —so far as the record goes—expressed dissent.

The terms in which these or concomitant powers were conveyed are

THE LAST TEN DAYS 207

known to us in some detail from a contemporary document of the first
importance, whose recovery we owe to a remarkable man.

During the years when Cola di Rienzo, before his famous tribunate
of 1347, was searching for and learning from the neglected documents
of ancient Rome, he came across a large bronze tablet, used by Pope
Boniface the Eighth in the construction of an altar in the basilica of St
John Lateran. In the letter in which he alludes to the discovery, written
a few years later to the Archbishop of Prague, he says that his attention
was arrested by an inscription engraved on the back of the metal tablet.
On studying it, he was delighted to discover that a reference in the text
to the granting of imperial prerogatives made it clear that, in the days
of Roman greatness, these had stemmed constitutionally from the
Senate and People of Rome. This was welcome grist to his mill. In the
spring of 1347, he arranged a grand meeting in the basilica. In its
centre a platform had been erected, upon which the venerable and
mysterious document was prominently exhibited in a suitable frame.
Rienzo, dressed in striking and exotic raiment (the scene is described
with vigour in the anonymous life of the tribune), then mounted the
stage and delivered an expository and not altogether accurate lecture
upon the text, with a homily driving home the lesson for his own day:
'*Signori,*' he cried, '*tanta era la majestate de lo Puopolo de Roma che allo*'
'*Mperatore dava l'auttoritate. Hora mone l'havemo perduta con nuostro gran
donno e vergogna.*' In 1576, the venerable relic was transferred to the
Palazzo dei Conservatori on the Capitol, though Gibbon, in the
penultimate chapter of his *History* penned in 1787, incautiously says
that it was still in the Lateran at that time, an error perhaps excusable
after the lapse of years since his short visit to Rome in October 1764.
The inscription recovered by the eager Rienzo contributed to his own
rise and fall, and perhaps to the course of Italian and European
history; and it certainly bulks large today amid the none too plentiful
evidence for the nature of the Roman principate.[81]

The document is a portion of the so-called *Lex de imperio Vespasiani* or
Lex regia. In its surviving form, it resumes under eight heads and a final
Sanctio ('Exemption from Penalty') part of the legislative work of the
period 21 December 69 to 1 January 70 inclusively. The formulation is
that of a law passed by the People, enshrining the language of the antecedent decree of the Senate, datable to 21 December or very shortly
afterwards. Vespasian is granted a number of powers, some already
possessed by Augustus, Tiberius and Claudius. The choice of precedents may seem strange, but Gaius and Nero suffered condemnation
of their memory, at least at this date: the status of Galba was not
determined until 1 January; and Otho and Vitellius seem to be
omitted as usurpers, though similar powers were certainly granted to
them, and only Vitellius' name is erased in the minutes of the Brethren

of the Fields. These powers include the right to make treaties, to summon the Senate, to refer matters to it for advice or decision, and to commend candidates for office, now without restriction of number. Of particular interest is the eighth clause, which copes with the delicate situation created by an emperor who had good reasons to insist that he had a legal title to the principate as from 1 July 69. The document guarantees the validity of acts performed by Vespasian himself or at his orders 'before the passage of the bill into law': a vague expression which might be conveniently explained away as bridging the time lag between the passage of the decree and that of the law, but which almost certainly serves to stop the much greater and more vital gap of six months. At Beirut, Vespasian had made a number of appointments and dispositions whose retrospective validation was absolutely necessary, and without this measure it might be claimed that they, like the coinage of money and the movement of troops, were treasonable in the autumn of 69.

Moreover, Vespasian could hardly arrive before the opening of the sailing season in 70, and he might well be detained longer in the East, until such time as the Jewish War was over and his return, and that of Titus, could be truly triumphal. It was therefore necessary that the power of convening the Senate and guiding its agenda (a power which he would have enjoyed without question, if present) should be reserved to his written communications and to his agent, Mucianus. Hence the peculiar language of the surviving third head:

and that when the Senate shall be held according to his will or authority, by his order or commission, or in his presence, the legality of all business transacted shall be no less established and guaranteed than if the Senate had been convened or were being held in accordance with the law.

The wording seems to be purposely designed to cover a number of possible situations in which the legality of business might be questioned by captious or malevolent critics; but among other things, this comprehensive third head, which forms an addendum to the second but, unlike it, makes no reference to precedents, gives Mucianus, technically only one *consularis* among many, the right to be heard and heeded as the mouthpiece of the absent Vespasian: it conveys in legal language the authority vested in his supporter by Vespasian in person when he called Mucianus his 'brother' and handed to him the ring by which he could set the imperial seal upon whatever documents must be issued. In fact, the clause presented the viceroy (and the emperor himself) with a large carte blanche. By it, the Flavians were enabled to control proceedings, even if—as the constitution allowed—the Senate were summoned by a praetor or tribune of the plebs. At all costs it was necessary to avoid the recriminations and witch-hunts that had followed the death of Nero and preceded the arrival of Galba. And such must certainly be expected when a stiff-necked republican like Helvidius Priscus was among the praetors of 70, and commanded a certain following, small but vocal, in refusing to recognize the institution of the principate. In January of the coming year, there is at least one example of this control of senatorial debate exercised by Domitian and Mucianus acting together, just as the latter settles a difficulty concerning the Praetorian Guard in virtue of his remit from the supreme commander. Under the arrangement now sanctioned, Domitian, soon to be urban praetor with consular power, and Mucianus as mandatory of the emperor, would be in a position of complete authority. When Vespasian in due course arrived, it would become even more obvious that the powers of the emperor were continuing to grow at the expense of the Senate, and at the end of his reign of ten years, it was discovered that during this time Vespasian had held eight consulships, Titus seven and Domitian five.

It must be regarded as highly improbable that a decree of the Senate such as is embodied in the *Lex de imperio* should have been so phrased merely at the suggestion of the Flavian leaders present in Rome on 21 December. It seems obvious that it was Mucianus who, in his December letter to the Senate, had foreseen the legal difficulties to which he might be exposed by the presence of a hostile faction in the chamber and a possibly uncooperative Antonius in the army; and he had made it clear to the consuls (and, among the senators, to the consul designate Valerius Asiaticus in particular), first that the special position of himself and Domitian should be provided for in a *Lex de imperio*; secondly, that any honours decreed to Antonius and Varus should give them no political status; and thirdly, that the two consuls designate should abdicate by the end of the year in favour of Vespasian and Titus, and the urban praetor designate in favour of Domitian. Valerius obediently carried out these wishes, by virtue of his right (together with that of the other consul designate) to be first to be called upon to express an opinion and formulate a motion at any meeting of the Senate.

The caution of Mucianus was fully justified by events. Already, in the recognition debate, Helvidius, who had made it his life's work to avenge his father-in-law Thrasea Paetus, Nero's victim, seems to have given notice of that continued campaign of opposition to the principate which was to win for himself and for his son notoriety and death. According to the account of Tacitus, which unhappily is broken by a lacuna, 'he expressed himself in language which, while paying respect to the new emperor, yet . . . complete frankness. The Senate applauded his words enthusiastically.' The historian's tribute is curious. Applause there may have been, but it was not so enthusiastic as to translate itself

H

into a vote against Vespasian's recognition. The proposals of the consul designate were accepted. Tacitus is clearly paying a polite tribute at this point to the memory of a man whose wife and daughter were known to him, and even in praising Helvidius at somewhat disproportionate length, he ventures upon a mild criticism: there were, he admits, some who felt that he was too concerned for his own reputation. In the *Agricola*, written some ten years earlier, he had expressed himself more trenchantly: the men of the Stoic opposition were conceited seekers after martyrdom, bringing ruin upon themselves without helping their country.

The consuls (or consul, if only the pro-Flavian Quintius Atticus was present) then raised the question of the composition of the senatorial deputation which should, according to protocol, wait upon the distant Vespasian. Valerius Asiaticus suggested that the delegates should, as usual, be chosen by lot. The proposal was supported by the powerful and eloquent Eprius Marcellus and accepted by the chamber—not, however, before Helvidius Priscus had again made himself conspicuous by suggesting an alternative: the choice of individuals by the magistrates under oath. This was an obvious move to pack the deputation and bring the influence of himself or like-minded opposition senators to bear upon the new ruler at the earliest date. In a second speech by Eprius Marcellus, the many objections to such an invidious course of action were put fully and convincingly. All senators, he pointed out, were qualified to perform an act of homage. The principate was a practical necessity; and, while one prayed for good emperors, one must take them as they came. He, like many other senators, had had to cooperate with Nero, difficult and repugnant as the task had been. But the new emperor was no youthful megalomaniac who needed philosophy tutors to keep him in order. He was a mature man, an old soldier, a *triumphator*, and the father of grown-up sons. It was not at all likely that he would welcome the officious promptings of designing politicians. It would be well to forget the Thrasea vendetta and remember that the Roman state depended upon the amicable cooperation of princeps and Senate.[82]

The issue, which had caused some heat, was closed by a vote in which the view of Valerius and Marcellus was supported by the moderates. The Senate also decreed the erection of a statue of Galba to mark the spot in the Forum where he had met his death. This suggestion, well meaning as it was, was eventually vetoed by Vespasian, in accordance with the policy that bygones should be bygones. That an emperor had been murdered in his capital should be passed over in discreet silence. Such reminders of tyrannicide were dangerous.

The Senate now turned to the question of finance. At an earlier point, it had been agreed that the Temple of Jupiter Optimus Maximus should

be restored. The cost would be enormous, and the praetors in charge of
the state treasury, reporting that the exchequer was in low water, asked
for a stringent limit on expenditure of all kinds. The consul designate
suggested that, in a situation where commitments were so heavy and
present resources so slight, it might be as well to leave the decision to the
emperor. Helvidius intervened for a third time, proposing that the
responsibility for restoring the building should lie firmly with the
Roman state, but that Vespasian's assistance should be asked. This
pedantic amendment the speakers that followed passed over in silence,
and it was later forgotten, except by Helvidius' biographer. It was, in
fact, a meaningless display of verbal ballistics. Finally, the tribune of
the plebs, Vulcacius Tertullinus, used his veto—the last recorded instance of the use of the tribunician veto in Roman history—to prevent
any discussion on such an important matter in the absence of the
emperor. The intervention was providential, for here at least, since he
knew nothing of the events of the last few days, Vespasian had given no
remit to Mucianus. Finally, another attempted witch-hunt was foiled
by postponement. Musonius Rufus attacked a brother philosopher for
securing the condemnation and death in 66 of Barea Soranus, a respected figure and governor of Asia. Once more the old feuds were being
revived. But the matter was shelved until the next meeting of the
Senate, which was likely to be in the following year. It was summoned
by Sextus Julius Frontinus, urban praetor designate: for, of the Vitellian
consuls, Simplex could hardly act and even his colleague Quintius
might seem to have compromised himself by admitting sacrilege and
arson.

While the Senate thus demonstrated the moderation and good sense
of most of its members, together with the vindictiveness of a few extremists, there were practical jobs to be done by the army. The most
urgent of these was the interception of Lucius Vitellius and his Praetorians. On the morning of 21 December, a large part of the Flavian
army moved along the Appian Way, the legions taking up a position
short of Bovillae, where the rise up to the outer slope of the Alban crater
begins. The cavalry were sent on to the high ground of Ariccia. There
was, however, no fighting. The six Praetorian cohorts were still some
twenty miles from Rome, near Lanuvio. Lucius Vitellius was a realist
as well as a man of action. To fight a battle which there was no chance
of winning, on behalf of an emperor who was dead, did not make sense.
He surrendered unconditionally and, perhaps conscious that in a certain sense he had failed his brother, seems to have taken no steps to save
himself from an inevitable fate. A long line of disarmed Vitellians,
hedged in by armed guards, trudged through the city, grim and un-
moved by the clapping and insults of the jeering mob. None of them
said anything that could earn him discredit, and in the hour of downfall

they preserved their dignity. Antonius had them placed in the Praetorian camp, where they would be under observation and heavily outnumbered by the ex-Othonian and Flavian troops. Lucius Vitellius was
then executed: he was too dangerous to survive, and the times too hard
for chivalry. He had shown great vigour during his brother's reign, and
while, as a senator in Italy, he had not been closely associated with
Aulus' rise, he was swept irresistibly away by his fall. But the problem
of the disposal of so many Praetorians was acute. It was to be solved
gradually by natural wastage and discreet individual discharges: such
a multitude of pampered troops was a dangerous luxury which Rome
could not afford.

There was still a confusion in Campania. Lucilius Bassus, granted
an unspecified position and soon to be reinstated as commander of both
the Italian fleets, was sent off with some cavalry to restore order. Petty
jealousies between the communities had flared, fanned by the naval
insurrection. The sight of the troops had a wonderfully calming effect.
The smaller towns which, voluntarily or not, had supported the
mutineers were, of course, not penalized. But Capua Vetere, enthusiastic in its attachment to Vitellius, had the strongly Flavian Third
Legion quartered upon it, and the wealthier families of the city suffered
severely by the necessity of purchasing immunity from billeting at a
high price. Thus the interests of peace, accommodation, retribution and
finance were simultaneously served. The only compensation that
Terracina enjoyed was that Vergilius Capito's slave, who had betrayed
the town to Lucius, was crucified, still wearing the knight's rings
presented to him by Aulus on the evening of 18 December.

Within Rome itself those Vitellian troops who had gone into hiding
had to be winkled out on information supplied by the populace, and the
process extended also to the environs of the capital. But Antonius and
Varus avoided acts of unnecessary violence when the fighting was over,
and this restraint, which Cremona had taught them, made them very
popular in a city which had feared the worst. When Mucianus finally
arrived about 25 December, however, the centre of power shifted decisively. For all their achievements, Antonius and Varus had to yield to
a man who was the emperor's confidant, carrying his instructions and
claiming the right to decide all things in his name. Those who wished
for promotion courted Mucianus and him alone. He, for his part, kept
himself well in the public eye, constantly moving from one palace or
villa to another. It was noted that he retained inside the city his armed
escort.

Mucianus himself had his problems. Of these perhaps the most delicate was the handling of the 18-year-old Domitian, who must be used
as a front man without being given too much of the power which he
was all too eager to exercise. We have already seen that, in his letter to

the Senate, Mucianus had suggested for Domitian the position that protocol seemed to demand. As the younger of the two sons of the new emperor, Domitian might conveniently become praetor (observance of normal age limits was usually disregarded in the imperial family) in the consulship of his father and elder brother, and Julius Frontinus was invited to abdicate the urban (senior) praetorship, in order to create a vacancy for him: such complaisance could be sure of a reward in due course. It was to avoid awkward conflicts of authority between Domitian and other praetors owing their election to Vitellius that the young man had been given an *ad hoc* 'consular power', enabling him, if necessary, to veto the administrative decisions of Praetorian or lesser magistrates. Mucianus, who could thus work partly through Domitian, partly as the recognized representative of Vespasian, seems to have accepted no specific office. For him, typically, the reality of power, military and political, was enough.

A second task was the need gradually to weaken Antonius Primus and Arrius Varus, by removing their formations to forts throughout the empire. Manipulating public opinion by court scribblers, Mucianus achieved his aims more skilfully than Antonius did by outspoken and impatient complaint. Men might feel sympathy with, and admiration for, the hero of the Flavian invasion, who had done more than any other single person to bring Vitellius down; but they acted in a manner which they thought acceptable to Mucianus and advantageous to their future careers.

When reasons of state seemed to require it, Mucianus could be ruthless. To him must be attributed responsibility for the death of another Dolabella. Gaius Calpurnius Piso Galerianus had kept out of political adventures (his father had been a friend of Claudius), but his good looks and youth, together with a distinguished name, made him the subject of popular gossip: idle tongues had earlier spoken of him as a possible emperor. There was little substance in this, but Mucianus took no chances. Within the walls of Rome Piso's end would have attracted attention: forty miles from the city, on the Appian Way, his veins were opened and he bled to death. On the other hand, Alfenus Varus, Vitellius' Praetorian prefect, managed to survive his cowardice and removal from office, though his colleague Julius Priscus committed suicide, not indeed from compulsion but from a sense of shame. Asiaticus, being a freedman, paid for his influence at the Vitellian court by suffering the execution appropriate to a slave, crucifixion. One can understand, while one deplores, a last severe decision taken by Mucianus: the death of Vitellius' son when finally, some months later, the unfortunate child was tracked down.

The old order had been swept away, or at least one set of leaders had been replaced by another. It was clear that Rome was to be ruled by men who knew what they wanted. To what extent and in what ways the new régime promised to prove superior to the Julio-Claudian dynasty would not be established until Vespasian himself arrived. For this event Rome was to wait many months. Yet the spirit of civil war had been exorcized or exhausted. Rising in Gaul and Spain, it had possessed Upper and Lower Germany and the Balkans, and finally traversed Egypt, Judaea, Syria and almost every province and garrison. The plague was now spent, the world purged.

In December 69, if we may trust Tacitus, the Senate looked to the past and the future with a sense of relief, even cheerfulness; bad as things had been, they might have been worse. Vespasian seemed likely, both from past knowledge of his career and from the tenor of his recent letter, to be a moderate and efficient ruler who, in due course, would be succeeded by an equally acceptable son. To the modern observer, the optimism seems (as it did to Tacitus, writing a generation after the event) a little misplaced. New men did not necessarily mean a new system. It was true, of course, that the empire had survived a violent convulsion substantially unimpaired. Two invasions across the Danube had been promptly and effectively repelled; piracy on the Black Sea had been rapidly suppressed; Cartimandua in Yorkshire had been saved, though with the prospect of prolonged fighting and the eventual necessity of advancing the frontier to Scotland. Even the catastrophic situation in the Rhineland—hardly yet appreciated in its full gravity— was not likely to endure when normality returned elsewhere. Dynastically, the application of adoption to the succession problem was an interesting experiment, not proved to be a failure by the fatal events of 15 January. In the military field, the endurance and efficiency of the Roman soldier had been demonstrated by battles fought against the toughest enemy: himself. Finally, the wide acclaim for Vespasian seemed to show that blind fate, or an ultimately beneficent providence, had chosen well in the end.

Against these positive gains must be set weaknesses starkly revealed. Financially the state was bankrupt. The rivalry between the garrisons of Spain, Germany, the Danube and the East had demonstrated the danger of allowing static formations to feel solidarity with the local populace. The Praetorians were an incubus. Weak, vacillating and elderly army commanders had been used by intriguing colonels. To us, the fundamental weakness of the Senate is more startlingly displayed by the events of 69 than it is by the mordant irony with which Tacitus recalls some of its more embarrassing predicaments. Repeatedly it lived up to the damning description of it by Tiberius as a body of men born to serve rather than to rule. As it was in 14, so it is in 69. Abhorring above everything a vacuum of power, it shows indecent haste in approving the choice of the army. Galba is accepted on the day of Nero's

death, Otho on the day when Galba dies. The news of Otho's death
leads immediately to the election of Vitellius. On 21 December Vespasian's authority is backdated to 1 July. Occasionally we hear of some
verbal sparring in the *curia*, but of any real process of selection and
rejection of those regarded as *capaces imperii* we have no evidence.
Verginius Rufus is certainly among these, his birth (if that still mat-
tered) lowlier than Galba's, but not noticeably inferior to Vespasian's.
Dolabella, exiled by Otho, is reluctantly executed by the mild Sabinus
on Vitellius' instruction: the Senate remains silent and passive. And
there were others thrown up in gossip fatal to themselves. The Senate
fails to give to Galba and his heir the vigorous support which might
have deterred even Otho. It gives no advice to Vitellius, and submits
obediently to the fatherly instructions of Mucianus. Tacitus' picture of
its members protesting loyalty to Galba and running to court his
murderer, or gazing in appalled terror over the dinner table at the
frightened Otho, or huddling helplessly together at Bologna and
Modena, scenes bordering admittedly on caricature, give us some in-
sight into one man's view of the typical behaviour under stress of the
sovereign body of which he was a member. Rienzo was right to point
out that the *Lex de imperio Vespasiani* shows that constitutionally all
power came now, as centuries before, from the Senate and People of
Rome. But outside Italy, the Roman people are a widely scattered local
aristocracy who, for purely mechanical reasons of time and space, are
unable to exercise any really democratic choice between imperial
candidates, or any real control over imperial policy: and the body
which should have done so, the Senate sitting in Rome, seems in our
eyes a group of courtiers, ciphers or bigots.

   The essential reasons for the weakness of the Senate are two. First,
many of its members owe to imperial patronage their past advancement,
and have a shrewd eye for what may prolong it in the future. Secondly,
the absence of political parties, as opposed to power-seeking factions,
means that outside the imperial favour no process of natural selection
for leadership exists. It is not that political parties are unthinkable in
first-century Rome. There are problems enough, sufficiently similar to
our own, to justify a polarization of political pressures. How rapidly
should citizenship be spread? What weight of taxation is appropriate to
a simple peasant economy, sustaining a fully-stretched governmental
structure? What can be done to extend the social services beyond the
pauperized mob of Rome? Where must money be profitably spent on
public works? Does current trade serve the real needs of society?
Should the empire's boundaries be advanced? On these and many
other questions public-spirited members of the Senate should have been
exercising their minds, and some no doubt did. That on the whole both
initiative and decision lie now with the emperor seems to mark the

change from the vigour of a young people to the resignation of middle or old age. The minds of the few active politicians are fascinated by a meaningless shibboleth, Liberty; and the senatorial opposition—not unfairly represented by Helvidius Priscus and Musonius Rufus—takes the form of a sterile republicanism, gazing backwards, seeking martyr-dom, contributing nothing to the well-being of living Romans. In the Long Year, both the strengths and weaknesses of the empire are made manifest, prognosticating the future and making some men fear the death of the Eternal City.

But it is easy, too, for us to exaggerate the impact of the political and military drama. There were many parts of the empire—Britain, much of Gaul, Greece, Anatolia, Upper Egypt and much of Africa and Spain, and even Italy—where the civil conflict was talked about rather than experienced. The Apulian cattle drovers still moved the herds from winter to summer pastures, the vine trimmers of Mantua still sang at their work, the farmer and his ox still warred with the earth. It took more than a few alarms to stop the beekeepers of Ostiglia moving their waterborne hives along the riverside luxuriance. In many a comfortable farmhouse you could admire the hams curing above the smoking hearth, and the poor peasant eked out his eggs and cheese with cabbage and leek that came from his garden, not the market town. In the *basses-cours* and by the whitewashed dovecots the poultry chattered and gobbled. At Cremona the October fair had not been cancelled because Antonius had invaded Italy. It remained a land of fruitfulness. For centuries now, relentless toil had forced the forests higher and higher up the mountainsides, extending over hill and plain the neat patterns of meadow, lake, watercourse, cornfield, laughing vineyards and grey files of olive. High up on Sila the woodman's axe rang and the great cattle grazed under forested heights. The famous army of geese marched to Rome, an annual invader from the English Channel. The highways were busy with traffic, the Mediterranean studded with flaxen sails carrying the goods of three continents. There were many senators and officers who maintained under bad or transient emperors the day-to-day business of a civilization ordered by custom, law and contract. Such were Gaius Rutilius Gallicus, judicial assistant governor of Asia, such Marius Celsus, faithful servant of Galba, Otho and Vitellius. One of the consuls of 69, Titus Flavius Sabinus, began his career under Nero, and pursued it under Otho, Vitellius and Vespasian. Quintus Vibius Crispus, friend of Vitellius, is prominent under Nero and Vespasian alike. And though Tacitus delights to record the alleged infamy of Asiaticus, he does not remind us of another imperial freedman: the accountant Tiberius Claudius, who occupied the same position of trust under Nero, Galba, Otho, Vitellius, Vespasian, Titus and Domitian.

The Long Year was over. The balance of good and evil could be struck, the accounts totalled and recorded. In prospect and retrospect, as December drew to its end, Romans had reason to feel thankfulness, if not optimism. The heart was still sound. The last peg had not yet been hammered home in the calendar. Though the shrine on the Capitol was dust and ashes, the day would come when the pontifex and the silent Virgin would climb the slope once more, to a new temple built on the old foundations.

On 1 January, A.D. 70, in the eight-hundred-and-twenty-second year of the City, the emperor Caesar Vespasian Augustus (then in Egypt) and Titus Caesar Vespasian (then in Palestine) entered office as consuls, the former for the second time.

Abbreviations and Notes

AE	*Année épigraphique*
AFA	*Acta Fratrum Arvalium*
AJP	*American Journal of Philology*
BCH	*Bulletin de correspondance hellénique*
BGU	*Berliner Griechische Urkunden*
BJ	*Bellum Judaicum*
CAH	*Cambridge Ancient History*
CIL	*Corpus Inscriptionum Latinarum*
CPJ	*Corpus Papyrorum Judaicarum*
CR	*Classical Review*
EJ	V. Ehrenberg and A. H. M. Jones, *Documents Illustrating the Reigns of Augustus and Tiberius*
GS	(T. Mommsen's) *Gesammelte Schriften*
ILS	*Inscriptiones Latinae Selectae*
JRS	*Journal of Roman Studies*
MAAR	*Memoirs of the American Academy in Rome*
MEFR	*Mélanges d'archéologie et d'histoire de l'Ecole française de Rome*
MW	M. McCrum and A. G. Woodhead, *Select Documents of the Principates of the Flavian Emperors*
Nash	E. Nash, *Pictorial Dictionary of Ancient Rome*
NC	*Numismatic Chronicle*
NH	*Natural History*
OGIS	*Orientis Graeci Inscriptiones Selectae*
Platner-Ashby	S. B. Platner and T. Ashby, *A Topographical Dictionary of Ancient Rome*
PW	Pauly-Wissowa, *Realencyclopädie*
REA	*Revue des études anciennes*
RhMus	*Rheinisches Museum*
RömMitt	*Mitteilungen des Deutschen Archäologischen Instituts, Römische Abteilung*
RRAM	(Magie's) *Roman Rule in Asia Minor*
S	E. M. Smallwood, *Documents Illustrating the Principates of Gaius, Claudius and Nero*
TAPA	*Transactions of the American Philological Association*
WF	*Wege der Forschung*

1 For a study of the portraits of Galba, Otho and Vitellius, see M. Gjødesen, *Meddelelser fra Ny Carlsberg Glyptotek* 16 (1959), 1–46; and of Galba, H. von Heintze, *RömMitt* 75 (1968), 149–53. Suetonius is confused on the date of Galba's birth; Hardy (Plut., *Galba*, p. 93) opts for 5 B.C., W. R. Tongue (*TAPA* 69, 1938, xlix) for 3 B.C.

2 An ambitious reconstruction of the forecourt of the Golden House is offered by E. B. Deman, *MAAR* 5 (1925), 115–26 and pl. 62.

3 Hungry chickens: Cic., *De Diuinatione* ii, 73. Shaded pronaos: Ovid, *Fasti* i, 71ff. with Frazer's commentary. Magliana: T. Mommsen, *Reden und Aufsätze* 270–93, esp. 291.

4 On the Seventh Legion and Galba's activities in Spain in 68, see *Legio VII Gemina* (Instituto Leonés de Estudios Romano-Visigóticos, León 1970). Pomponius Rufus: MW 31 and M. Raoss, *Epigraphica* 20 (1958), 46–120, esp. 104.

5 On Macer see K. R. Bradley, 'A Publica Fames in A.D. 68', *AJP* 93 (1972), 451–8. A date for Galba's arrival in Rome can only be argued from the mention of Narbonne, reached by the deputation about the beginning of August; on 13 October a statue of Liberty Recovered was dedicated in the palace: *ILS* 238 = MW 30.

6 The appointment of Agricola as investigator into deficits in the temple treasuries is one example of Galba's attempts to rectify the malpractices of Nero's reign.

7 For some of the literature on the population of the empire, see *Der kleine PW*, s.v. 'Bevölkerung' (Heichelheim). Estimates for Rome vary from 250,000 to 1½ million (listed by F. G. Maier, *Historia* 2, 1953–4, 318–61, esp. 321f.). For a recent conservative estimate see J. E. Packer, *JRS* 57 (1967), 80–95 and *MAAR* 31 (1971), 74–9 (attacked in *JRS* 63, 1973 279–81). Thirteen miles: Pliny, *NH* iii, 66.

8 On the speed of travel there is abundant evidence and an enormous literature: I cite only W. Riepl, *Das Nachrichtenwesen der Altertums* (Leipzig-Berlin, 1913); L. Friedländer, *Sittengeschichte Roms*10 I (1922), 333–42; L. Casson, *Ships and Seamanship in the Ancient World* (Princeton, 1971); and C. Préaux, 'Le Règne de Vitellius en Egypte' in *Mélanges G. Smets* (Brussels 1952), 571–8.

9 The soldiers' annual oath: Pliny, *Ep.*, x, 52 with Sherwin-White's note.

10 Antonius Naso: MW 355, 421.

11 The standard work on divination is A. Bouché-Leclercq, *Histoire de la divination dans l'antiquité* (Paris 1879–82). On the Piacenza bronze 'liver', see G. Körte, *RömMitt* 20 (1905), 348–77 and pls. xii–xiv.

12 Subrius Dexter: MW 337. The site of Liberty Hall is much disputed: T. Mommsen, *GS* v, 60–2; and E. Welin, *Studien zur Topographie des Forum Romanum* (Lund 1953), 179–219, esp. 194, places it at a point later covered by Trajan's Forum.

13 The Basin of Curtius: Platner-Ashby, s.v., Nash2 i, 542ff.; G. Lugli, *Roma antica: il centro monumentale* 156; Welin, op. cit., 75ff. The fig tree is illustrated on the Plutei of Trajan: Nash2 ii, 176f.; 399.

14 Mucius Scaevola: Livy, *Ep.* lxxxvi.

15 On the unsatisfactory nature of Tacitus' famous obituary in *Histories* i, 49, 2–4, see E. Koestermann, 'Das Charakterbild Galbas bei Tacitus' in *Navicula Chiloniensis, Festschrift für Felix Jacoby* (Leiden 1956), 191–206 (= V. Pöschl, ed., *Tacitus* (WF), Darmstadt 1969, 413–31).

16 On the Horrea Sulpicia, see G. F. Rickman, *Roman Granaries and Store Buildings* 1971, esp. 167.

17 Customs dues: S. J. de Laet, *Portorium* (Brugge 1949). Digne: Pliny, *NH* iii, 37.

18 The military coin issues: H. Mattingly, 'The "Military" Class in the Coinage of the Civil Wars of A.D. 68–9', *NC* 12 (1952), 72–7; C. Kraay, 'Revolt and

Subversion; the so-called "Military Coinage" of A.D. 69 Re-examined', ibid., 78–86. But the coins were surely minted not in 'South Gaul' but at Lyon; and I doubt whether their purpose was 'to be smuggled into Rome, put into circulation there, and thus subvert the loyalty of both troops and civilians'. The Fides Praetorianorum coins may imply a bribe already offered by Vitellius to his troops in Germany: the promise that any who wished would be enrolled in the Guard.

19   The date of departure from the Rhine can only be argued from an elaborate calculation of distances and times for which this is not the place; and the same is true for other incidents in the movements of Valens, Caecina and Vitellius.

20   *educatrices Augusti nostri*: CIL xiii, 5138 = E. Howald and E. Meyer, *Die römische Schweiz* 233.

21   Mons Vocetius: another and perhaps more likely identification is the Ütliberg west of Zürich: A. Deman, 'Tacite, *Histoires* i, 67–68' in *Hommages à Max Niedermann* (Brussels 1956), 90–101; he also places at Zürich the fort whose pay was stolen.

22   The Great St Bernard: Strabo iv, 6, 7; cf. PW Supplement-Band VII, 407 and G. Walser, *Itinera Romana* (Bern 1967) i, 44.

23   Jars: Strabo v, i, 12.

24   Nero's 'liberation' of Greece: P. A. Gallivan, *Hermes* 101 (1973), 230–4. False Neros: D. Magie, *RRAM* ii, 1422n; K. Holzinger, 'Erklärungen . . . der Offenbarung Johannis . . .' in *Sitzungsberichte der Akad. der Wissenschaften in Wien* 216, 3 (1936); P. A. Gallivan, 'The False Neros: a Re-examination', *Historia* 22 (1973), 364f. Asprenas: B. Levick in *Anatolian Studies* 17 (1967), 102f. and pl. xia has published an inscription (*AE* 1967, 492) from Pisidian Antioch referring to him and dated 71.

25   The Esterzili inscription: CIL x, 7852 = *ILS* 5947 = MW 455; cf. T. Mommsen, *GS* v, 325–51.

26   Dalmatia: CIL iii, 9973; and 9938 (= ILS 5951 = MW 451) with J. J. Wilkes, *Dalmatia*, 1969, 214ff.

27   The Aurelian Way repaired by Nero: S 352. Suedius Clemens: MW 339, 405 and 476. A drink made of barley: Strabo iv, 6, 2.

28   Vestricius Spurinna: see Pliny's letters *passim*, with Sherwin-White's commentary.

29   Much of the narrative of chapters 4 and 5 is discussed in detail in *JRS* 61 (1971), 28–51.

30   A plausible supplement: *Histories* i, 90, 3, *profectus Otho ⟨Flauio Sabino⟩ quietem urbis curasque imperii Saluio Titiano fratri permisit.*

31   Galerius Trachalus: greatly admired by the young Quintilian: x, 1, 119; xii, 5, 5.

32   Virgil's carrier: *Catalepton* x, where the boy poet describes the votive tablet of the retired muleteer, in which he was represented with reins and comb, in the chapel of the Castors (Dioscuri). The poem is a delightful parody of Catullus, written shortly after the publication of *Phaselus ille, quem uidetis, hospites . . .*

33   For a description of Roman troops marching *impediti*, see *BJ* iii, 115–26 (tr. Williamson, Penguin, pp. 180f.); and for illustrations, the reliefs of Trajan's Column, published in standard editions by Fröhner (1872), Cichorius (1896–1900) and Lehmann-Hartleben (1926).

34   Gaeta inscription: CIL x, 6087 = *ILS* 886 = EJ 187. There is an illustration of the mausoleum in the *Enciclopedia dell' Arte antica* (Rome 1958–73), iii, 724. A convenient and authoritative recent guide to Roman Lyon is that of A. Audin, *Lyon, miroir de Rome dans les Gaules* 1965.

35   Veleia inscription: *ILS* 2284 = MW 386.

36   Philostratus, *Life of Apollonius* v, 13.

37 Streets needing repair: *ILS* 245 = MW 412.

38 A small sacrifice: *AFA*, first half of June: *ob* [*uictoria*]*m faction. Venet. porcam et a[gnam . . .*

39 Chills and malaria: with the remarks of *Histories* ii, 93 and 99 may be compared the discussion of W. H. S. Jones, *Malaria and Greek History* (Manchester 1909).

40 A Nereid: Statius, *Sil.* iii, 2, 33. The Pharos of Alexandria: H. Thiersch, *Pharos* (Leipzig-Berlin 1909); M. Asin and M. L. Otero, *Proc. British Academy* 19 (1933), 277–92; C. Picard, *BCH* 76 (1952), 61–95. For the graceful epigram of Posidippus relating to the lighthouse, see A. S. F. Gow and D. L. Page, *The Greek Anthology: Hellenistic Epigrams* i, p. 169 (no. xi) and ii, pp. 489–91. The poet declares that the lighthouse is visible from an infinite distance: Josephus, *BJ* iv, 613 says that the light could be seen at a distance of up to thirty-seven miles, and Mr T. Ireland, of the Department of Navigation at Leith Nautical College, confirms the accuracy of this figure if we accept (from our Arabic source) that the structure was 135·7 metres high and if we place our imaginary observer 50 feet above sea-level with good conditions of visibility.

41 An encyclopaedic work on the city is P. M. Fraser's *Ptolemaic Alexandria* (Oxford 1972). Piazza del Popolo obelisk: *ILS* 91 = EJ 14.

42 Irresponsible excesses: for the exuberant behaviour of the Alexandrian mob in the theatre and the hippodrome, cf. E. K. Borthwick, *CR* 86 (1972), 1–3.

43 *BJ* ii, 487–98.

44 *OGIS* 669 = MW 328 = S 391; cf. B. Chalon, *L'Edit de Tiberius Julius Alexander* (Olten-Lausanne 1964); tr. N. Lewis and M. Reinhold, *Roman Civilization* ii, 98. The papyrus version, which reproduces the first fourteen lines of the inscription with slight discrepancies, is *BGU* vii, 1563 (from Philadelphia in the Fayum).

45 For a recent study of the portraits of Vespasian and his family, see G. Daltrop, U. Hausmann and M. Wegner, *Die Flavier* (in the series *Das römische Herrscherbild*) (Berlin 1966). Vacuna: Hor., *Ep.* i, 10, 49; the Roccagiovine inscription is *CIL* xiv, 3485 = *ILS* 3813 = MW 432.

46 Oenoanda: *ILS* 8816 = MW 258 = S 243a. Antalya: S 243b.

47 Euphrates: Pliny, *NH* v, 83; elephant: viii, 6; monkeys: viii, 215; goats: viii, 202; teeth: xi, 107; leather pipe: v, 128; plane tree: xii, 9.

48 Alans: Josephus, *BJ* vii, 244; Ammianus Marcellinus xxi, 2, 12ff.; D. Magie, *RRAM*, ii, 1418f. At *Histories* i, 6, 2 we should read *in Alanos* with T. Mommsen, *Römische Geschichte* v, 394n (= tr. *Provinces of the Roman Empire* 1886, ii, 62n).

49 *BJ* iii, 398–404.

50 5 June: *BJ* iv, 550. My understanding of πεμπτῃ Δαισίου μηνός rests upon the (ancient) table of equivalences published by Kubitschek in *Denkschriften der k. Akad. d. Wissenschaften in Wien* 57, 3 (1915), 12 and on the belief that a date important in Roman history would have been reported by Josephus according to the Macedonian (i.e. Julian) calendar: so E. Schürer, *History of the Jewish People*, tr. (Edinburgh 1890), I, 2, pp. 233f.; cf. p. 376. The supposition that Josephus was using the Tyrian calendar here leads to the dating 23 June (and to the previous year 68, inappropriate in the context, and found incredible by W. Weber, *Josephus und Vespasian*, Berlin, etc., 1931, 156f.).

51 Vitellius did not so regard 1, 2 or 3 January: *AFA* under 1 May.

52 The papyrus fragment: *P. Fouad* 8 = MW 41 = *CPJ* 418a. On Fronto and Peducaeus, see p. 127.

53 T. Mommsen, 'Die Dynastie von Kommagene', *GS* iv, 81–91. For interesting evidence of Roman occupation of the Euphrates frontier in this area, see *ILS* 8903 = MW 93 with V. Chapot, *BCH* 26 (1902).

54 For some details of Eastern promotion, see G. W. Houston, 'M. Plancius Varus', *TAPA* 103 (1972), 167–80, esp. 177n40.

55 L. Peducaeus: *P. Oxy.* xxii, 2349; A. Stein, *Die Präfekten von Ägypten* (Bern 1950), 39f.; R. Syme, *JRS* 44 (1954), 116.

56 Nero's regulation about wills: Suetonius, *Nero* 17.

57 The Fondi inscription: *CIL* x, 6225 = *ILS* 985 = MW 2741; cf. *AE* 1966, 68.

58 20 August: the date must be calculated on the basis of distances and marching speeds, as indicated in the text.

59 The Vitellian cohorts seem to have been engaged on routine bridge-building. The many wide rivers of northern Italy called for the maintenance of a number of pontoon bridges.

60 The doubts that obscure Saturninus' career are expounded by R. D. Milns in 'The Career of M. Aponius Saturninus', *Historia* 22 (1973), 284–94.

61 The Vedennius stone: *CIL* vi, 2725 = *ILS* 2034 = MW 375; Helbig, *Führer*[4] i, 275f. On Roman artillery in general see the works of Dr E. W. Marsden, *Greek and Roman Artillery: Historical Development* 1969; and *Technical Treatises* 1971.

62 Palisaded crown: Aulus Gellius v, 16, 17.

63 Valens' route northwards: *JRS* 63 (1973), 296. For a map of Pisa Port, see PW, s.v. 'Volaterrae'.

64 Umbrian prosperity: to Spoleto and its territory it may be possible to attribute the comparatively dense population of 23,000 (R. Duncan-Jones, *The Economy of the Roman Empire*, Cambridge, 1974, pp. 273–4): 17,850 plus slaves.

65 Cerialis: for a recent view of his career, see A. R. Birley, 'Petillius Cerialis and the Conquest of Brigantia', *Britannia* 4 (1973), 179–90.

66 The old circular harbour; de la Blanchère, *MEFR* 1881, 322ff.

67 Rembrantesque setting: Rembrandt's painting in the Swedish National Museum, 'Claudius Civilis makes the Batavians swear to rise against the Romans', depicts the scene, on which see *Konsthistorisk Tidskrift* 25 (1956), 3-92. The work, with which one may compare a number of preliminary sketches, was offered in vain to the city fathers of Amsterdam.

68 The Roman historian's principles: as recorded by Orosius, *Historiae adversum paganos* vii, 10, 4.

69 Vetera: the older standard accounts (especially important is H. Lehner, *Vetera*, Berlin-Leipzig 1930) should now be supplemented by H. von Petrikovits, PW, s.v. 'Vetera'.

70 The main (south) gate of Vetera: with Lehner's reconstruction (op. cit., Abb. 23).

71 A poor soil: Strabo xi, 2, 12.

72 cf. *P. Graec. Vindob.* 25787 (cf. H. Gerstinger, 'Neue Texte aus der Sammlung Pap. Erzherzog Rainer in Wien', *Anzeiger d. öst. Ak. d. W., phil.-hist. Kl.*, 1958, nr. 15, pp. 195–202). The text, if it is properly taken to record the words of Vespasian, seems to refer to an occasion early in 70.

73 A. Rowe, 'A visit to the Soma', *Bull. J. Rylands Library* 38 (1955), 139–55; A. Bruhl, 'Le Souvenir d'Alexandre et les Romains', *MEFR* 47 (1930), 202–21.

74 Every eye: Pliny, *NH* xxxiv, 24.

75 The foundations of the temple: *CAH*, pls. iv, 92a.

76 *ILS* 984 = MW 97 (Marquardt, *Privatleben*[2] 244n).

77 MW 405; G. R. Watson, *The Roman Soldier* 1969, pp. 103 and 193; Macrobius i, 10, 1.

78 Martial x, 23, 5–8.

79 The cellars of the Capitoline Temple: Aulus Gellius alludes to the *fauisae Capitolinae*, ii, 10.

80 Tampius Flavianus also was probably involved in repelling the invasion: *ILS* 985 = MW 274 mentions *ornamenta* and the taking of hostages from the enemy, a *Tran[sdanauuianis]*. Cooperation with Mucianus in the autumn to restore the

Danube frontier position might well account for the favour he continued to enjoy in Vespasian's reign despite his connection with Antonius.

81 Letter to the Archbishop of Prag: no. xxxv in A. Gabrielli, *Epistolario di Cola di Rienzo* (Rome 1890), p. 165. The scene in the Lateran is described in the lively and anonymous Life (*c.* 1358) to be found in Muratori's *Antiquitates Italiae Medii Aevi* (Milan 1740) iii, coll. 400ff. and since then separately in other editions including that of A. M. Ghisalberti (Florence, etc., 1928), Capitolo Terzo. The tablet is now in the Stanza del Fauno of the Capitoline Museum (Helbig[4] ii, 220f.). Text: *CIL* vi, 930 = *ILS* 244 = MW 1. It has generated an enormous debate, for which see *inter alios* G. Barbieri in de Ruggiero, *Dizionario Epigrafico* iv (1957), 750–8. Rienzo's homily: 'Gentlemen, so great was the majesty of the Roman people that it gave the emperor his authority. Today, however, we have lost this privilege, to our great discomfiture and shame.'

82 Eprius Marcellus: MW 271–3.

Index

Page numbers in bold indicate major references

Wellesley, Kenneth.
    The long year A.D. 69 / [by] Kenneth Wellesley. —Boulder,
Colo., Westview Press [1976]
        xvi, 234 p., leaf of plate. [8] p. of plates : ill., maps, plans, ports. ; 24 cm.
                                                                    GB76-02744

        Bibliography: p. xiii.
        Includes index.
        ISBN 0-236-40001-0 : £6.95

        1. Rome—History—Civil War, 68-69.   2. Galba, Servius Sulpicius, Emperor
of Rome. d. 69.   3. Otho, Marcus Salvius, Emperor of Rome, 32-69.   4. Vitellius, Aulus, Emperor of Rome, 15-69.   5. Vespasianus, Emperor of Rome, 9-79.
I. Title.